Sade

Sade

The Libertine Novels

John Phillips

LONDON • STERLING, VIRGINIA

First published 2001 by Pluto Press
345 Archway Road, London N6 5AA
and 22883 Quicksilver Drive, Sterling, VA 20166-2012, USA

www.plutobooks.com

British Library Cataloguing in Publication Data
A catalogue record for this book is available from the British Library

Library of Congress Cataloging in Publication Data
Applied for

ISBN 0 7453 1504 6 hardback
ISBN 0 7453 1598 4 paperback

10 09 08 07 06 05 04 03 02 01
10 9 8 7 6 5 4 3 2 1

Designed and produced for Pluto Press by
Chase Publishing Services, Fortescue, Sidmouth EX10 9QG
Typeset from disk by Gawcott Typesetting Services
Printed in the European Union by TJ International, Padstow, England

To my good friend, Gaëtan Brulotte, in gratitude for his inspiration and support over the last decade.

Contents

Preface

In preparing this book, I have used the most accessible editions of Sade's works in both French and English. These editions are listed in the first section of the bibliography, and all page references given immediately after quotations in the text are therefore to these French and English editions. Of the six primary texts which form the subject of the book, only *La nouvelle Justine* is currently unavailable in English, so translations from this text are my own, as are all unacknowledged translations of the secondary literature.

The reader is advised that I have sometimes found it necessary to follow the practice of a number of other Sade critics, notably Angela Carter and Lucienne Frappier-Mazur, in using so-called 'obscene' language descriptively or denotatively. In so doing, I have not consciously set out to shock or to transgress the norms of academic language, but to avoid inaccurate, clumsy and even coy-sounding euphemisms and circumlocutions.

I should like to thank Arrow Books and Grove Weidenfeld who were kind enough to provide on request free copies of editions of the novels in English. Among the publishers that I approached, only Oxford University Press, who publish the most recent translation of *Les Infortunes de la vertu*, refused me this modest facility. My thanks also to all who have encouraged me to write this book and have helped smooth the path to publication, in particular the Research Committee of the Humanities Faculty at the University of North London for giving me the six-month sabbatical which enabled me to complete it more or less on time; Gaëtan Brulotte, David Coward and Peter Cryle for supporting the project at its early stages; my commissioning editor at Pluto Press, Anne Beech, for her invaluable suggestions and unflagging enthusiasm; and all those friends and colleagues too numerous to mention here, who have in their various ways influenced my thinking about Sade over the last decade.

John Phillips
London
February 2001

1

Introduction

This book has two main aims: firstly, and most importantly, to introduce the Marquis de Sade's most controversial works of fiction to a new generation of readers, especially in the English-speaking world; secondly, to attempt to recuperate these works from the margins of eighteenth-century literature, to which they have for too long been relegated by censoring discourses, ranging from the puritanical to the politically correct.

Sade was the author of a large number of novels (many of which are perfectly respectable), of plays (all conventional in style and content), journals, letters and a few essays, but those writings upon which the Marquis's sulphurous reputation rests, and which have been of particular interest to critics as much as the general reader are the four 'libertine' novels composed over a twelve-year period from 1785 to 1797, known as *Les 120 Journées de Sodome*, *Justine*, *La Philosophie dans le boudoir* and *Juliette*.[1] There has certainly been much critical interest since the 1960s, most of this coming from French intellectuals, whose promotion of Sade has had some impact on American universities but very little on universities in the UK or elsewhere in the English-speaking world. Consequently, while a handful of advanced studies have appeared – mostly in the United States – in recent years since Sade's writings have been legally available to the public in unexpurgated editions, there has not been an introductory guide in English which could provide accessible readings of his four libertine novels.[2] This critical gap is no doubt explainable in terms of a reluctance on the part of many university teachers to expose their younger charges to Sade's work, so that, while some graduate literature and humanities programmes are beginning to require a reading of Sade as a philosopher if not as a novelist, his appearance on undergraduate courses is still rare.

This absence of Sade at less advanced levels of study is of course reflected in the literary manuals and histories that accompany them: if these primers mention Sade at all, it is usually in dismissive tones. This book therefore represents an attempt to make the study of Sade accessible to a wider circle of English speakers, including the student of literature at any level as well as the more general reader, by providing individual introductory analyses of the four gospels of Sadean libertinage, and situating each work in its historical, political and philosophical context, as well as in the author's own personal trajectory. After focusing on each of the novels individually in the following four chapters, I devote a final chapter to my overarching theme. Ranging over all four novels, Chapter 6 explores the hypothesis that the Sadean project is essentially that of a quest for an impossible object, formulated unconsciously as a transcendence not of the soul but of the body.

Notwithstanding my general thesis, this book was conceived essentially as an introductory study, rather than an ideologically driven polemic defending Sade against the various charges that have been levelled against him in the past.[3] I have therefore not set out to address in any depth or detail the vexed question of the 'pornographic effect' (in other words, does the representation in writing of sexual crimes lead to their enactment in the real?). Although my reader will find references to the question, especially in Chapters 2 and 5 where it is raised by the text itself, the complexities of the issues surrounding it, coupled with the lack of conclusive scientific evidence relating to it, place it well outside the scope of an introductory study. The question, when it does arise, is left open and readers are implicitly invited to form their own conclusions.

At a time of creeping intellectual conservatism in the West, induced by economic as well as cultural imperatives, the contemporary reader of Sade will be directly confronted with issues of sexual violence, paedophilia, sadomasochism, fetishism and perversion that politically correct discourses tend to repress or address only in sanitised form. This reader will certainly be horrified by the violence of Sade's text and, above all, by its objectification of human beings, by images of the darker side of our nature that we would prefer not to acknowledge: the inhumanity of man (or woman) to man (or woman), the utter selfishness of lust, the tyranny of an ego that is unfettered by laws or lacks the humane influences of socialisation. The horrific rapes and burnings of Kosovo or the primitive and unfeeling treatment of orphans and handicapped children in Romania after Ceaucescu bear a stark testimony to the existence of this darker side. Confronting it in the fictions of Sade may just help us to some kind of understanding of a potential for cruelty that his libertines tell us we all possess.

The reader will also perhaps be surprised that the same fictions challenge norms of age, gender and sexuality, presenting women as sexually autonomous and undermining modern culture's binary distinctions between young and old, male and female, hetero- and homosexuality.

Certainly many have found and will continue to find his libertine works abhorrent, but nowadays most will wish to confront, not censor, him. Yet, censorship can take far more subtle forms than outright banning: as we have already seen, the exclusion of a writer from courses of study or literary histories or the shelves of public libraries can be just as effective in keeping him out of the public domain. While writing this book, I was struck by the number of young people of my acquaintance – all intelligent and well-informed individuals – who had never heard of the Marquis de Sade. Before turning in this introductory chapter to his literary and philosophical ideas and finally reviewing the critical background, I shall therefore summarise the known facts of his existence. Who or what, then, was the 'divine Marquis'?

Biographical Details

There are as many Sades as there are biographies of him, in that every biographer is ideologically motivated to present a particular version of his life, thought and attitudes. Given that the sources of information are almost entirely confined to letters written by Sade himself from prison or by others who took up positions on his behaviour, any attempt to write about the Marquis de Sade's life runs an exceptional risk of fictionalising further that which has already been fictionalised a hundred times. The conflation of the life with the work, or worse, the work's standing in for the life, helps to perpetuate the myth that masks any truth that there might be: myth of Sade the vivisector, child murderer, and woman beater, myth of Sade the apostle of freedom (Apollinaire's accolade to Sade as 'the freest spirit who ever lived'), myth of a genius unrecognised and misunderstood. Awareness of the dangers will not necessarily prevent us from creating yet another Sade myth – there is no such thing as total objectivity – but it might help us to do more justice to the complexity of the Sadean phenomenon.

Donatien Alphonse François de Sade was born in 1740, the son of Jean-Baptiste Joseph François, Comte de Sade, lord of Saumane and Mazan, cavalry officer and diplomat, and of Mlle Maillé de Carman, a lady-in-waiting and poor distant cousin of the Princesse de Condé. The main influences on Sade's young life were his father and his paternal uncle, the Abbé Jacques François de Sade, who were both active debauchees: the lustful Abbé enjoyed liaisons with a number of society women and even visited some of the more notorious Parisian bordellos, while the bisexual Count was on one occasion arrested for accosting a young man in the Tuileries Gardens. At the same time, both were highly cultured men. Sade's father was a close friend of Voltaire's and himself wrote verses, while Donatien's uncle in particular had a fine and extensive library which, alongside the classic authors, included all the major works of contemporary Enlightenment philosophy as well as a fair sample of erotic writings. As Donatien spent much of his early childhood at the family château of Saumane in Provence in the care of his uncle, he had plenty of time to become well acquainted with this library of free-thinking authors.

The future writer and roué grew up, then, in a world of progressive ideas and libertine tastes. It was also a predominantly masculine world. When he was not in the company of his father and uncle, Donatien's early education was divided between the Jesuit college of Louis-le-Grand in Paris, which he attended alongside other boys of the French aristocracy and haute bourgeoisie between the ages of ten and fourteen, and a young preceptor by the name of Abbé Amblet, who taught him reading, arithmetic, geography and history. From the evidence of Sade's own later correspondence, Amblet was a gentle and highly intelligent man, and the only male member of the child's entourage who was not a libertine. From the Jesuits, Sade acquired a taste for rigorous intellectual enquiry, the debating skills of classical rhetoric and, above all, a lifelong passion for the theatre. The Jesuits' enthusiasm at this time for both sodomy and corporal punishment may also have helped shape the young Marquis's nascent sexuality.

As for his mother, she appeared to take very little interest in her only child. Her relative absence from his childhood is often seen by critics as the possible source of the mother hatred that permeates Sade's adult writings, although a number of 'mother substitutes' did flit in and out of little Donatien's life. These were his paternal grandmother and five aunts who doted on the only boy in the family, showering him with gifts and indulging his every whim – behaviour that, as the Marquis himself was later to admit, only served to increase his natural tendencies to arrogance and self-centredness. Donatien was by all accounts a handsome young lad with blue eyes and curly blond hair, and his aunts were just the first in a long line of female relatives and family friends who would be seduced by the future libertine's charming looks and sensitive character.

At the age of 14, Sade was sent to a prestigious military academy to train for service in the light cavalry regiment of the king's guard. The Comte de Sade was keen for his son to embark on a military career and only a year later was able to pull enough strings to get his son a sub-lieutenantship. The Carabineers only took tall, well-built men (the minimum height was five feet four inches, which was considered well above average in the eighteenth century), and Donatien was only five feet two, but the Count was able to call in a favour from the brigade's commander-in-chief. It was the end of 1755 and the eve of the Seven Years War. During the next few years, Donatien distinguished himself in action against the British, successes that he would later attribute less to courage than to a natural aggressiveness.[4]

Perhaps though, this aggression was less a natural trait than a defensive reaction to the lack of affection shown to him by his parents. The Count became thoroughly disenchanted with his son's increasingly spendthrift and promiscuous ways during his army years, and Donatien tried unsuccessfully on a number of occasions to regain his favour. This state of affairs was exacerbated in 1762 by the death of a grandmother, the dowager Marquise de Sade, whom he adored.

When the war came to an end in 1763, the now 22-year-old Marquis left one dissolute life as a soldier for another as a Paris socialite, much to the exasperation of his now destitute father who determined to find him a wife and a dowry without delay, and quickly came up with the daughter of a senior Paris judge. Of about the same age as Donatien, Renée-Pélagie de Montreuil came from the recently ennobled bourgeoisie rather than from the traditional aristocracy to which the Sade family proudly belonged, but the Montreuils were well connected and wealthy, and offered a substantial dowry for their eldest daughter. Renée-Pélagie was a plain girl and of no great intellect, though independent-minded and possessing a strength of character that would prove an enormous asset in the years to come. She would indeed remain utterly devoted to her husband during all the trying times ahead. Her mother, the Présidente de Montreuil, was a formidable woman who would also play a significant role in the Marquis de Sade's destiny. At first, the Marquis refused point blank to marry the Montreuil girl on the grounds that he was deeply in love with another woman. Then a second, potentially more serious, problem presented itself. Just before the planned wedding, Donatien discovered that he was infected with venereal disease. After a number of delays, however, the wedding ceremony finally took place on 17 May 1763.

The young couple were initially housed by the Montreuils, either in their Paris house or in their château in Normandy, and for a while all was domestic peace and harmony. It was at this time that Sade began to put on plays, allocating parts to his wife and even his mother-in-law, indulging an interest in the theatre which had been awakened during his school days by the Jesuits and would last throughout his life. This was the quiet before the first storm of Sade's libertine career: only five months after the wedding, the impetuous Marquis was arrested for the crime of debauchery and imprisoned at Vincennes. It appears from police records that, having paid a 20-year-old Parisian whore named Jeanne Testard to spend the night with him, Sade had shocked her religious sensibilities with talk of masturbating into chalices and thrusting communion hosts into women's vaginas, and had then frightened her with whips and other weapons into committing a number of similar sacrilegious acts. She had, however, refused to let him bugger her (not surprisingly, since sodomy was a capital offence in eighteenth-century France). Sade's first spell of imprisonment lasted only three weeks. On 13 November 1763, the king ordered his release on condition that he reside at the Montreuils' château in Normandy and keep out of mischief.

In 1764 the Marquis was given permission to move back to Paris. The next couple of years saw him fall in and out of love with three women, all actresses whom he met while frequenting the theatrical milieu. One might conjecture that this succession of painful amorous experiences eventually had a desensitising effect on Sade's emotional character. The last of these paramours, a Mademoiselle Beauvoisin, even accompanied him as his wife to La Coste, where the Sade family owned a castle and land. Sade enjoyed a feudal-style relationship with the villagers of La Coste, who for the most part remained loyal and even affectionate towards their lord and master throughout the turbulent decades to come. For his part, Sade was deeply attached to the property, which sits on a hill overlooking magnificent rolling scenery in the west of Provence, and made up his mind to live there permanently with his real wife and family. In 1766, he began extensive renovations, planting groves of fruit trees and enlarging the private theatre that he had already started building in the castle the previous year. On the list of the building work was the construction of a secret apartment, in which he would house his growing collection of erotic and anti-clerical books, as well as a number of oddities, including a large collection of enema syringes.

In January 1767, Sade's father died at the age of 65. This was a traumatic event for Donatien who had been very close to the Count, in spite of their many quarrels. Perhaps it was as a mark of fondness and respect for his father's memory that Sade never assumed the title of Comte but continued to refer to himself as Marquis. Later that year, he returned to Paris for the birth of Louis-Marie, the first of Pélagie's children who would survive into adulthood. Back in the capital, it was not long, however, before the young husband's extramarital activities were causing fresh scandals.

On Easter Sunday in 1768, Sade picked up a 36-year-old beggar named Rose Keller and, on the pretext of needing a cleaner, took her to a little country house he had rented at Arcueil. Once there, he locked the woman up, ordered her to strip and whipped her, pouring what felt to her like molten wax into her wounds. Keller later managed to escape from the house and report her experience to the police. Sade was duly arrested and taken to the royal prison at Saumur, where he was held for a fortnight before being transferred to Pierre-Encize, another royal prison near Lyons. His valet was allowed to accompany him to Pierre-Encize because he was suffering from a bad attack of haemorrhoids and needed someone to help change his dressings daily.[5] After a hearing at which Sade categorically denied any intention of causing Keller any serious harm (the medical evidence in fact supported his defence) and claimed that the woman was a prostitute who had accepted money for sexual purposes, he was fined and released after a few months' imprisonment on the condition that he return to Provence and remain there until further notice.[6]

Around this time, the huge debts that Sade incurred to pay for his sexual pleasures and also for the amateur theatricals at La Coste were beginning to change his mother-in-law's view of him, a process that would eventually culminate in her outright hostility, which would in turn prove his undoing. But the single event that probably did most damage to his relationship with La Présidente was the love affair with his wife's youngest sister, Anne-Prospère de Launay, who was as beautiful as Renée-Pélagie was plain. Fresh from her convent schooling and still dressed as a nun, this pretty and by all accounts flirtatious 20-year-old must have represented to Sade all the taboos that his fictional characters would take such pleasure in breaking: virginity, incest and religion. The two would soon be thrown together by the consequences of another major scandal.

On 22 June 1772, Sade and his valet, Latour, set off for Marseilles to obtain a much needed loan. It was not long, however, before they were looking to spend the money Sade had just borrowed in France's southern city of sin. In humorous self-disguise, the two men swapped names – Sade calling his servant Monsieur le Marquis, while Latour addressed his master as Lafleur (which would later be the name of a valet in *La Philosophie dans le boudoir*) – and organised a session of debauchery with four young prostitutes, ranging in age from 18 to 23. The session included acts of flagellation and sodomy, but, most memorably for the girls, they were asked to swallow pastilles containing cantharides (or 'Spanish fly'), a well-known aphrodisiac, although the intention on this occasion was to cause flatulence, the effects of which Sade found particularly arousing.[7] One of the girls became ill and complained to the authorities that Sade had tried to poison her. Less than a week later, a warrant was issued for the two men's arrest, and on 9 July the police arrived at La Coste to take them into custody. But they were too late. An actor in Sade's theatre company having warned them of the allegations made in Marseilles, Sade and Latour had already fled, accompanied this time by the ravishing Anne-Prospère. In spite of Renée-Pélagie's attempts to bribe the whores into withdrawing their accusations, the two men were found guilty of all charges and condemned to death *in absentia* (sodomy alone, we remember, carried the death sentence at this time), and on 12 September their bodies were symbolically burned in effigy. By now, the three runaways had reached Italy, Sade travelling under the pseudonym of the Comte de Mazan.

This was the first of three Italian trips that Sade undertook between 1772 and 1776 in his attempts to escape French justice. These journeys prompted him to write his first major literary work, *Voyages d'Italie*, a sort of travelogue with philosophical and historical commentaries, which would not be published until 1795 but which represented an important stage in his formation as a writer and thinker. On the one hand, the travel perspective enabled Sade to develop a theme to which he would return repeatedly in his libertine fiction and which would come to form the basis of his opposition to the absolutism of religious morality: the cultural and historical relativity of human mores. On the other hand, in their increasing improbability, events in the Marquis de Sade's life were beginning to resemble the picaresque adventures of the typical eighteenth-century hero of fiction and so would also provide ample inspiration as well as geographical and cultural material for the novels he would write in the 1790s (*Justine* and *Juliette*).

During this four-year period, Sade played an extended cat and mouse game with the French authorities. He was arrested in Chambéry in December 1772 by order of the King of Sardinia and detained at the sixteenth-century fortress of Miolans. Renée-Pélagie did all she could to obtain his release, but the Montreuils exercised their influence to keep him behind bars. His devoted wife was even refused permission to visit him and, on one memorable occasion, was reduced to dressing as a man in order to gain access to the prison! On 30 April 1773, however, Sade managed to escape by crawling through a kitchen window and in the autumn of that year he finally made his way back to La Coste, where he was able to spend a few quiet months with Renée-Pélagie. The following January, a loyal villager warned Sade of an impending police raid on the château – an expedition commissioned by a mother-in-law who would never forgive him the seduction of her youngest daughter – and the fugitive Marquis was once again forced to flee. By March, he was heading down the Rhône for Marseilles, dressed as a priest! (Given the vehemence of Sade's anti-clerical views, this is one of a number of ironies that seemed to punctuate Sade's career as an outlaw. Others include the names of towers in which he was imprisoned: 'Grande Espérance' or 'Great Hope' at Miolans and 'La Liberté' in the Bastille.) At the instigation of Mme de Montreuil, warrants for Sade's arrest were issued and reissued over the next few years. Before the first extended period of Sade's imprisonment which began in 1777 and was to last until the Revolution, there was one more scandal which greatly assisted La Présidente in her vigorous campaign to get her embarrassingly wayward son-in-law permanently locked up. This was known as the 'Little Girls' affair.

During a period of prolonged residence in hiding at La Coste between 1774 and 1775, the Marquis had hired five girls and a young male secretary for the winter. It was Anne Sablonnière, a young woman of 24, otherwise known as 'Nanon', who helped find the girls and was as a consequence later alleged to have acted as procuress. There was undoubtedly some truth in this, in that the intention had almost certainly been to organise a little harem for sexual purposes, which included flagellation and sodomy.[8] In addition to the six youngsters and Nanon, there was also Renée-Pélagie's maid, Gothon, a young girl from a Swiss protestant family. In January 1775 Sade was accused of having abducted the five young girls. This situation was exacerbated in the spring of that year by Nanon's giving birth to an illegitimate child and claiming that Sade was the father. This affair was hushed up in a manner which does not reflect well on the Sade or the Montreuil families, who succeeded in pulling enough strings to get her arrested for an alleged theft of three silver plates and locked away in a house of detention at Arles where she would remain for three years. Her baby died of neglect at La Coste at the age of ten weeks. As for the five girls, four of them were sent off to various nunneries to keep them quiet, while one chose to stay with Renée-Pélagie as a scullery maid. Nevertheless, the whole business of the 'little girls' had done his reputation considerable damage and, fearing another police raid on La Coste, Donatien headed for Italy again. It was a full year before he felt safe enough to return to Provence.

Settling down once more in the reassuringly familiar feudal surroundings of the château, Sade began to recruit young girls again. These included a pretty 22-year-old named Catherine Treillet, whom he nicknamed Justine.[9] Her father, a local weaver, gradually became concerned about the goings-on at La Coste and decided to bring his daughter back home by force. When the daughter refused to go with him, he became violent and fired at the Marquis. This incident obviously had legal repercussions which contributed to a fateful decision. In his legal battle with Treillet, Sade determined to seek satisfaction in the Paris courts, and on 8 February 1777 he and Renée-Pélagie arrived in the capital, where he learned that his mother had died three weeks earlier. Regardless of the circumstances, this was a perfect opportunity for Madame de Montreuil to dispose of her family's black sheep once and for all, and within a week of his arrival in Paris Sade was arrested by his nemesis, Inspector Marais, and imprisoned in the fortress of Vincennes. He would not be released for 13 long years.

The following year, the verdict imposed on Sade and his valet for the Marseilles 'poisoning' was in fact annulled by the court at Aix, but, to his horror, Madame de Montreuil was able to have a new *lettre de cachet* issued to keep her son-in-law detained.[10] On the return journey from the Aix appeal to the prison at Vincennes, Sade effected another of his Houdini-like escapes. As they stopped to rest at a coaching inn in Valence, the resourceful Marquis managed to give his guards the slip and made off into the surrounding countryside. While Inspector Marais and his officers searched the inn and outbuildings, Sade headed for La Coste, which he reached on foot at eight o'clock the next morning. His freedom was short-lived, however, for, just six weeks later, Marais stormed the château with a detachment of ten armed men and brutally rearrested the Marquis, escorting him in ignominy back to Vincennes.

This fleeting taste of liberty was the only interruption in a 13-year period of detention, initially at Vincennes and then in the Bastille to which Sade was transferred in February 1784. To fill the long days and evenings, he read voraciously, gradually amassing a varied and extensive library which included the classics he had read as a child (such as Homer, Virgil, Montaigne, La Fontaine, Boccaccio), works of Enlightenment philosophy by Buffon, La Mettrie, d'Holbach, Diderot, Rousseau and Voltaire, and, of course, volume upon volume of drama and fiction by Beaumarchais, Marivaux, Voltaire, Defoe, Rousseau, Shakespeare and many others. Some have conjectured that, if it had not been for this protracted period of imprisonment, the Marquis de Sade would never have become a serious author, for it was in the solitude of his prison cell that he began to write in earnest, producing a remarkable number of works in a relatively short time. So prolific, in fact, was the Marquis's literary output that in 1788 he was able to compose a comprehensive catalogue of his works, listing no fewer than eight novels and volumes of short stories, 16 historical novellas, two volumes of essays, an edition of diary notes and some 20 plays. From this canon of writings, only a small number survived the storming of the Bastille in 1789, so the following remarks naturally apply to these alone.

All the plays and two important works of prose – the lengthy epistolary novel, *Aline et Valcour*, and the slightly risqué but conventionally written philosophical short story, *Les Infortunes de la vertu*, which would form the basis of the full-length obscene novel, *Justine*, that Sade would publish after the Revolution – conformed in every sense to accepted literary norms, but, with the exception of *Les Infortunes*, none of these has been considered by critics to be of special literary value. On the other hand, of the libertine works composed during these prison years, the novel, *Les 120 Journées de Sodome*, written between 1782 and 1785, and a philosophical essay with strong libertine overtones, *Dialogue entre un prêtre et un moribond* or *Dialogue between a Priest and a Dying Man* (1782) represent important milestones in Sade's evolution as a writer and thinker. Indeed, in their total disregard for the conventions of form as well as of content, the obscene works that he began to produce in prison in the 1780s and completed for publication in the 1790s are of considerably more interest than anything else he wrote.

When the Revolution came, Sade's watchword was expediency. In the months and weeks immediately preceding the storming of the Bastille on 14 July 1789, crowds of increasingly restive Parisians were in the habit of gathering underneath its walls. Sade quickly saw that the present unrest offered his best chance of freedom in 13 years and, improvising a megaphone from a long metal funnel that he used to empty his slops into the moat, he bellowed to the throngs below that the guards were about to cut the prisoners' throats. This provocative act immediately got Sade moved to the lunatic asylum at Charenton, a few miles south of Paris, where he could do no more harm. Ten days after the funnel incident, however, the citizens of Paris took his advice and invaded the fortress, murdering the governor and plundering or destroying those manuscripts and other personal possessions that Sade had not previously been able to smuggle out of the building. The lost works included *Les 120 Journées de Sodome*. He had to wait until the following

April before finally being set free thanks to the abolition by the new National Assembly of *lettres de cachet*, the legal means by which Sade and so many others had been held without trial for indefinite periods under the *ancien régime*.

Therefore, on April Fool's Day, Sade was thrust into the turbulent theatre of revolution, a balding and obese man of nearly 50 with not a single penny in his pocket. Renée-Pélagie, who had remained utterly devoted to her husband throughout most of his time in prison, had by this time resolved to live alone in a Paris convent and had steadfastly refused to see him. It was not long, though, before the Marquis's old magnetic charm was able to rescue him from dying of starvation in the streets. That summer, Sade met the woman who would take his wife's place as loyal companion, if not as lover. Constance Quesnet, a 33-year-old former actress, who was separated from her husband and had a six-year-old son, would remain at his side for the rest of his life. Nicknamed 'Sensible' or 'Sensitive' by Sade because of her highly strung temperament, Constance was a modestly educated but gentle, loving and intelligent woman, who brought a much needed calming presence into Donatien's life. The couple scraped a living on her small allowance, while Citizen Louis Sade, as he was now obliged to style himself, tried to get his plays performed at the Comédie Française and other leading Paris theatres. These efforts were largely unsuccessful, however, and Sade's increasingly straightened circumstances (brought about by years of mounting debts and the seizure of his lands under the Revolution) drove him to publish between 1790 and 1800 'well-spiced' novels that he hoped would sell well: *Justine ou les Malheurs de la vertu* in 1791, *La Philosophie dans le boudoir* in 1795, *La Nouvelle Justine* and l'*Histoire de Juliette* in 1797.[11] Only *Aline et Valcour*, published in 1795, and *Crimes de l'amour*, a collection of short stories which appeared in 1800, were sufficiently 'respectable' to be published under his own name. Citizen Sade was determined to make money, although in fact, for reasons which have more to do with the prevailing climate of taste in the 1790s than with anything else, the first *Justine* alone achieved best-seller status.

Although remaining an aristocrat and a monarchist at heart, Sade nevertheless managed to survive the Revolution and the Terror of the Robespierre regime by playing the revolutionary game. This he did admirably, throwing himself energetically into local activities and penning well-received patriotic speeches. Indeed, for a former aristocrat, his rise to prominence as a revolutionary was remarkable. He became secretary, then president, of his section for a brief period, and was eventually appointed one of the section's 20 judges, positions which he could very easily have exploited to avenge himself on the Montreuils, whose death warrants he was asked to sign. However, being a lifelong opponent of the death penalty, Sade saved his in-laws and many others from the guillotine. Such 'inaction' was to have its consequences. On 8 December 1793, Sade was arrested for counter-revolutionary activities. He was charged with having sought admission to the king's royal guard in 1791, although this accusation was merely a pretext for the removal of a man whose judicial moderation was viewed by the architects of the Terror as unpatriotic and whose atheism was no longer fashionable. Robespierre's cult of the Supreme Being was now the prevailing credo.

Shuttled from prison to prison during the early months of 1794, Sade finally ended up at Picpus near Vincennes, a well-appointed former convent. It was here, from his cell window, that the *ci-devant* or 'former' Marquis watched as many of his fellow aristocrats mounted the steps of the guillotine, which had been moved to the Picpus location from Place de la Révolution (the present-day Place de la Concorde) because of the stench of blood, their corpses piled into a mass grave that had been dug in the prison gardens. A large lead urn placed under the guillotine to collect the blood was emptied at Picpus every evening. He would later write that the sight of the guillotine did him 'a hundred times more harm' than his imprisonment in the Bastille ever did. Sade himself escaped the guillotine thanks to bureaucratic confusion. In July 1794 his name appeared on a list of prisoners to be collected from Paris jails for judgement and execution that day, but as he failed to respond when his name was called, he was marked down as absent. Within a short time, the political climate had changed again with Robespierre's own fall from grace and execution, and Sade was freed on 15 October 1794.

For the next five years, Sade and Constance lived a from-hand-to-mouth existence. When the writing failed to bring in sufficient income to keep them afloat, Sade would write desperate letters to his lawyer, Gaufridy, begging him to send him money, though to little avail. By 1799, the former nobleman and landowner was even reduced to working as prompt in a Versailles theatre for 40 sous a day. Eventually, under the strict new censorship laws of the Bonaparte regime, Sade's reputation as the author of the 'infamous *Justine*' caught up with him, and on 6 March 1801, he was arrested at his publisher's. For the first time in his life, he was imprisoned for his writings and, with no powerful voices raised in support of his release, he would remain in detention until his death in 1814. Less than two weeks after his arrest, the Sade-Montreuil family arranged for the Marquis to be transferred to the Charenton asylum, where he had briefly stayed in 1789, in surroundings far more salubrious than any of the Paris prisons. The authorities justified Sade's continued detention and move to an insane asylum by inventing the medical diagnosis of 'libertine dementia', although in no sense could Sade be described as demented. The arrangement was one of pure convenience for the family. With their father out of the way, the Marquis's two sons would have a better chance of finding suitable brides.

Under the enlightened management of François de Coulmier, however, Charenton offered the ageing and indigent Marquis a number of distinct advantages. The family was obliged to pay for his accommodation, which was by no means spartan. He had an expensively furnished two-room flat, with agreeable rustic views, a library of several hundred volumes, and the freedom to walk in the gardens whenever he liked. It was the social and intellectual life at Charenton, however, which proved especially agreeable. Constance was allowed to move into the asylum with him, there were frequent dinner parties, and Sade enjoyed a stimulating, if at times tempestuous, relationship with the asylum director. The latter was progressive enough in his views to believe in the therapeutic value of theatre; consequently, for the first time in his life, Sade was given free rein to indulge his greatest passion. A full-size theatre was built to house an audience of 300, and the Marquis was given complete control of the rehearsals and performances of plays, which obviously included works written by himself. All of the plays performed at the asylum were wholly conventional in character (unlike the psychodrama experiments represented in Peter Weiss's 1960s play, *Marat-Sade*) and were enacted by Sade, Constance and other inmates with the support of professional actresses brought from the capital. Productions were highly successful and attracted large society audiences.

In addition to these enjoyable dramatic ventures, Sade wrote four more novels at Charenton, of which only three have survived: *Adélaïde de Brunswick, princesse de Saxe, événement du XI siècle, l'Histoire secrète d'Isabelle de Bavière, reine de France,* and *La Marquise de Gange,* all conventional historical narratives.

It seems, however, that the libertine flame in Sade was not completely extinguished during his declining years. From the autumn of 1812 until his death two years later, a 16-year-old girl named Madeleine Leclerc, whose mother worked in the asylum, visited Sade on a regular basis. The arrangement was certainly a financial one, although there may also have been a romantic involvement of some sort. One wonders how Constance must have felt about the situation. It is one of the greatest paradoxes of the Marquis de Sade's life that imprisonment not only provided the opportunity for literary and dramatic creation, but this time also made it possible for him to indulge his libertine urges with total impunity.

Sade died on 2 December 1814 at the age of 74. His last will and testament had directed that his body be buried without ceremony or headstone on land he had purchased at Malmaison, near Épernon. Acorns were to be sown around the spot so that 'the traces of my grave will disappear from the surface of the earth as I trust my memory will disappear from the memory of men, except for those few who were kind enough to love me until the last, and fond memories of whom I take with me into my grave'. In complete disregard of these wishes, however, Sade's corpse was given a full religious funeral by his younger son, Armand, and buried in the Charenton cemetery, with a

Christian cross casting its holy shadow over his grave, a bitterly ironic close to the story of this amoral libertine, staunch atheist and fierce opponent of all religions, whose entire work can nevertheless be seen in terms of an unconscious desire to found a new religion – the cult of the body.

Literary Ideas

In *Reflections on the Novel* (*Idées sur les romans*), composed as a preface to the short story collection entitled *Crimes de l'amour* published in 1800, Sade attempts to provide a review of the novel from classical times, via the troubadours of medieval Europe to late sixteenth- and seventeenth-century Spain and France, before evaluating leading novels of the eighteenth century. The essay shows how well-read Sade was and offers some insight into the fundamentals of Sade's literary ideas, many of which were highly perceptive, but the playful and at times combative tone makes it hard to view it as an objective survey. There is, for instance, the predictable denial of authorship of *Justine*, and a notable omission in the list of novels discussed. Choderlos de Laclos's brilliant portrait of libertine wickedness, *Les Liaisons Dangereuses* (1782), may have directly inspired several of Sade's own compositions (*Aline et Valcour, La Philosophie dans le boudoir*) and perhaps the Marquis felt unable to acknowledge a work that had influenced him so strongly. Joan De Jean suggests that this omission is all the more surprising given the essay's concern to demonstrate the originality of the French novel, with the work of the French troubadours and Mme de Lafayette's seventeenth-century masterpiece, *La Princesse de Clèves*, as the genre's founding models.[12] If, however, we believe that Sade had personal reasons for excluding a novel which he cannot fail to have read, given its prominence, the omission is perfectly logical. His intention, after all, was to represent himself and no one else as the natural heir to the tradition initiated by the troubadours, subsequently developed by Lafayette, and in his own century by Rousseau. Sade's main aim in writing this essay was to persuade the reader to take him seriously as a conventional writer.

Having summarily judged past practitioners of the genre (praise for Boccaccio, Cervantes, Mme de Lafayette, Marivaux, Richardson, Fielding, Prévost, Crébillon, Voltaire, and especially Rousseau, contempt for the improbabilities of the English Gothic Novel and for the base style of his contemporary fellow countryman, Restif de la Bretonne),[13] Sade prescribes his own rules of good practice, all of which he managed to break during the course of his own novel-writing career: the novelist must strive to be convincing, if not truthful (his own novels are filled with improbable and even surreal elements); he must not interrupt the main plot with tangential episodes or narrative diversions (the Sade narrative is typically fragmented in structure and regularly punctuated with lengthy dissertations); he should avoid the 'affectation' of moralising – only the characters are permitted to make moral statements, and then, only if circumstances require them to do so (the whole purpose of the Sade dissertation, which is often supported by detailed authorial footnotes, is to comment on moral, religious, as well as political issues); he should not adhere slavishly to rules (the structures of *Les 120 Journées de Sodome* in particular are dictated by an obsessive preoccupation with symmetry and numbers).

Underlying these rules are two essential principles, which are transparently self-justificatory: the writer must be personally inspired and must reflect nature's laws. The first of these principles is clearly a sort of post-rationalisation of Sade's own experience. De Jean's analysis is again perceptive:

> To revitalize the moribund novel, Sade calls for a uniquely personal source of inspiration, an act of revenge for victimization. And, since only misfortune can indicate to the writer the proper perspective from which to study the human heart, Sade implies that the prison cell is the ideal place in which to compose a novel.[14]

As for the role of nature in the inspirational process, this is seen to justify the portrayal of vice as triumphant over virtue, which is characteristic of all Sade's fiction, and especially of the libertine novels. To understand why, we need to be familiar with his principal philosophical ideas.

The Religion of Atheism[15]

If atheism needs a martyr, then I am ready

Michel Delon, a leading contemporary Sade critic, has rightly observed that there is no single explicit philosophical system in Sade, but a number of warring and at the same time complementary ideas, and that the critic can merely attempt to throw light on the implicit and unconscious problematic underlying Sade's text.[16] This problematic, which is essentially one of ambivalence, turns around the whole question of religion and the associated belief in transcendence. However, before exploring the unconscious motivations which drive the text, let us begin with a brief summary of the conscious philosophical position, as expressed both by the characters of the fiction and by the author himself in his personal correspondence.

Sade's atheism was heavily influenced by the work of two materialist philosophers of the Enlightenment: La Mettrie's *L'Homme Machine*, published in 1748, and d'Holbach's *Système de la nature*, which appeared in 1770. Materialism rejected belief in a soul or afterlife, reducing everything in the universe to the physical organisation of matter. According to La Mettrie, scientific observation and experiment are the only means by which human beings can be defined, and this method tells us that man is quite simply a machine, subject to the laws of motion like any mechanism of eighteenth-century science. The sole purpose of existence, in this scheme of things, is pleasure – a doctrine espoused with relish by so many of Sade's libertine characters. Baron d'Holbach views the human being as a collection of atoms, so that even the conscience has a material origin, acquired from our education and experience. His system does not, therefore, allow for free will, since all our decisions are determined by our personal interest. For him, all morality is a matter of social utility or pragmatism. Sade described *Système de la nature* as the true basis of his philosophy and a book that he would be prepared to die for, and indeed he lifted whole passages from it practically verbatim to place in the mouths of his protagonists as they railed against the various dogmas of religion.

Although these writers provide Sade with the essentials of his thinking, and he certainly plagiarises from them liberally, it is also possible to identify features of his philosophy that are peculiarly his own. The most important of these is his conviction that every human being is utterly alone. This *isolisme* helps to explain the lack of expression in his work of any fraternal feeling: if we are fundamentally cut off from all others, then self-interest can be our only motivation. Sade wants to abolish the social, not merely in the form of the *ancien régime* society which he constantly attacks, but in the guise of any society worthy of that name, that is, one based on a code of ethics which protects the individual while observing what Rousseau called 'the general will'. The feminist critic Jane Gallop is right to take Georges Bataille to task for ignoring the communities of Sade's fictional world (for instance, the Society of the Friends of Crime in *Juliette*) when postulating Sade's *isolisme*, but what *she* misses is that these communities are in no real sense societies of the kind envisaged by the eighteenth-century *philosophes*, because they are exclusive or elitist groups – clubs would be a better word – formed within and to the detriment of an existing society. They may observe a 'general will' enshrined in a set of prohibitive rather than permissive rules, but their main mission or purpose is to maximise the gratification of individual members within the wider social framework surrounding them. In this sense, they may be thought of as 'anti-societies'. They are certainly not communities, as these imply elements of fraternity, fellow-feeling and a mutual support springing from sympathy or affection. Their fundamental instinct is egotism, not human compassion.[17]

The self-interest at the heart of Sade's thinking, which makes possible the unfeeling exploitation of others, is justified because it is 'natural'. Since nature treats us all equally and so does not allow for any special cases, we are free to dominate others; indeed, in doing so, we are conforming to nature's wishes expressed in the universal 'law of the jungle', according to which the strong survive at the expense of the weak. All laws are therefore inimical to nature's plan, since they are designed to protect the weak, and neither God nor morality has any meaning in a universe governed entirely by natural forces. Nature in fact needs crime in order to preserve a necessary balance (for instance, for the purposes of population control). Any absolute distinction between good and evil breaks down because the preservation of this natural equilibrium will have different requirements in different societies and at different times. There are thus no moral absolutes, but only culturally and temporally relative values. On the shifting sands of Sade's moral universe, reason alone is man's guide. As the seat of prejudice, emotion can never be trusted. On the other hand, reason can only operate on the basis of physical sensations:

> Toutes les idées intellectuelles sont tellement subordonnées à la physique de la nature que les comparaisons fournies par l'agriculture ne nous tromperont jamais en morale.[18]

> All intellectual ideas are so greatly subordinate to nature's physical aspect that the comparisons supplied to us by agriculture will never deceive us in morals.

Taking materialism to its logical extreme, Sade locates reason in the body, and the Sadean body being entirely subordinated to sexual desires, only these desires make any sense – a notion encapsulated in Curval's starkly anti-intellectual dictum in *Les 120 Journées de Sodome* that it is better to fuck man than to try to understand him!

The laws of nature are the only laws to which we are subject, and these do not obey any ordering intelligence – nature is blind. It is this dependency on forces which are arbitrary but also unpredictable that elicits an ambivalent response from the Sadean hero. While, on the one hand, nature justifies all his crimes (which in fact cease to be crimes because they are simply necessary to the natural order), nature completely lacks either rationale or compassion, either reason or emotion. In the psychoanalytic perspective of Melanie Klein, nature is an absent mother, a 'bad breast', stirring up feelings of longing but also of resentment and hatred, and prompting a power struggle by the child against its parent. Like the Kleinian infant, Sadean man thus experiences an intense desire to destroy the absent and yet all-powerful and all-nurturing maternal breast that nature represents to him. But nature is infinite, and if man is to best nature, then he too must achieve the power and status of infinity. As we shall see in the final chapter, this quest for infinity, for a transcendence that will challenge mother nature's monopoly on power is a dominant and recurring theme in the Sadean text.

Reception of Sade's Work

No introduction to the writings of the Marquis de Sade would be complete without some discussion of their reception by readers and critics, and a guide to the most useful and accessible criticism currently available in English. I therefore propose to end this chapter with a brief account of modern Sade criticism, but such a survey needs to be prefaced with a few cautionary remarks.

'Put a pen in Satan's claw [...] and he could do no worse,' wrote the celebrated author, Louis-Sébastien Mercier, of Sade's *Justine* at the end of the eighteenth century. From the Revolution to the present day, from the outright condemnation typified by the Mercier *boutade* to the clandestine adulation of nineteenth-century writers and poets such as Flaubert and Baudelaire to the twentieth century's gradual rehabilitation and lionisation of Sade as a martyr of free thinking, the history of the reception of Sade's work is that of a succession of myths. Most of these myths, such as those referred to at the beginning of this chapter, are based on a confusion between the author and his characters, projecting images from fiction on to biography. Even the positive myth of Sade as rebel and liberator created in this century by Apollinaire and the Surrealists is a travesty of the truth because it ignores the reactionary and opportunistic streaks in the Marquis's personality. These mythical projections are most damaging, however, because they focus our attention on the writer, inviting us to read the work in terms of the life. This is, indeed, the danger run by any critic who provides a biographical account of a writer alongside of, or as a prelude to, textual analysis. It is quite a different matter, however, to read some, though not all, levels of the text as an expression of authorial desire, or as reflecting (though not explained away by) aspects of lived experience, and this is the approach which I have tried to adopt in this book. In this sense, a summary of Sade's life hopefully provides a necessary historical backcloth against which to situate some features of the writing (events of the revolutionary years are an obvious example here) as well as an elementary psychological portrait which may throw light on others. But in the chapters that follow, it is always the text rather than the life which I take as the starting point of analysis. Neither, of course, should any work of criticism be allowed to displace the text as primary focus. As an introduction to Sade's libertine fiction on the other hand, this book must try to help readers find their way through the baroque and often bewildering labyrinths of Sade criticism.

The Sadean text is an excellent weather-vane of the changing forms and priorities of literary criticism since the eighteenth century. In fact, as one of the few eighteenth-century writers to interest modernists like Roland Barthes, Michel Foucault and Jacques Derrida (Jean-Jacques Rousseau in Derrida's work is the other obvious example), Sade is almost unique in having excited the interest of critics and reviewers almost non-stop since the publication of *Justine*. One would have thought that this distinction alone would have guaranteed his work a place in the pantheon of French literature. However, even in France, most encyclopaedias and manuals on the subject which are largely intended for the general reader or the novice student are still reluctant to mention Sade's name, let alone devote space to any discussion of his novels. In the UK in particular, Sade has excited very little interest, whether within or outside the academy. Fortunately, a small but assiduous band of mainly French scholars has kept the flame of interest in Sade alive, and in the twentieth century there have been occasional bursts of critical adulation, first by the Surrealists in the 1920s and 1930s, later by the Structuralists and the *Tel Quel* group. Those who can read French and have a special interest in the fascinating subject of Sade's reception from his lifetime until the 1970s will find Françoise Laugaa-Traut's *Lectures de Sade* especially informative.[19] Given the limitations of space and the probable requirements of the majority of modern readers, I shall confine the following observations to works of Sade criticism which have appeared since the 1950s when the novels began to be more widely available to the general public.

In 1947, the first volumes of Jean-Jacques Pauvert's edition of Sade's *Complete Works* appeared in Paris. This edition and the trial of which it was the subject proved an important landmark in the reception of Sade's work, which had been repeatedly seized and prosecuted in the past. After the Pauvert trials of the late 1950s, Sade began to be more widely read, a development that culminated in the publication of paperback editions from the 1970s onwards. In the 1990s, Sade's writings finally achieved the status of classical literature by being published in the prestigious *Pléiade* series. *The Complete Works* have also been reissued since 1986 under the editorship of Pauvert and Annie Le Brun.

With the increasing availability of the work from the late 1940s onwards came increased critical attention in France. Jean Paulhan, Pierre Klossowski and Maurice Blanchot had already published important studies which sought understandably to rehabilitate Sade at a time when his works were not legally available.[20] Even then, Sade criticism of the late 1940s and early 1950s was certainly not universally favourable. Both Albert Camus and Raymond Queneau, for example, were highly critical of Sade from a political perspective, Queneau seeing the concentration camps of Hitler and Stalin as prefigured by his ideas.[21] In 1951, Simone de Beauvoir published the first feminist analysis of Sade in her remarkable essay, 'Must we burn Sade?'[22] De Beauvoir shifts her ground somewhat between a view of Sade's literary talents as second rate and praise of his flashes of insight and political scepticism, but her essay undoubtedly helped to place Sade at the top of the intellectual agenda in France and to mount a defence of the publication of his work in the Pauvert court case.[23] Defence witnesses included Jean Paulhan, André Breton, Jean Cocteau, and not least Georges Bataille, who in 1958 published his highly original exploration of eroticism and transgression, *L'Érotisme*, which contained a lengthy philosophical essay on Sade, entitled 'L'homme souverain de Sade'.[24] Readers new to Sade criticism will find the writings by Klossowski and Bataille somewhat rebarbative in style (although their influence has been significant) and are advised to consult summaries of their work in English. Pauvert's eventual acquittal on appeal in 1958 led to the relaxation of book censorship for adult readers (though not minors). In the 1960s, English editions of Sade's collected works finally appeared in the US published by Grove Press between 1965 and 1968 and in the UK by Arrow Books. These translations have not been superseded to date and, with the exception of *La nouvelle Justine*, are therefore the source of all English quotations from Sade's novels in this book.

The last 40 years have proved to be a period of sustained critical interest in Sade. In the 1960s and 1970s, leading French intellectuals turned their attention to the Sadean corpus: Roland Barthes, Michel Foucault, Jacques Lacan, Gilles Deleuze and Philippe Sollers all wrote enthusiastically about Sade's literary and philosophical legacy, and there were outstanding monographs by Marcel Hénaff, Philippe Roger, Béatrice Didier and Angela Carter.[25] During the last 20 years, Annie Le Brun, Michel Delon, Chantal Thomas, Lucienne Frappier-Mazur and Jane Gallop in particular have contributed important new studies to Sade scholarship[26] which are all available in English. Sade has also been the subject of university colloquia and literary and philosophical journals: among the latter, *Yale French Studies* (1965), *The Divine Sade* (1994) and *Paragraph* (spring 2000) might be found particularly useful by the English reader.[27]

In the 1960s and 1970s, much of this criticism focused exclusively on the text, rejecting the assumption that behind the text is a living author: the Structuralists, for example, treated Sadean libertinage as secure within linguistic boundaries, eschewing the moral problems that would immediately present themselves if Sade were to be read as the expression of a personal agenda or in the context of a political and social reality (an approach typified by Roland Barthes, for whom 'shit, when written, has no smell'). In the post-structuralist period of the 1980s and 1990s, psychoanalysis of the text avoids this problem to some extent by 'bracketing off' the author as a person and substituting the author as a textual construction. It then becomes possible to speak of a 'textual unconscious' and 'authorial desire' without implying any judgements relating to the man himself, about whom, in any case, we still know far too little.

It is indeed the very indeterminacy of Sade's text that helps to explain his fascination for the Postmodernists. Via myriad, often conflicting, voices (of narrator, character and authorial footnote), the writing constantly plays hide and seek with the reader on the subject of politics, moral responsibility, and even religious and transcendental issues. In the words of du Plessix Gray,

> One of the most maddening and modernist aspects of Sade's writing is that he has programmed himself to foil most methods of decoding and typification. Having robbed us of all the traditional pacts of trust between reader and writer, having also cracked, through his excesses, any traditional critical grid through which we might evaluate him, he forces us to play his own game, which works through principles of fluidity, indeterminacy, and sadomasochistic traumatization.[28]

More recently, Annie Le Brun, editor of Pauvert's late 1980s edition of the *Complete Works*, latter-day Surrealist, vociferous anti-feminist and ardent champion of Sade, has sought to break with the modernist tradition that has tended to view the writing as pure discourse and, in her words, to 'put the body back into the text', re-establishing the links between words and things, and making unequivocal identifications. In her brilliant and controversial exegesis of Western art and culture, *Sexual Personae*, Camille Paglia also rejects the notion that there is no person behind a text (an idea which she describes as the 'most pernicious of French imports') and presents Sade essentially as a realist whose unromantic, anti-Rousseauist view of nature as 'pagan cannibal, her dragon jaws dripping sperm and spittle' has exiled him from the history of Western literature and philosophy.[29] While acknowledging that the indeterminacies of Sade's text contribute in no small measure to its appeal as literature, my own focus on the Sadean body combines textual (psycho)analysis with Paglia's and Le Brun's more eclectic, more sexual and ultimately more personal reading.

Many conventionally biographical studies of Sade have appeared in the last 20 years, most of them available in English. I particularly recommend those by Maurice Lever, Donald Thomas, Laurence L. Bongie and Francine du Plessix Gray.[30] Bongie's 'biographical essay' is a well-researched and entertainingly written example of that rare thing, a biography hostile to its subject, while du Plessix Gray's more balanced portrait of Sade as a family man as well as a libertine rake is both excellent scholarship and a rattling good read.

Finally, Roger Shattuck's *Forbidden Knowledge* (1996) must be mentioned.[31] Challenging the recent rehabilitation of the Marquis de Sade, the book argues strongly for the moral responsibility of writers and puts Sade's novels on trial for their pernicious influence on twentieth-century child murderers. Shattuck raises powerful arguments relating to the effect of pornography on the vulnerable, the amoral and the already depraved, arguments based on scientific research of dubious value, but which nevertheless need to be addressed.

A Provisional Conclusion: Reading Excess

In many horror novels and films, men and women are mutilated and killed by predators who need to kill to survive ('vampire' stories, the *Alien* films) or by supernatural entities embodying the abstraction of evil (*The Exorcist*, the *Omen* books and films). We understand and tolerate a motive, which, whilst it repulses and terrifies us, nevertheless springs from a kind of rationale. On the other hand, horror narratives depicting sexually motivated murders tend to provoke the strongest negative reactions and, at the very least, to live longest in our cultural memories (Hitchcock's *Psycho* is probably the best example of this type in mainstream cinema). Similarly, the sex monsters of Sade's fiction, who mutilate and kill for sexual gratification, are beyond all sympathy or understanding, because unless sex is directly linked to procreation we are conditioned to see it as selfish and gratuitous. The sexual criminal is far worse than the vampire or even the deranged serial killer, whose humanity has been diseased by psychosis. The sex maniac kills for sexual pleasure alone and so is intolerable according to a moral code which is firmly rooted in a puritanical hatred of any form of hedonism. It is, in Sade's writing, the sexual motive which we find especially unbearable rather than the crime of murder itself, abhorrent though this may be.

Not surprisingly, it is his vain call to Robespierre for the creation of public bordellos which has been found by many to be his most subversive proposal. If once we can overcome our distaste for self-gratification *per se*, if, with Bataille, we can see the thirst for pleasure as an end in itself, then it becomes possible to read Sade in the same way that we read an Anne Rice or a Stephen King novel or watch a David Cronenberg movie – with a mixture of shock and excitement bordering on *Schadenfreude*, but without the guilt associated with the sexual prejudices of a largely Christian tradition. As with the violent contents of the horror genre, there are even strategies for the containment of the reader's repulsion, one of which is laughter. Reading Sade as an essentially comic writer prevents us from reading him simultaneously either as a writer of horror or as a sadistic pornographer.[32] Moreover, the Sadean text is probably most subversive and certainly most entertaining when read in this way. Like some dark comic strip caper set in the Gothic dungeons of eighteenth-century French châteaux, his libertine fictions marry the obsessiveness of farce (all bottoms and exaggerated body parts) with the gore of horror, both 'fantasy' genres situated at some distance from the real.

It would, of course, be highly reductive to insist on any single reading of Sade's novels to the exclusion of all others. Sade is a writer of many voices – self-contradictory, provocative, reassuring, conservative, revolutionary, scandalous, censorious, and many more. This plurality gives birth to a multilayered text that is in turn sexy and repugnant, poetic and vulgar, philosophical and physical, belligerent and conciliatory, misogynist and emancipatory, horrific and comic. But if Sade's work is to be summed up in one word, this word would not be 'sexual' or 'comic' or even 'sadistic', it would be 'transgressive'. As it systematically transgresses all sexual, social, religious and moral norms, his writing repeatedly and earnestly insists on the exquisite pleasure to be derived from this transgression.

The essential interest of Sade's writing lies less in its literary qualities (although, as the analysis of the novels demonstrates, these are certainly not lacking) than in its transgressive power generating the relentless movement of the narrative towards excess. This excess may be repulsive and shocking, fascinating and fantastic, and comic at the same time. As creatures of such excess, characters like Gernande (and there are many of them) are essentially adult fairy-tale figures: a giant vampire who can come only when he sees blood squirt from the veins of a beautiful young woman, but whose penis is no bigger than a three-year-old's, Gernande is a black comic creation, with echoes of Bluebeard, the giant from *Jack and the Beanstalk* and the satyrs of mythology. Some of Grimm's fairy tales in their unbowdlerised versions are just as horrifying as *Juliette* at its most extreme (although lacking the Sadean text's sexual content). The witch in *Hansel and Gretel* who bakes children alive for her dinner is, after all, no less human-seeming than the demonic Saint-Fond or the appalling Noirceuil. Books are not corrupt, only people are. If Bruno Bettelheim can argue that the sanitised Disney versions of fairy tales are at worst positively harmful and at best ineffectual as educational material because the child is not offered the opportunity to confront horror from the safe distance of fantasy, then it should also be possible to argue that the dark writings of the 'divine Marquis' enable adult readers to purge the need to look into the furthest recesses of the human psyche.[33] The entire horror genre from Poe to King serves the same need, but no one has ever suggested that murderers like Brady and Hindley were inspired by fictitious monsters from fairy tales or Gothic horror stories.[34]

Sadean excess is a wholly comprehensible response to the excessive circumstances in which the writer found himself during the latter half of his adult life. At the same time, had he not spent those long years in prison, Sade may never have become the great novel writer he became. He was the *enfant terrible* of his time, beyond the pale both philosophically and politically, a naughty boy put out into the corridor, excluded from society for most of his adult life. In general, then, it was only in this 'corridor' that he was able to act at all, mainly, of course, through his various writings.

During his earlier years he may have been guilty of minor sexual misdemeanours, but then so were many other young French aristocrats of the time. What seems likely was that he committed none of the monstrous crimes of which his fictitious characters are guilty. In any case, although it may contain strongly personal elements, the literary work is not reducible to the status of mere biography, nor is biography of any use in establishing the quality of the work. In the end, the writing and our responses to it are all that remain. Each time we read *Justine* or *Juliette,* we do so against our own unconscious fears and our own unspeakable desires. In the Sadean house of fantasies and horrors are our best dreams and our worst nightmares. Sade's libertine novels are ultimately worth reading because of the light they cast into the darkest corners of human desire and because, at the very edge of sanity beyond the real and its moral dimensions, they offer us safe, imaginary spaces of cathartic play.

2

In the Cathedral of Libertinage: *Les 120 Journées de Sodome*

a book that in a sense towers above all other books in that it represents the truth of man's fundamental desire for freedom that he is obliged to contain and keep silent

Georges Bataille
La Littérature et le mal, p. 81

One hundred and twenty days of Sodom. A hundred and twenty. One relentlessly following the other. The very title suggests excess, a criminal orgy of sexual deviance protracted well beyond the normal limits of human endurance. It seems to contain and at the same time to proclaim the dearest preoccupations of a prisoner whose sexual activities were necessarily confined to the onanistic and the fantastic, and whose suffering was greatly increased by a repeated failure to discover the term of his imprisonment. The title, then, on the one hand suggests the cryptic and symbolic significance of numbers, which we know to be a common feature of the Sadean text; it also represents time as duration, to be endured, a time period conceived not as a whole but in terms of its many parts. Time as an intolerable succession of days on end is, however, simultaneously made tolerable by the sodomy with which it is not only juxtaposed but made synonymous: the 120 days are days *of* Sodom, every moment of them filled with and defined by Sade's favourite sexual activity.[1]

The notion of divine retribution which the biblical connotations of the word 'Sodome' invoke seems directly and provocatively to be challenged in the title by the very repetition and regularity of what a Christian would consider to be one of the most heinous of sexual crimes – a crime which in Sade's time merited the death penalty: sodomy not just once but repeatedly, on countless occasions, from moment to moment, from day to day, from week to week, from month to month, a ritualistic and extreme event, a trial of endurance to outperform the mere ten days of Christ's passion which it seems ironically to echo. The most sulphurous-sounding of Sade's works, then, a title whose boldness and open depravity is probably more responsible than any other for the Sade myths: Sade the invert, Sade the godless, Sade the master of extremes.

It is hardly surprising, therefore, that among those who know the author only by reputation, there is a tendency to think of the *120 Days* as his final work, as the peak of a steep curve of ever more pornographic writing. This impression will seem to be confirmed by a reading of the introduction to the work, where the narrator proudly describes his narrative as '[le] récit le plus impur qui ait jamais été fait depuis que le monde existe' (p. 76) / 'the most impure tale that has ever been told since our world began' (p. 253). In fact, it was his first long work of fiction. Its unfinished nature perhaps fuels this particular misapprehension. The dramatic circumstances surrounding its composition and eventual loss must also have contributed to the creation of a mythical status for the work. Sade had started it in prison on 22 October 1785, writing in microscopic handwriting on long narrow rolls of paper which he glued together into a roll that was eventually 49 feet long, kept hidden in a hole in the wall of his cell in the Bastille. In the ironically named Tower of Liberty where his cell was located, he wrote every evening after dinner for three hours or more, taking only 37 days to produce a novel-length draft of the first of four sections and detailed notes for the remaining three.

When he was suddenly moved from the Bastille ten days before it was stormed in the Revolution of 1789, he became separated from this rudimentary manuscript and in fact never saw it again. When the Bastille was taken, the work was discovered and found its way into the hands of the Villeneuve-Trans family, remaining in their possession until its sale in around 1900 to a German collector. In 1904, the German psychiatrist, Dr Iwan Bloch, under the pseudonym Eugen Dühren, published the first edition of the work limited to 180 copies. The father of modern Sade studies, Maurice Heine, acquired the manuscript on behalf of

Vicount Charles de Noailles in 1929 and provided a much revised version in the early 1930s, but this was an equally limited print run, this time of less than 400 copies, reserved for the members of the *Société du Roman Philosophique*.[2] Both of these early editions were aimed at those doctors and scientists working in the new field of sexology who saw the novel as providing the first known encyclopaedia of sexual aberrations, predating the work of Freud and Krafft-Ebing by more than a century. Dühren considered the work to be an important scientific resource for anyone studying the 'sociology of love', whilst for Heine,

> It was the bold initiative of the Marquis de Sade which, beginning in 1785, imposed the modern approach to the classification of sexual facts on the basis of an ethico-social conception [...] The similarity between (the content) and modern observations is clear justification of the precursor who broke the pretentious monopoly theologians had established where such matters were concerned.[3]

Sade's own admission that he wept tears of blood at the loss of the work has also probably helped to give the impression that this was his most important and therefore most mature undertaking.[4] Although his first and not his last work, however, the *120 Days* is for many, quite simply the foundation stone of the Sadean edifice,[5] containing many of the features which would become characteristic of his novel-writing: a passionate concern with order and categorisation, a preoccupation with numbers, the uniquely Sadean rhythm of orgy following dissertation or narrative, of practice following theory, and above all, the encyclopaedic mission to 'say all' in the area of human sexuality. The work represents an audacious attempt to catalogue all known sexual perversions (or 'passions', as Sade called them), and in both conception and form clearly seems inspired by Boccaccio's *Decameron*.[6] For both Gilbert Lély and Maurice Heine, *Les 120 Journées* is quite simply Sade's literary masterpiece.

The work is set in the first decade of the eighteenth century during the last years of the reign of Louis XIV, not, as Stuart Hood seems to think, in the Thirty Years War (1618–48).[7] Errors like Hood's remind us to what extent the most shocking book of all literature has so often been read with less attention than it deserves, even by the most inspired of Sade critics – Angela Carter also believes it to be set 'in the seventeenth century'.[8] This misreading of the historical setting is regrettable because it misses an important point. The novel's four libertine protagonists are wealthy enough to embark on a murderous four-month orgy thanks to the huge profits they have made from Louis XIV's expansionist wars. As in all Sade's narratives, the violence depicted in *Les 120 Journées* is framed by a violent historical context, one sufficiently long ago to be 'just outside the collective memory of the writer's contemporaries', as Joan De Jean puts it,[9] but nevertheless a past not too distant to suggest an underlying critique of the entire contemporary period, that is, of a century whose rulers all share some responsibility for the impoverishment and ruin of both the Sade family and the French nation. In a negative image of Rousseau's fraternal utopia, the libertines form a pact cemented by their wealth and influence. Right from the start, Sade distances himself from his characters, holding up a mirror to a corrupt society in which money is power:

> Les guerres considérables que Louis XIV eut à soutenir pendant le cours de son règne, en épuisant les finances de l'État et les facultés du peuple, trouvèrent pourtant le secret d'enrichir une énorme quantité de ces sangsues toujours à l'affût des calamités publiques qu'ils font naître au lieu d'apaiser, et cela pour être à même d'en profiter avec plus d'avantages. (p. 5)[10]

> The extensive wars wherewith Louis XIV was burdened during his reign, while draining the State's treasury and exhausting the substance of the people, none the less contained the secret that led to the prosperity of a swarm of those bloodsuckers who are always on the watch for public calamities, which, instead of appeasing, they promote or invent so as, precisely, to be able to profit from them the more advantageously. (p. 191)

The four main actors and orchestrators of the four-month orgy which forms the main subject matter of the novel represent the four sources of authority and power in eighteenth-century France (the nobility, the Church, the courts and high finance), and their largely negative portrayal reinforces the impression gained by the reader in the opening lines that one of Sade's aims is political satire. The portrait of the leading libertine of the four, the Duke de Blangis, reads as a strong critique of privilege:

> Le duc de Blangis, maître à dix-huit ans d'une fortune déjà immense et qu'il a beaucoup accrue par ses maltôtes depuis, éprouva tous les inconvénients qui naissent en foule autour d'un jeune homme riche en crédit, et qui n'a rien à se refuser: presque toujours dans un tel cas, la mesure des forces devient celle des vices, et on se refuse d'autant moins qu'on a plus de facilités à se procurer tout. (p. 12)

> The Duc de Blangis, at eighteen the master of an already colossal fortune which his later speculations much increased, experienced all the difficulties which descend like a cloud of locusts upon a rich and influential young man who need not deny himself anything; it almost always happens in such cases that the extent of one's assets turns into that of one's vices, and one stints oneself that much less the more one has the means to procure oneself everything. (p. 197)

Now a 50-year-old Bluebeard figure who has already killed his mother, sister and three of his wives, Blangis not only possesses all the vices that one would associate with libertinage – 'faux, dur, impérieux, égoïste, également prodigue pour ses plaisirs et avare lorsqu'il s'agissait d'être utile, menteur, gourmand, ivrogne, poltron, sodomiste, incestueux, meurtrier, incendiaire, voleur' (p. 13) / 'treacherous, harsh, imperious, barbaric, selfish, as lavish in the pursuit of pleasure as miserly when it were a question of useful spending, a liar, a gourmand, a drunk, a dastard, a sodomite, fond of incest, given to murdering, to arson, to theft' (p. 198) – but he is a coward to boot: 'Un enfant résolu eût effrayé ce colosse et dès que, pour se défaire de son ennemi, il ne pouvait plus employer ses ruses ou sa trahison, il devenait timide et lâche' (p. 18) / 'a steadfast child might have hurled this giant into a panic [...] as soon as Blangis discovered he could no longer use his treachery or his deceit to make away with his enemy, he would become timid and cowardly' (p. 202). His brother, a bishop, aged 45, has earned his criminal spurs by murdering two young children for their money. Unlike Blangis, whose penis is twelve inches long by eight inches in circumference, the bishop has a 'very ordinary, even little' member, hardly qualifying him for the 'stud' status one might expect of a male libertine – but then he does belong to the Catholic clergy that Sade detested so intensely. The 53-year-old financier, Durcet, too, has an 'extraordinarily small' penis and the breasts and buttocks of a woman. He poisoned his mother, his wife and his niece in order to inherit their wealth. The Président de Curval, a magistrate of 60, as repulsive physically as he is morally, also owes his fortune to debauchery and murder: 'entièrement blasé, entièrement abruti, il ne lui restait plus que la dépravation et la crapule du libertinage' (p. 22) / 'entirely jaded, absolutely besotted, all that remained to him was the depravation and lewd profligacy of libertinage' (p. 206).

While the bishop and Durcet suffer from inadequately sized genital equipment, Curval has difficulty achieving erection, although his infrequent orgasms are as explosively violent as those of the permanently priapic Blangis. Sade himself experienced problems ejaculating, and yet his orgasms had the violent character of epileptic fits. This sexual idiosyncracy is perhaps reflected in the sexual portraits of his four protagonists, who represent the two extremes of virtual impotence (Curval) and the fantasy of unlimited potency (Blangis whose ejaculatory abilities seem almost superhuman). Both libertines shriek like banshees when reaching orgasm.

As Raymond Jean points out, the book presents the reader with a gallery of social types as physically and morally unattractive as the four libertines: bankers, lawyers, magistrates, priests, courtiers, landowners, military officers; all old, rich and powerful, they represent a wide cross-section of the ruling classes, whom Sade had every reason to hate. In this work, if not in Sade's later novels, libertinage is certainly not painted in seductive colours.

The bishop is an inveterate sodomite and even his three bisexual friends display a marked preference for sodomy with their own sex. The duke alone finds pleasure in vaginal intercourse. Despite this, three of the debauchees have married the daughter of one of the others, in a perverse parody of the bourgeois patriarchal system of marriage, according to which fathers marry off their daughters to the sons of other wealthy men in order to obtain property and other financial interests. As the bishop cannot marry and therefore cannot participate properly in the system of exchange, his daughter is regarded as common sexual property by the others. Sade thus simultaneously undermines the family structure and the incest taboo which, according to structural anthropologists, Marcel Mauss and Claude Lévi-Strauss, is designed to promote the material and other benefits of exogamy (or the marrying of women outside the family group).

According to Lévi-Strauss, 'Exchange – and consequently the rule of exogamy which expresses it – [...] provides the means of binding men together, and of superimposing upon the natural links of family the henceforth artificial rules [...] of alliance governed by rule.'[11] Blangis, Curval and Durcet have all enjoyed and continue to enjoy relations with their own daughters, while exchanging them with the other two as a means of strengthening ties between them. Incest, a familiar Sadean theme, may transgress religious and societal taboos, yet it in no way damages the exchange value of the women involved.[12] These daughter-wives share their victim status with a harem of 28 others: 16 young boys and girls aged between 12 and 15, eight 'studs' in their twenties, known as 'fuckers', chosen for the herculean size of their penis and their sexual potency, and four ugly and depraved old women. While the youngsters are selected for their superlative beauty and virginity, and are dressed in costumes that accentuate their sexual availability, the old hags are repulsive in the extreme. Such contrasts form the basis of Sadean eroticism, as we shall see presently.

Last but certainly not least among the orgy's participants are four *historiennes* or storytellers, three cooks and three kitchen servants. As providers of all the food and alcohol consumed, the cooks enjoy a special status which insures them against all harm and, indeed, they number among the small band of survivors eventually allowed to return to Paris. So too do the storytellers, whose role and importance is central to the work. Duclos, Champville, Martaine and Desgranges are all prostitutes of many years' experience. Their function is to narrate and describe down to the last detail scenes of sexual perversion which will subsequently be enacted by the listening libertines.

Although the harem of sexual victims includes males, women and girls are seen to undergo the worst treatment, especially the four spouses, and the libertines are forever rehearsing theories of female inferiority to justify their use of them as objects of pleasure and exchange. Somewhat stereotypically, it is the homosexual bishop who is seen to hate and despise women most, expressing sentiments which the author–narrator appears implicitly to support:

> l'évêque qui abhorrait [les femmes] se livra à toute la haine qu'elles lui inspiraient. Il les ravala à l'état des plus vils animaux, et prouva leur existence si parfaitement inutile dans le monde qu'on pourrait les extirper toutes de dessus la terre sans nuire en rien aux vues de la nature, qui, ayant bien trouvé autrefois le moyen de créer sans elles, le trouverait encore quand il n'existerait que des hommes. (p. 357)

> the bishop who abhorred [women] gave vent to all the hatred they inspired in him. He reduced them to the state of the vilest animals, and proved their existence so perfectly useless in this world that one could extirpate them from the face of the earth without in the slightest countercarrying the designs of Nature who, having in times past very surely found the means to create without women, would find it again when only men were left. (p. 511)

'Une langue de femme n'est bonne qu'à torcher un cul' (p. 263) / 'what the devil is a woman's tongue good for if not to wipe assholes?' (p. 422) he tells Duclos, the female narrator, whose tongue is employed to tell stories on command for men and who is herself, therefore, an arse-licker of sorts. Like Juliette, the storytellers may escape the victim status of most other women in Sade's world partly because, as narrators, they are projections of the author in the text, but also because, again like Juliette, they are whores who are, as the feminist critic, Jane Gallop, puts it, 'aggressively, scandalously at the disposal of the master's whim, being interpreters of that whim'.[13] On the other hand, the choice of female narrators is characteristic of the eighteenth-century novel, and even of libertine writing, in which it carries appreciable erotic advantages. Quoting Joyce McDougall, Lucienne Frappier-Mazur interprets this eroticism in psychoanalytic terms:

> Sade seeks to appropriate the feminine, and writing demands a passage through the feminine – be it a phantasy of incest with the mother, a rivalry with the maternal as genitor, or a descent into the Kristevan abject [...] the choice of women historians or of Juliette as storytellers and spokespersons betrays the survival of a 'secret relationship, basically an anal-erotic and anal-sadistic one, between mother and child' introducing the mother as a complicitous witness to the perverse staging, and ending in the phantasy of a phallic writing, which finds its metaphor in the simulacrum and in fetish objects.[14]

Against the hatred of women in general and the maternal in particular, identifiable so often at the surface of the Sadean text, Frappier-Mazur's analysis thus suggests the possibility of a lingering unconscious erotic dependency on the mother.

The orgy takes place in a remote castle, the château of Silling, owned by one of the debauchees, located on a high peak in the depths of the Black Forest. Sade emphasises Silling's total inaccessibility, 'une retraite écartée et solitaire, comme si le silence, l'éloignement, et la tranquillité étaient les véhicules puissants du libertinage' (p. 55) / 'a remote and isolated retreat, as if silence, distance, and stillness were libertinage's potent vehicles' (p. 235). Silling offers no hope of rescue or survival to those unfortunates captive within its impenetrable walls and womb-like security to their nefarious captors. Completely cut off from the outside world for the four winter months of their protracted orgy, Sade's four libertine protagonists realise a universal unconscious fantasy of unlimited power over others:

> Il était chez lui, il était hors de France, dans un pays sûr, au fond d'une forêt inhabitable, dans un réduit de cette forêt que par les mesures prises les seuls oiseaux du ciel pouvaient aborder, et il y était dans le fond des entrailles de la terre. (p. 61)

> [He was at home] He was out of France, in a safe province, in the depths of an uninhabitable forest, within this forest in a redoubt which, owing to the measures he had taken, only the birds of the air could approach, and he was in the depth of the earth's entrails. (p. 240)

Nature itself conspires to consolidate this geographical security when a huge quantity of snow falls in the surrounding valley, strengthening the castle's isolation and smothering the cries of both torturer and victim:

> On n'imagine pas comme la volupté est servie par ces sûretés-là et ce que l'on entreprend quand on peut se dire: «Je suis seul, ici, j'y suis, au bout du monde, soustrait à tous les yeux et sans qu'il puisse devenir possible à aucune créature d'arriver à moi; plus de freins, plus de barrière.» (p. 251)

> Ah, it is not readily to be imagined how much voluptuousness, lust, fierce joy are flattered by those sureties, or what is meant when one is able to say to oneself: 'I am alone here, I am at the world's end, withheld from every gaze, here no one can reach me, there is no creature that can come nigh where I am; no limits, hence no barriers; I am free.' (p. 412)

In this, more than any other of his works, Sade was creating the fantasy of total licence as an antidote to the restraint of his own circumstances. Writing in his cell in the Bastille every evening, Sade created an exaggerated libertine utopia in his unfettered imagination to make up for the physical freedoms he had lost. This utopia of total sexual and ethical licence is indeed only possible in the imaginary world conceived in and framed by prison walls. In this sense, the *120 Days* may be, as De Jean puts it, 'the ultimate work of prison literature'.[15]

Models for Silling are to be found, therefore, in the prisons of Vincennes and the Bastille itself where the work was composed, but also in the various provençal castles owned by the Sade family, especially La Coste, which was Donatien's preferred dwelling. For some critics, Silling is identical in construction to the La Coste château, where the young marquis had already spent so much of his time, and where he was known to have conducted a number of real-life orgies. There was even a special room there, equipped with 'mechanical devices' and other objects of a compromising nature, that Sade's lawyer, Gaufridy, was eventually required secretly to remove and destroy.[16] Despite such exotic features, however, there is nothing Gothic about the Sadean château, real or imaginary. Silling is a completely functional location, with no frightening dark spaces or gratuitous luxuries, where everything is designed for the protection and subsistence of the resident libertines and the satisfaction of their perverse sexual desires. Maurice Heine calls it a 'laboratory for research in experimental debauchery'.[17] There are separate dormitories and closets for each of the different classes of resident according to a scrupulous set of rules (see below), and a main hall designed in the semicircular shape of an amphitheatre to facilitate the narration of stories and the communal orgiastic activities that these stories are intended to promote:

> Il était d'une forme demi-circulaire, dans la partie cintrée se trouvaient quatre niches de glaces fort vastes et ornées chacune d'une excellente ottomane; ces quatre niches par leur construction faisaient absolument face au diamètre qui coupait le cercle, un trône élevé de quatre pieds était adossé au mur formant le diamètre, il était pour l'historienne [...] elle se trouvait alors placée comme est l'acteur sur un théâtre, et les auditeurs placés dans les niches se trouvaient l'être comme on l'est à l'amphithéâtre. (p. 58)

> Its shape was semicircular; set into the curving wall were four niches whose surfaces were faced with large mirrors, and each was provided with an excellent ottoman; these four recesses were so constructed that each faced the center of the circle; the diameter was formed by a throne, raised four feet above the floor and with its back to the flat wall, and it was intended for the storyteller [...] she was placed like an actor in a theater, and the audience in their niches found themselves situated as if observing a spectacle in an amphitheater. (pp. 237–38)

The victims sit on steps below the throne and within easy reach of the four libertines in their respective recesses. On either side of the throne stands a column to which victims can be attached and on which hang instruments of 'correction' and torture. Closets lead off from each recess, providing the individual libertine with a space for activities which he would rather conduct in private. The principal space of the novel is, nevertheless, both public and theatrical. The amphitheatre is designed so that the libertines can see and hear everything that occurs in every corner, in the other recesses as much as in the throne area; debauchery here is above all a shared activity, in which to be seen is as important as to see. Acting out their own desire, the four protagonists are also audience to that of others. What is staged at Silling in this theatre that is so emphatically cut off from the real world is the unreality of desire, but also its very *mise en scène* or representation, as narration itself becomes the dominant subject of the work. We shall return to the all-important place occupied by storytelling later. First, however, we need to look at broader stylistic and structural considerations.

The Prison-House of Number

Michel Foucault and Roland Barthes saw Sade's writing as marking the culmination of the classical age: the lightning bolt that splits Justine's body asunder (see Chapter 4) is seen by them as emblematic of this rupture with classicism.[18] Yet, as De Jean persuasively demonstrates, the preoccupation with symmetry and numerical precision above all, together with the work's emphasis on claustrophobic confinement, make *Les 120 Journées* far more classical than modern. For De Jean, Sade is inescapably classicism's heir in a number of important respects. Firstly, the opening repeats the pattern established by that most classical of French novels, *La Princesse de Clèves*, which begins by situating the novel in the last years of a reign. The setting is not, therefore, ahistorical, as some have claimed. Secondly, style and structure are informed by a 'contained and single-minded vision': the classical utopia is a fortress. De Jean contrasts this stylistic and structural containment with what she calls the 'picaresque dispersal' of *Justine* and *Juliette*.[19] This classical modelling has implications for the reader's role, to which we shall return later. First, we shall examine how the entire framework of *Les 120 Journées* is dictated by order and systematisation.

Number and symmetry dominate the structure and meanings of *Les 120 Journées* to an obsessive degree. In all Sade's writing, symmetry governs the constructions of the living tableaux, in which men and women are sexually linked to each other as in a chain or rosary beads, or the human towers of circus acrobats. In *Les 120 Journées*, these tableaux enjoy multiple permutations in pursuit of the ambition, expressed in the introduction, to cover all possible perverse scenarios, and of course, numerical is as crucial as physical symmetry. Among the round figures that shape all events in the work, the figure four holds a special place.[20] Four libertines have planned an orgy that is scheduled to last 120 days or four months, during which they will hear about and themselves enact 600 'passions' or perversions (Maurice Heine calls them 'modes of the libido') at the rate of 150 per month or five per day. These passions will be narrated by four storytellers, one for each month and for a different class of perversions, which are to be illustrated by 'case histories' of an increasingly violent nature, from the 'simple passions' of November via the 'passions de seconde classe ou double' of December, and the 'passions de troisième classe ou criminelles' of January, to the 'passions meurtrières ou de quatrième classe' of February.

Sade in fact only completed Part 1, but wrote detailed notes for the remaining three parts. These notes reveal a veritable mania for listing: there are lists of victims to be whipped, lists of rules governing the distribution of the victims' virginity and the type of virginity (vaginal or anal) owned by each of the four libertines, the date of defloration, etc., and most memorably, the final tallies of casualties and survivors. The victims' days are literally numbered according to a systematically planned timetable of torture and execution. On the last day, there will remain 16 survivors, organised in four groups of four. The fundamental structural principle of the work is, therefore, that of gradation and acceleration until a crescendo of murderous violence is reached in the final part. The work thus has the rhythm of a long and slow masturbation. Sade's aim is to cover all conceivable sexual manias, in other words, to produce a veritable encyclopaedia of sex.

As we have already seen, the four libertines are also accompanied by four spouses, four old women, eight boys, eight girls and eight fuckers. The latter were selected by four procuresses to recruit women and four pimps for men, while the overall planning had taken place at four supper parties held every week at four different country houses located at four different extremities of Paris. In a lengthy introduction, the author–narrator divides up each day into a rigid calendar of events, the most important of which is the daily narration of stories for four hours between six and ten o'clock in the evening. During this time, a 'quatrain' of two boys and two girls sit opposite each recess tied to each of the four libertines by a garland of artificial flowers. 'Story time' is followed by exactly four hours of orgy from ten until two in the morning, when all retire to their allocated rooms. Numbers play a determining role in many other aspects of the narrative, in particular as a means of defining and expressing the progressive increase in violence: 'Il fouette une fille neuf jours de suite, à cent coups le premier jour, toujours en doublant jusqu'au neuvième inclus' (p. 446) / 'He flogs a girl, giving her one hundred lashes the first day, two hundred the second, four hundred the third, etc., etc., and ceases on the ninth day' (p. 592). Peter Cryle shows how almost every aspect of the sexual acts represented is measured numerically, whether it be the size of penises and clitorises, the distance that sperm is thrown or even the numbers of turds produced by victims. Again, the figure four predominates, either on its own or in fractions or multiples – 'The unit of time for noncopulative erotic activities is usually a quarter of an hour [...]' – while penis dimensions are invariably four, eight or twelves inches exactly: 'What the sexual giant and the sexual dwarf have in common, in Sade's world, are foursquare organs' and turds invariably come in fours.[21]

What, then, are we to make of this obsession with arithmetical symmetry and especially with the figure four? Cryle tells us that the same figure is found in *Justine*:

> The Sadian rule, alluded to in *La nouvelle Justine*, is that wherever four wicked people are gathered together, they are likely to achieve the fullness of villainy. The circle thus formed is not the magic circle formed by a group of three [...] The Sadian circle is a stable one, an unremitting frame that adds to the virtues of the foursquare *those of perfect enclosure.*[22]

The menacing connotations of the figure four could not be more apt in the context of *Les 120 Journées*, in which even the reader feels trapped by the sense of claustrophobia generated by the repetitiousness of structure. The events of every day at Silling follow the same monotonous pattern, regulated by the clock, a monotony reflected in the repetition of set linguistic formulae at identical points in the narrative of each chapter: 'Duclos [...] reprit ainsi le fil de sa narration' (p. 111) / 'Duclos [...] resumed her narration in this wise' (p. 285), 'Duclos reprit en ces termes' (p. 154) / 'Duclos began to speak' (p. 324), 'on fut essayer de trouver dans quelques heures de repos des forces nécessaires à recommencer' (p. 200) / 'in a few hours of repose they sought to find the strength necessary to starting out afresh' (p. 365), 'La nuit vint mettre un peu de calme à tant d'intempérance, et rendre à nos libertins et des désirs et des forces' (p. 240) / 'Night came at last to restore some measure of calm to so much intemperance, and to restore as well our libertines' desires and faculties' (p. 402), 'chacun fut se coucher et prendre dans les bras de Morphée les forces nécessaires à resacrifier de nouveau à Vénus' (p. 257) /

'everyone retired to bed, and in Morpheus' arms recovered the strength requisite to make further sacrifices to Venus' (p. 418), etc. As regards the more general preoccupation with numerical symmetry, it is clear from Sade's correspondence during the 1780s that he read secret and symbolic meanings into the use of numbers by his wife and others,[23] and it is certainly not the case that this is his only work to have a significant numerical structure or in which numbers play a meaningful role: *La Philosophie dans le boudoir,* for instance, has seven characters in seven dialogues, while the symmetries of the Sadean orgy are well known.

From a general point of view, then, numbers have a semantic as well as a structural function in the Sadean text. Some have rightly suggested that the obsession with order that they represent (including its inversion) is partly the product of Sade's rigid formation in a Jesuit school, followed by his experiences of prison life.[24] For Éric Bordas, the reader's imagination is circumscribed within the temporal and spatial confines of the text just as the bodies of the characters are imprisoned within Silling Castle.[25] What the manic use of numbers manifests above all, therefore, is the need to control the textual expression and readerly consumption of a sexual imaginary that might otherwise destroy the mind in which it originated. The larger process of classification which numbers serve is, after all, a means of normalising the abnormal: to categorise sexual perversions is to define linguistically and to assert logical mastery over the seething chaos of the erotic imagination which is thereby rendered harmless as yet another object of study alongside the natural sciences. In the *120 Journées*, Sade's obsession with counting translates itself into lists of characters, the most striking being the closing list of those who perish and those who survive from each class of victim.[26] As Marcel Hénaff points out, a manic preoccupation with listing is one of the determining traits of obsessive behaviour and a manifestation of an anal character (see below).[27] What is being measured in such lists is not so much the content of the list itself as the subject's mastery of it. Desire cannot, perhaps, be fully understood, but counting the different forms it takes provides the subject with the satisfying illusion of control.

The author–narrator's controlling anality manifests itself also in a compulsive and inflexible gradation of the 600 passions, which prevents a mixing of activities from different 'classes' of sexual perversion and which leads to the need to explain the many omissions that this necessitates:

> [...] il se porta sur-le-champ à des excès avec elle qu'il nous est encore impossible de dire. Le lecteur qui voit comme nous sommes gênés dans ces commencements-ci pour mettre de l'ordre dans nos matières nous pardonnera de lui laisser encore bien des petits détails sous le voile. (p. 87)

> [...] he lost not an instant doing to her things too excessive for us to describe as yet. The reader will notice how hampered we are in these beginnings, and how stumbling are our efforts to give a coherent account of these matters; we trust he will forgive us for leaving the curtain drawn over a considerable number of little details. (p. 265)

> [...] il y fut encore en état d'y procéder à mille autres horreurs toutes plus singulières les unes que les autres, mais que l'ordre essentiel que nous nous sommes proposé ne nous permet pas encore de peindre à nos lecteurs. (p. 162)

> [...] he was again able to commit a thousand fresh horrors, each more extraordinary than the other, but not, we regret, to be described to the reader, or rather not yet, for the structure of our tale obliges us to defer them. (p. 331)

Cryle argues that having to recount 'whole series of mediocre episodes' in order 'not to diminish the impact of the greater' and the frequent justification of ellipses in the narrative are significant weaknesses, although he does concede that 'something is certainly gained by the presence of secret spaces', and that the gradual unfolding of activities may be perceived as erotic in itself.[28] Such holes in the narrative are, in my view, however, not simply reducible to a matter of poor narrative technique. While the concealment of certain details early on undoubtedly serves the work's graded structure, one is forced to ask why Sade chose this structure in the first place. In Chapter 6, I will suggest that the tension between concealing and revealing which such a structure generates has unconscious motivations related to the Sadean quest for transcendence. Here, I shall focus discussion on the anally retentive nature of the graded approach, and on the relevance of this feature to the structure and sexual contents of *Les 120 Journées*.

Before proceeding with this discussion, we first need to consider a precise and detailed definition of terms:

> Freud's second stage of libidinal development, occurring approximately between the ages of two and four, is known as the anal-sadistic stage or phase, and is characterised by an organisation of the libido under the primacy of the anal erotogenic zone. The object-relationship at this time is invested with meanings having to do with the function of defecation (expulsion/retention) and with the symbolic value of faeces. The anal-sadistic stage sees the strengthening of sado-masochism in correlation with the development of muscular control. [...] In his article on 'Character and Anal Eroticism', Freud had already linked character-traits surviving in the adult – the triad constituted by orderliness, parsimony and obstinacy – with anal eroticism in the child. [...] In 1924 Karl Abraham suggested that the anal-sadistic stage should be broken down into two phases on the basis of two contrasted types of behaviour *vis-à-vis* the object. In the first of these phases anal eroticism is linked to evacuation and the sadistic instinct to the destruction of the object; in the second, by contrast, anal eroticism is connected to retention and the sadistic instinct to possessive control. [...] How should the link between sadism and anal eroticism be understood? The suggestion is that sadism, being essentially bipolar (since its self-contradictory aim is to destroy the object but also, by mastering it, to preserve it) corresponds *par excellence* to the biphasic functioning of the anal sphincter (evacuation/retention) and its control.
>
> At the anal stage, the symbolic meanings of giving and withholding are ascribed to the activity of defecation; in

this connection, Freud brings out the symbolic equation: faeces = gift = money.[29]

The character both of Sade the man and of his writing corresponds in many salient respects to the above definitions of anality, which may therefore help to throw considerable light on the preoccupation with order and symmetry that informs the structures but also the sexual thematics of *Les 120 Journées*. Sade's biographers and critics have long noted the anal-retentive features of his personality. Sylvie Dangeville speaks of his truly neurotic relationship with money, as revealed by his letters to Gaufridy,[30] and Sade's many letters to his wife from prison, in which demands for food, clothing and other articles grow ever more extravagant and exacting, bear adequate testimony to his fussiness and obstinacy. This correspondence also displays a veritable mania for numbers, for instance, in the scrupulous records he kept of his masturbations.[31] These aspects of his personality are clearly reflected in the tight structures of the narrative and also in the many rules to which the libertines, as well as the victims, are subject. These rules help to generate a tension between freedom and restraint, similar to that between retention and release that underlies the anal character. Of particular interest here is the thematic preoccupation in *Les 120 Journées* with defecation and the rules that accompany it, which seem to constitute a literalisation of the metaphorical and symbolic anality described by Freud and identifiable in the work's narrative structures.[32] Moreover, the link between excrement and money is especially illuminating in the context of what Bernard Noël calls Silling's 'economic totalitarianism', according to which human bodies and their waste products are just so much merchandise.[33] On a purely erotic level, the thematic of defecation in the novel is most closely related to the second phase of anal eroticism described by Abraham, in which retention and sadistic control are foregrounded.

In addition to the detailed examples of coprophilia and coprophagia narrated by Duclos in the first month (her tales focus on the eating of turds produced by female prostitutes) and emulated by her libertine audience (during the narratives of the fourteenth day, for example, Curval shits into the fourteen-year-old Sophie's mouth), there are strict rules governing the defecation of the spouses and other victims. The latter are brutally punished if their chamber pots are found to be full in the mornings, and there are similar consequences if they are found to have wiped their bottoms without permission. Eventually, it is forbidden to shit anywhere, or even to fart, except directly into the mouth of a libertine. Just as details of stronger perversions are withheld until a time deemed appropriate for their revelation, so the defecation of victims is placed under systems of sadistic control by the libertines which ensure the retention of faeces until a similarly appropriate time. Thus, the anality of the structure reflects itself in and is reflected by the sexual thematics of the text. Everything has a value in a society in which even human waste becomes a part of the process of barter and exchange, as victims buy freedom from pain with their shit.[34]

Apart from the violent and murderous passions of the unwritten Parts 2–4, coprophilia is probably the most transgressive activity represented in *Les 120 Journées*, and for Sade, it is transgression that is the basis of all eroticism: what excites the duke and his friends is the *idea* of breaking taboos: 'ce n'est pas l'objet du libertinage qui nous anime, mais l'idée du mal,' declares Blangis to unanimous approval, 'c'est pour le mal seul qu'on bande et non pas pour l'objet' (p. 199) / 'it is not the object of libertine intentions which fires us, but the idea of evil, and that consequently it is thanks only to evil and only in the name of evil one stiffens, not thanks to the object' (p. 364) – a notion echoed by Duclos, who speaks of 'cette flamme libertine qui ne manque jamais de paraître chaque fois qu'on brise un frein' (p. 320) / 'that libertine flame which never fails to appear every time one violates some prohibition, abolishes some restraint' (p. 476). Other transgressive acts depicted in Duclos's stories and promptly re-enacted by the libertines include urine-drinking, armpit-smelling, saliva-swallowing, fart-swallowing, nostril-licking, the drinking of menstrual blood, and corpse-fucking. Some of these activities, the last two for example, are transgressive because they infringe societal and religious taboos, but all share with coprophagia the conquest of natural feelings of repulsion. Sade inverts aesthetic norms, replacing the sweet fragrances of youth and beauty with the foul-smelling and the ugly as the basis of sexual attraction[35] – bombarded as we are in our culture with images of the eternally young and the physically perfect, some readers might find the Sadean aesthetic a refreshing contrast:

> [...] tandis que des objets de la plus grande beauté et de la plus extrême fraîcheur sont là sous leurs yeux, prêts à satisfaire leurs plus légers désirs, c'est avec ce que la nature et le crime ont déshonoré, ont flétri, c'est avec l'objet le plus sale et le plus dégoûtant que nos deux paillards, en extase, vont goûter les plus délicieux plaisirs ... (p. 161)

> [...] even though objects of the greatest beauty and in the best condition are there before their eyes and ready to brave anything in order to satisfy the least of their desires, even so it is with what Nature and villainy have dishonored, have withered, it is with the filthiest and least appetizing object our two rakes, presently beside themselves, are about to taste the most delicious pleasures ... (p. 330)

> – Eh! sacredieu, dit Curval, est-il donc besoin d'être jeune et jolie pour faire couler du foutre? Encore un coup, c'est dans toutes les jouissances la chose sale qui attire le foutre, ainsi plus elle est sale et plus il doit voluptueusement se répandre. (p. 183)

> 'Ah, by God!' said Curval, 'will you now say that youth and pretty looks are indispensable to an elicitation of fuck? Why, once again 'tis the filthy act that causes the greatest pleasure: and the filthier it be, the more voluptuously fuck is shed.' (p. 349)

Transgressive activities generate an excitement associated with any extreme behaviour, but sometimes it is the contrast between the beautiful and the ugly that is found sexually arousing – as when a very pretty young girl shits or vomits into the libertine's mouth. The greater the contrast, the greater the pleasure, a principle that most of us will not be able to follow to the Sadean extreme. Although many readers will be aroused by the description of some of these transgressive acts and will even be inspired to include them among their own sexual practices (fellatio, cunnilingus, *soixante-neuf* and even 'golden showers' can provide hours of fun if you've never tried them!), most will wish to draw the line at shit-eating or violence. Both are excessive forms of behaviour that are more likely to distance the reader from the text than to stimulate his desire. Admittedly, any feelings of disgust that the reader might have are perhaps lessened to some degree by the representation of turds in the text as the source of gastronomic as well as erotic pleasure. Indeed, the emphasis on the former might well be said to attenuate the latter. Peter Cryle suggests that the aestheticisation of turds as food amounts to the denial of excrement as waste matter.[36] The special diet of the victims ensures turds that melt in the mouth: 'ils étaient plus moelleux, plus fondants, d'une délicatesse infiniment plus grande' (p. 303) / 'they were more mellow, softer, dissolved more readily, had an infinitely more subtle flavor' (p. 461), while the knight of Malta of Duclos's story keeps a veritable larder of turds, maturing like cheeses. Despite this culinary recuperation, however, praise of the turd's gastronomic delights might provoke a humorous but rarely erotic response.

Beatrice Fink stresses the metaphorical and symbolic significance of excrement in *Les 120 Journées* within the wider thematics of consumption which she places at the very centre of the novel. *Les 120 Journées*, she reminds us, is 'the story of a magnificent meal of 600 courses'. In addition to the frequent restorative collations enjoyed by the libertines, and washed down by liberal quantities of alcohol (orgiastic excess is always accompanied by and partly dependent on over-indulgence at the table), eating is dominant in the work's sexual repertory, in which 'sucking, licking and devouring' are commonplace activities, and both coprophagy and cannibalism play an important symbolic role in a gastronomic scenario whose profound significance is related to Sadean megalomania:

> Le culte et la divinisation de l'excrément constituent une satire de la religion; ensuite, rôle central dans la combi-

> natoire qui permet de se manger indéfiniment les unes les autres, de se manger soi-même, de se manger à travers d'autres [...] Fantasmagories de l'insatiable libertin qui actualise son désir par l'introjection, son rêve de toute-puissance par l'anéantissement de l'autre en le privant de nourriture ou en le mangeant. J'absorbe, donc je suis.[37]

> The cult and the deification of excrement constitute a satire of religion and also play a central role in the scheme which allows the libertines to eat each other, or themselves, or to eat themselves through others [...] fantasies of the insatiable libertine who realises his desire through introjection, and his dream of omnipotence by depriving the other of food or by eating him in order to annihilate him. I absorb, therefore I am.

Readings such as Fink's draw on psychoanalytic theory to emphasise the excremental's symbolic meanings. Awareness of this symbolism, as of the text's obsessive preoccupation with symmetry and numbers, has a derealising effect for the modern reader, focusing his attention on process rather than on erotic content. Indeed, it is *the mise en scène* of this process, the very performance of pornographic storytelling at Silling that occupies centre stage, the features of which now deserve some consideration.

We have spoken already of the theatricality of the setting and of the centrality of the *mise en scène* of narration: the *historiennes* hold the stage for most of the time, relating episodes experienced or witnessed by them which illustrate the 600 passions to be covered, and provoking the libertines to act out what they have heard, in ironic illustration within the text of 'the pornographic effect': as intradiegetic listeners, the four friends effectively substitute for the male reader, showing him what to do.[38] However, the reader is distanced from the text by not being addressed directly, in addition to being distanced from the action narrated in that text by the storytelling situation. This distancing inevitably has the effect of diminishing the erotic impact on the reader. Furthermore, these 'embedded' narratives are framed by the author's controlling narration which, far from seeking to arouse the reader located outside the text, contains frequent references to the narrative process within it. There are the many lists – of characters, of errors that the author intends to correct ('Omissions que j'ai faites dans cette introduction' (p. 84) / 'Omissions made in the Introduction', 'Fautes que j'ai faites' (p. 425) / 'Errors I have made'), warnings to the reader of what is to come – 'je conseille [...] à tout dévôt de laisser là tout de suite [cet ouvrage] s'il ne veut pas être scandalisé [...]' (p. 37) / 'I advise the overmodest to lay my book aside at once if he would not be scandalized [...]' (p. 219) – and instructions on how to use the work, in the manner of a foreword to a school textbook:

> Sans doute, beaucoup de tous les écarts que tu vas voir peints te déplairont, on le sait, mais il s'en trouvera quelques-uns qui t'échaufferont au point de te coûter du foutre [...] choisis et laisse le reste sans déclamer contre ce reste, uniquement parce qu'il n'a pas le talent de te plaire [...] Quant à la diversité, sois assuré qu'elle est exacte, étudie bien celle des passions qui te paraît ressembler sans nulle différence à une autre et tu verras que cette différence existe [...]
>
> Au reste, on a fondu ces six cents passions dans le récit des historiennes. C'est encore une chose dont il faut que le lecteur soit prévenu; il aurait été trop monotone de les détailler autrement et une à une sans les faire entrer dans un corps de récit. Mais comme quelque lecteur peu au fait de ces sortes de matières pourrait peut-être confondre les passions désignées avec l'aventure ou l'événement simple de la vie de la conteuse, on a distingué avec soin chacune de ces passions par un trait en marge, au-dessus duquel est le nom qu'on peut donner à cette passion. Ce trait est la ligne juste où commence le récit de cette passion, et il y a toujours un alinéa où elle finit. (pp. 76–7)

> Many of the extravagances you are about to see illustrated will doubtless displease you, yes, I am well aware of it, but there are amongst them a few which will warm you to the point of costing you some fuck [...] choose and let lie the rest without declaiming against that rest simply because it does not have the power to please you. [...] As

> for the diversity, it is authentic, you may be sure of it; study closely that passion which to your first consideration seems perfectly to resemble another, and you will see that a difference does exist [...]
>
> We have, moreover, blended these six hundred passions into the storytellers' narratives. That is one more thing whereof the reader were well to have foreknowledge: it would have been too monotonous to catalogue them one by one outside the body of the story. But as some reader not much learned in these matters might perhaps confuse the designated passions with the adventure or simple event in the narrator's life, each of these passions has been carefully distinguished by a marginal notation: a line, above which is the title that may be given the passion. This mark indicates the exact place where the account of the passions begins, and the end of the paragraph always indicates where it finishes. (pp. 254–55)[39]

This self-reflexivity acts like the number symmetry to de-realise and de-eroticise the text, moving the focus away from sexual desire to writing and discourse. Overall, in fact, *Les 120 Journées* functions inefficiently as a work of pornography, since, as we have seen, the reader's interest is constantly displaced from any erotic effect to the ways in which sexuality is represented through linguistic, arithmetical and other formal structures. Moreover, on one level, the work reads as a parody both of the dictionary as a genre (immensely popular in the eighteenth century, the *Encyclopédie* itself being the most obvious example) and of the scientific method.[40] For Philippe Roger, what Sade is attacking above all in his introduction is the scientific claim to the coldness of objectivity: this work, on the contrary, will aim to 'get the reader hot' ('échauffer le lecteur').[41] Despite this aim, however, parody and eroticism are essentially incompatible, as Jean-Marie Goulemot points out: 'Since parody supposes a reading on two registers, it is fundamentally opposed to erotic writing, which is always strictly conditioned and self-sufficient.'[42] Related to this parodic effect, the general pedagogical character of the work equally detracts from its effectiveness as an erotic text.[43] The whole novel after all is an extended lesson: subtitled 'L'École du libertinage' / 'The School of libertinage', it functions as a catalogue of perversions, brilliantly exemplifying modern teaching methodology according to which theoretical explanation is immediately followed by detailed illustration and finally student participation in practical experimentation. There is, as Goulemot points out, nothing particularly new about this – 'The narrative recounted by the "historiennes" in the *Cent-vingt journées de Sodome* is merely a variation on the pedagogical and excitatory use of erotic literature so much a topos of other works in the genre'[44] – although Sade's 'calendar'-style format gives the lesson a rather original framework.

If the reader will find it hard to respond to the work erotically, as the reader of pornography might, what then is his position? The narrator is sometimes on intimate terms with his reader, who, in the introduction to the work, is addressed as 'tu' as well as 'vous' and always as 'cher lecteur' / 'dear reader' or 'ami lecteur' / 'friend reader'. (Sade addressed even himself in the polite 'you' form of 'vous'!) The reader, in other words, is not just a mate but a soulmate. Some have argued that the narrator sidles up to the reader in this way the better to control him. For instance, Joan De Jean develops a well-argued case against readerly freedom in *Les 120 Journées*. For her, there are just two voices in the text: a voice of liberation and a voice of control, and the controlling voice is characteristic of the classical tradition. The very material nature of the manuscript itself, she maintains, is rebarbative to the reader, 'a narrative without margins, almost without paragraphs, with few of the divisions or ruptures that conventionally serve to break the flow of narrative for readerly consumption, a text without the *failles* Barthes considered essential to readerly *jouissance*'. As for the reader aides, these are the 'very antithesis of modernism' in that, rather than liberating the reader, they actually have the effect of keeping demands on him to a minimum:

> *The 120*'s author/narrator refuses to allow the reader to forget or to become confused. In the process, he also attempts to deny him any interpretive freedom [...] *the 120*'s authorial dictator moves to take over the reader's space.

De Jean sees the master teacher's voice in the discourse itself which is not really a dialogue but a 'continuous and depersonalised flow' to use Philippe Roger's expression:

> The fact that all those in power sound alike and speak with the same language restrains the reader's urge to identification and projection. The dominant discourse in *The 120* is a monolithic force that seeks to hold Sade's reader in check, to turn him into the victim of the master who has thought of everything [...] The narrator holds out to the reader the freedom to use any of the encyclopedic building blocks he may find useful to construct his own encyclopedia. He then makes it clear that as he has arranged them, these blocks form a complete and perfectly ordered entity.[45]

Peter Cryle similarly refers to 'forms of disciplined erotic response inscribed thematically in the text' which function as part of a 'closed circularity of modelling' to which the reader is also subject: the libertines control the storytellers who are given very precise instructions on what to say and when to say it; the former then model their behaviour on the stories which they themselves have commissioned.[46] There is obviously considerable merit in these arguments, particularly with regard to the existence of a single authorial voice in the Sadean narrative. But instead of accepting the passive role seemingly inscribed for him into the text, the reader is perfectly capable of resisting the text's totalitarianism. The multiplicity of narrative voices, moreover, helps to decentre the source of narratorial authority in the text. Even the main narrator (who is not of course to be confused with the author, Sade) claims to be non-omniscient, not to know everything about the behaviour of his characters:

> Des propos on passa aux actions, le duc s'échauffa, et je ne sais ni pourquoi ni comment, mais on prétendit que Thérèse porta quelque temps ses marques. (p. 272)

> For from words they passed to deeds, the Duc got hot again, and I don't know just why it happened or how, but

> they say Thérèse bore the marks of his affection for weeks. (p. 431)
>
> [...] il m'a toujours été impossible de découvrir ce qui se passait dans ces infernaux cabinets. (p. 361)
>
> [...] I have never been able to discover what went on in those infernal closets. (p. 514)

Many such protestations of ignorance on the author's part may simply be devices required by the gradation of the passions, although the phrasing of the second of the above examples suggests a permanent inability to disclose.[47] Whatever their authorial motivation, these ellipses have a positive liberating effect on the reader, who must have recourse to his imagination in order to fill in the gaps.

Such aporia, together with the many references and addresses to the reader during the course of the narrative, help to create a text that is fundamentally reader-centred.[48] This 'reader-centredness' makes it hard to believe that the work was never intended to be published, as some critics have suggested.[49] Indeed, at the end of Part 1, an observation by the author suggests that Sade anticipated staggering publication in several successive volumes: 'nous ne ferons pas attendre la seconde [partie] au public, si nous voyons qu'il accueille bien la première' (p. 423) / 'for whose second part we will not keep the public waiting if to our consideration it has kindly received what we have chronicled so far' (p. 569). The warning notices posted early in the text ensure that the reader is not taken by surprise, and the recapitulatory tables and thumbnail sketches of the characters are user-friendly *aides-mémoire* designed to assist rather than control readings of the text. Most importantly, as with any dictionary or encyclopaedia, the modern reader used to zapping and sound bites can dip in and out of the work as he pleases. The narrator–chef offers his diners a sexual menu of 600 different dishes, from which they can order a meal to suit their own tastes. Despite the house rules there is nothing to prevent the reader from skipping passages that he dislikes (there being no conventional plot developments in each chapter that require the reader's attention), especially in Parts 2–4 the lists of which are even more episodic and fragmented than the completed chapters of Part 1. This work may not deliver the *jouissance* promised by the author, then, but it does offer the reader the opportunity to learn how others have achieved it.

Conclusion

In the end, *Les 120 Journées* does not fit easily into any literary category or genre: not perhaps a novel in the strict sense of the word (there is no sustained plot development), not exactly theatre either (although containing many theatrical elements), and too much of a commentary on the process of erotic writing to be successful as erotica per se (for some, the work is, in any case, more about violence than about sex). And despite its undoubted similarity to the modern sexology manual, and its pretentions to the status of a scientific study, there are those who refuse to see it as a precursor to the work of Freud or Krafft-Ebing. Chantal Thomas rightly argues, for example, that, while Freud and Krafft-Ebing view any departure from normality as unhealthy, Sade actively advocates this.[50] Yet, Sade's first major work will prove to be a little of all of these things for those readers imaginative enough and broad-minded enough to make the necessary links.

Les 120 Journées de Sodome may not be the most compelling of the Marquis's writings – it is perhaps just too obsessive and repetitive, lacking the imaginative sweep and philosophical depth of *Juliette* or *Justine* – but it does have innovative features: the performativity of narration, the staging of the pornographic effect, as words and images are seen to give rise to acts, are of undeniable interest in the context of both critical theory and the current debate concerning the influence of pornography. For the Sade scholar, it is the nursery of Sadean philosophy and thematics, containing seeds that Sade's later works will nurture and grow to maturity. The Society of the Friends of Crime and the Sainte Marie-des-Bois episodes in *Juliette* and *Justine* respectively, for example, clearly represent attempts to reconstruct aspects of the lost work.

As regards influence beyond the Sadean corpus, the work has arguably had more impact than any of Sade's other writings. Its influence on modern literature is indisputable though perhaps less easy to document than that on twentieth-century cinema. Luis Buñuel's 1930 film *L'Âge d'Or* was heavily inspired by it.[51] The film constituted a savage attack on both the Catholic Church and conservative politics, depicting Christ as an absurd and ineffectual figure who preaches submissiveness and is unable to prevent murder. The controversy that surrounded it eventually led to the disruption of a screening in Paris by the extreme right who rioted in the cinema, smashing seats and throwing ink at the screen, and to its banning for over 50 years until 1981. *The 120 Days* was also the model for Pier Paolo Pasolini's extraordinary political allegory, *Salò* (1975), named after the small town in Northern Italy where the Germans installed Mussolini as a puppet ruler during the Second World War.[52]

While such de-historicising adaptations represent dangerous misreadings of a work that is not reducible to any political ideology, nonetheless, it is perhaps for the warnings it sounds beyond the purely literary dimension that *Les 120 Journées de Sodome* is most valuable: the concentration camps of the last century might have been modelled on Silling Castle, while Sade's four fictional Frankensteins come to life in our post-industrial society as the high-tech criminals who turn themselves and the rest of us into simulacra, reducing humans to body parts and the body to its machine functions. To read Sade against the background of our own monstrosity is sometimes the most frightening thing of all. Indeed, this is what makes Sade unreadable for some: not the obscenity or even the sadism, but the sheer hopelessness of his vision of the world and of human nature.

3

… and the Word was Made Flesh: *La Philosophie dans le boudoir*

Published in 1795, shortly after Sade's release from Picpus, *La Philosophie dans le boudoir* fizzes with self-confidence and is by far the most light-hearted (some have called it the least cruel) of his libertine works. The language is certainly obscene and there are moments of sadism, but these features are counterbalanced by a tongue-in-cheek and often self-reflexive humour that is both verbal and physical. The work also operates on a number of complex levels – dramatic dialogue, philosophical and political polemic, literary parody, Chaucerian farce – which make it Sade's most innovative and, at the same time, most accessible piece of writing.

At one important level, the work reads as a savagely ironic denunciation of Robespierre's 'virtuous republic', founded on repression and the guillotine. *La Philosophie* was begun during Sade's confinement in the Picpus sanatorium in 1794, in a room from which he could see the guillotine and its operations. (It had by now been moved from the Place de la Concorde because of complaints about the smell of blood.) Its victims were even buried in the grounds of the sanatorium, '1,800 in thirty-five days', and Sade's letters leave little doubt that the horror of this spectacle marked him profoundly. As Donald Thomas puts it,

> If Sade had watched the afternoon executions, the last moments of the victims and the spouting of blood as the heads were severed before the faces of those who were soon to take their turn, it must have occurred to him that nothing in his fiction had yet equalled such ghastliness.[1]

Not surprisingly, then, *La Philosophie dans le boudoir* is strongly satirical in character and conception (a feature of Sade's writing that has often been underplayed), in appearing to justify vice and, above all, murder, on the grounds that such things are good for a republic. Set some time between 1789 and 1793, the work positions itself unambiguously in the middle of the French Revolution and can be read as a powerful critique of its aims and methods. *Français, encore un effort, si vous voulez être républicains*, a polemical pamphlet intercalated in the middle of the work, is itself, on one level, a pastiche of the many political and philosophical *libelles* or underground pamphlets circulating in the revolutionary period. Chantal Thomas points out that the freedom of the press, announced in August 1789, led to a veritable explosion of journalism and pornographic publications, and that these *libelles*, which had been heavily censored under the *ancien régime*, now proliferated both in Paris and in the provinces.[2] But the work's main impact has always been as sexual pedagogy. Here, Sade was almost certainly influenced by two earlier models. The first of these was *L'École des Filles*, produced by Michel Millot and Jean l'Ange in 1665. Published in England in 1688 as *The School of Venus*, this relatively innocent tale concerns the sexual education of a young girl by her older female cousin. The second, Nicolas Chorier's more sexually explicit *L'Académie des dames* of about 1660, consists of a number of dialogues in which one young woman instructs another in the art of love-making. The similarly dialogic form of *La Philosophie dans le boudoir* is obviously a development of Chorier's technique.[3]

Unlike its predecessors, however, Sade's title promises to take the reader into a specifically feminine space, which is also associated with physical relaxation (though not with sleep), the word *boudoir* (mistranslated in English editions as 'bedroom') meaning an elegant salon into which ladies can retire (*Petit Robert*). The title itself, therefore, seems to sum up the whole Sadean project, which is to bring the body, in particular the female body, back into philosophy.[4] The work's subtitle, 'ou les instituteurs immoraux'/ 'or the immoral teachers', reflects the author's growing boldness at this time, explicitly acknowledging its immoral content. Suggesting its status as possibly the first modern work of sex education for young girls, the subtitle also implies the legitimisation of bodily desires within an accepted framework of instruction – the school classroom – while the adjective 'immoral' undermines this legitimacy, announcing with titular pride the illicit pleasures associated with the sexual corruption of innocence. The binarism of both title and subtitle encapsulates the two dominant impulses in Sade: the intellectual and the erotic, the mind and the body, the proselytising and the transgressive.

The text is also introduced by an epigraph, which has been much commented upon, and a dedicatory foreword. The epigraph, 'La mère en prescrira la lecture à sa fille' / 'Mothers will prescribe the reading of this work to their daughters', is an ironic echo of the epigraph to a pornographic and anti-monarchist pamphlet that had appeared four years earlier in 1791 with the fussy title, *Fureurs utérines de Marie-Antoinette, femme de Louis XVI, Au manège. Et dans tous les bordels de Paris*: 'La mère en proscrira la lecture à sa fille' / 'Mothers will *proscribe* the reading of this work to their daughters.' As Chantal Thomas observes, the irony of 'uterine fury' is cruel when one thinks of the play's tragicomic *dénouement*, in which the young heroine sews up her mother's vagina to prevent her from 'giving her any more little brothers and sisters'.[5] Sade's epigraph also, of course, draws attention to a central theme of the work, the antagonism between mothers and daughters, which the violence of the final scene brings bubbling to the surface. We shall return to this scene later. Angela Carter claims that the word 'proscribe' in fact appears in the second edition of Sade's obscene playlet, and she sees this vowel change as evidence of vacillation on the author's part:

> He acknowledges to the full the mutual antagonism between mother and daughter. But should the mother or the daughter be enlightened as to the nature and extent of this antagonism? Which one of them should have the benefit of the lesson? Or should they both?[6]

Probably because she was unaware of the existence of the 1791 pamphlet, Carter thus seems to ignore the line's ironic charge which is almost certainly all that the author intended, but her analysis does nevertheless identify reception of the work as an issue of some importance.

The dedication 'Aux Libertins' / 'To Libertines' addresses the work to 'Voluptueux de tous les âges et de tous les sexes' / 'Voluptuaries of all ages, of every sex', and goes on to break such readers down into three groups: 'femmes lubriques' / 'lewd women', 'jeunes filles' / 'young maidens', and 'aimables débauchés' / 'amiable debauchees'. Each group is encouraged to emulate a character from the play. 'Lewd women' should model themselves on the voluptuous Saint-Ange in taking pleasure as their only law; 'jeunes filles trop longtemps contenues dans les liens absurdes et dangereux d'une vertu fantastique et d'une religion dégoûtante' / 'young maidens, too long constrained by a fanciful Virtue's absurd and dangerous bonds and by those of a disgusting religion' are instructed to imitate the 'fiery' Eugénie, Sade's young heroine, and destroy the precepts taught them by their 'imbecile' parents, while 'aimables débauchés, vous qui, depuis votre jeunesse, n'avez plus d'autres freins que vos désirs et d'autres lois que vos caprices' / 'amiable debauchees, you who since youth have known no limits but those of your desires and who have been governed by your caprices alone' are told to study the 'cynical' Dolmancé, whose lechery and gratification of the senses knows no bounds. Clearly, the implied reader is, for the most part, already corrupted, and there is no attempt to win over the morally sensitive, no pretence of a defence of virtue (as in the dedication to the first published version of *Justine*, which had appeared four years earlier).[7] The imperatives addressed to this reader have become less wheedling, more imperious: 'nourrissez-vous de ses principes' / 'nourish yourselves upon (this work's) principles', 'n'écoutez que ces passions délicieuses' / 'harken only to these delicious promptings', etc.

By 1795, it seems, Sade's need to be accepted by the moral majority, if not his fear of the censor, had vanished. Like the *Justine* and *Juliette* volumes, *La Philosophie dans le boudoir* was certainly published anonymously and, like them, the place of publication alleged to be Holland, essential precautions at this time for any works containing obscene material, but all the works appearing from the mid-1790s onwards seem to project a defiance absent from Sade's earlier published writings. Is this change of attitude attributable to an optimism born of a greater personal freedom? We should remember that Sade narrowly escaped the guillotine in 1794 and was released the same year following Robespierre's own execution; there was also more political liberty under the less repressive five-man Directory which succeeded Robespierre. Another explanation might be found in the increasingly desperate financial situation of a Citizen Sade, who had lost all the lands and property associated with his former aristocratic title. Whatever the reasons for this new-found boldness, I argue in the next chapter that it has some negative consequences for his novel-writing – consequences which by their very nature cannot be said to affect the dramatic dialogues of *La Philosophie dans le boudoir*. With increasing age – Sade is now 55 years old and has spent over 13 of his best years behind bars – it is possible, too, that a painful awareness of the brevity of youth leads him more and more to throw caution to the winds. Take whatever pleasures you can in this sad world, he urges the reader in the foreword's closing lines – one indication among many to be found throughout Sade's writings of their intensely personal origins. Mme de Saint-Ange reiterates the point in her instruction of Eugénie:

> Profite du plus heureux temps de ta vie: elles ne sont que trop courtes, ces heureuses années de nos plaisirs! Si nous sommes assez heureuses pour en avoir joui, de délicieux souvenirs nous consolent et nous amusent encore dans notre vieillesse. Les avons-nous perdues? ... des regrets amers, d'affreux remords nous déchirent et se joignent aux tourments de l'âge, pour entourer de larmes et de ronces les funestes approches du cercueil ... (p. 71)

> Profit from the fairest period in your life; these golden years of our pleasure are only too few and too brief. If we are so fortunate as to have enjoyed them, delicious memories console and amuse us in our old age. These years lost ... and we are racked by bitterest regrets, gnawing remorse conjoins with the sufferings of age and the fatal onset of the grave is all tears and brambles ... (p. 221)[8]

This devil-may-care attitude does, at least, unambiguously answer the question of intended reception raised by Angela Carter: *La Philosophie dans le boudoir* is a work to be read by 'young maidens', willing to be debauched, and certainly as much by female as by male libertines of all ages, but there is no mention of the maidens' pious mothers. As the pubescent pupil of Dolmancé and his friends, to whom almost all the speeches are addressed, Eugénie essentially functions as the reader's representative within the text. We are thus led to identify with her youthful rebelliousness and open-mindedness, as well as with the perspectives of her gender. The now middle-aged author's fantasies are focused on a youth to which he no longer belongs and whose passing he bitterly regrets, and, as always, it is a young female that takes centre stage. Like Justine, Eugénie is a virgin, but unlike her, she is not just willing but eager to experience sexual pleasure. This time, Sade creates a young female with whom he can directly identify and who symbolically represents his own lost and lamented youth.

The actors of this obscene tragicomedy are all fit, healthy and, above all, young, Dolmancé at 36 being the eldest of the whole group. Even Eugénie's mother, the devout yet beautiful Mme de Mistival, is 32 'at the most'. Apart from Dolmancé, an active and passive sodomite, described as 'le plus profond séducteur, l'homme le plus corrompu, le plus dangereux' (p. 25) / 'the most profound seducer, the most corrupt, the most dangerous man' (p. 191), the other libertines are all under 30. Eugénie, whose sexual initiation is the pretext for the party, is a delicious young virgin of 15. (Her father, himself a well-known libertine and one of the richest merchants of Paris, has given permission for all that both daughter and mother are to undergo.) The bisexual Mme de Saint-Ange, who will play a leading role in Eugénie's debauchery, is 26. Her brother, the Chevalier de Mirval, is at 20 the youngest of the libertines, and his youthful vigour seems emblematic of a sexual athleticism, which is also enhanced by the extraordinary size of his penis: 'Ah! ma chère amie, quel monstrueux membre!' cries Eugénie on seeing it for the first time, 'A peine puis-je l'empoigner!' (p. 136) / 'Oh, dearest friend, what a monstrous member! ... I can scarcely get my hand around it!' (p. 261).

He prefers women, but can be persuaded to engage in sodomy with 'an agreeable man' like Dolmancé. In addition to these five principals, there are two minor characters: Augustin, a young gardener of 'about eighteen or twenty', who is even more impressively endowed than the Chevalier, his member measuring 14 inches in length and having a circumference of eight and a half, and Lapierre, Dolmancé's similarly well-equipped but syphilitic valet.

Seven actors who, in the course of seven 'dialogues' or scenes, will re-enact Christianity's founding myth, inverting its central message as the Eve-like Eugénie's rejection of God and her passage from sexual innocence to sexual knowledge are celebrated rather than lamented.[9] As we shall see, it is the pious mother, not the sacrilegious and debauched daughter, who is finally expelled from this perverse paradise of the body. Like its mythical model, their own Eden is a 'delightful boudoir', a privileged and almost timeless space isolated from the outside world, but, unlike the Christian version, the joys associated with it are physical, not spiritual. The only serpent is Augustin's delightfully monstrous penis – 'Allons, Eugénie,' Dolmancé warns his fascinated pupil as the gardener is about to ejaculate, 'le serpent va vomir son venin' (p. 148) / 'Look sharp, Eugénie, mind, the serpent is about to disgorge its venom' (p. 268) – and Eugénie and her mentors display an awareness of their nudity that is completely without shame.

Indeed, this nakedness is not merely a state of undress, but a total laying bare of the human body, as Eugénie is given an advanced lesson in male and female anatomy, both external and internal. The typically Sadean rhythm of dissertation alternating with orgy, of theory immediately put into practice, follows pedagogically sound principles, of which Rousseau would have approved.[10] Though Dolmancé's lesson contains some erroneous and largely male-centred notions of female biology – for example, that male sperm are alone responsible for the creation of life – Sade's text here displays a remarkable knowledge of the female body and of female sexual response, and some, though not all, of the views on sexuality that it contains appear strikingly modern. Women can only orgasm through stimulation of the clitoris, Saint-Ange implies when she tells her pupil, 'là gît toute la sensibilité des femmes' (p. 43) / 'there lies all a woman's power of sensation' (p. 204), and she expresses pro-abortion sentiments with which many a twenty-first century feminist would sympathise: 'nous sommes toujours maîtresses de ce que nous portons dans notre sein' (p. 115) / 'we are always mistress of what we carry in our womb' (p. 249).

There is also enlightened advice on contraceptive methods of the time (contraception, Eugénie is persuaded, is far preferable to abortion). Options range from mechanical methods (the use of dildos, sponges, condoms) to natural methods (hand relief, fellatio, cunnilingus, 'sixty-nine'). Among the latter, masturbation and sodomy, which the 'absurd' doctrines of Christianity have held to be mortal sins, are seen to be especially helpful. The defence of sodomy as universally practised by both sexes is found throughout Sade's writing and was revolutionary on both a political and a religious level at a time when the act was a capital offence. As for masturbation, Eugénie is given accurate and detailed lessons in the best techniques for both men and women that would not be out of place in a modern sex education manual. Again, Sade's view was startlingly enlightened for a century in which semen loss was widely believed to cause syphilis (which by now had reached epidemic proportions) and self-abuse directly linked to insanity. In 1760, a Swiss physician, Samuel Auguste André David Tissot, had published *Onanism, or a Treatise upon the Disorders Produced by Masturbation*, in which onanism was described as a pathology leading to illnesses of all kinds and eventually death.[11]

The positive advocacy of both sodomy and masturbation derives from the central theme of Sade's philosophy of sexuality: the enjoyment of sex for its own sake rather than for the purposes of procreation, a view running counter to the entire Christian tradition but that Dolmancé claims to be intended by nature. Does nature not allow the loss of sperm in all kinds of situations, other than for propagation? If women's sexual function is solely reproductive, why is their reproductive capacity limited to such a relatively short period in their lives? Clearly, argues Dolmancé, it is natural for human beings to have sex for pleasure alone. Now, it is true that throughout his entire work Sade expresses an intense dislike of the reproductive aspects of femininity that many have sought to explain in terms of a negative Oedipus complex, and we shall examine this theory in more detail in the discussion of the final scene. Whatever the impulses behind it, however, this view of sex as a source of pleasure, free of guilt and unshackled by the Christian institution of marriage, was especially liberating for women. If women have been created by nature 'to fuck' and 'be fucked from morning till night' ('fouts, en un mot, fouts' pp. 68–9 and 'se faire foutre du matin au soir' p. 73), then they were obviously not intended to be monogamous: 'Les femmes ne sont pas faites pour un seul homme: c'est pour tous que les a créées la nature' (p. 176) / 'Women are not made for one single man; 'tis for men at large Nature created them' (p. 286), and what men have called the 'crime' of adultery is a natural right.[12]

A paradisiacal space of sexual freedom for women as well as for men, therefore, the boudoir becomes a kind of model state and, like all states, it has to have a constitution, embedded in philosophical thought: hence the pamphlet, *Français, encore un effort, si vous voulez être républicains*, whose hundred or so pages form the centrepiece of the work. Dolmancé, who just happens to have been out and bought this pamphlet, hot off the press, at the Palais de l'Égalité, reads it out in response to a question from Eugénie about whether morals are necessary to government.

The pamphlet temporarily suspends the fiction of the dramatic dialogues and takes us outside the text, so to speak, and into the politics of the French Revolution. This part of Sade's text, at least, is firmly rooted in its historical context. In a sense, the insertion of the pamphlet into an anonymously published work of fiction provides a further protective barrier against discovery. Sade is thus able to express his views on topical ideas and events from a position of relative safety. On the other hand, although the author of the pamphlet is not named, there are knowing winks to the sympathetic reader who would have no difficulty in recognising the author of *Justine*, if not Sade himself behind the rhetorical first person: 'j'expose les idées qui depuis l'âge de raison se sont identifiées avec moi [...] je ne m'adresse qu'à des gens capables de m'entendre, et ceux-là me liront sans danger' (p. 218) / 'I set forth the ideas which, since the age when I first began to reason, have identified themselves in me [...] I address myself only to people capable of hearing me out, and they will read me without any danger' (p. 311). This somewhat defensive caveat recalls the attacks on Sade provoked by the publication four years earlier in 1791 of *Justine ou les Malheurs de la vertu*. Sade thus plays a coy game of hide-and-seek with the reader,[13] concealing authorship of both the pamphlet and the work in which it finds itself behind anonymous publication, while teasingly challenging those readers, familiar with his writing and unshocked by it, to identify the man from his ideas.

Some have tried to ignore this inserted monologue, alleging that it disturbs the play's structural harmony. Gilbert Lély, for example, contemptuously refers to it as 'cet ample morceau, intercalé arbitrairement dans un ensemble édifié d'exquise façon' / 'that lengthy piece, arbitrarily inserted into an exquisitely constructed whole'.[14] A recent English translation omits it altogether. This critical blindness is, however, probably due to the utopian and often contradictory nature of the arguments that the pamphlet contains, and to the fact that it repeats many of the ideas already raised in preceding dialogues. The polar opposite point of view, expressed by Béatrice Didier, who praises the pamphlet's eloquence, calling it 'one of the finest texts of our revolutionary literature' is just as inaccurate.[15] The fact is that, despite its many positive features and its strongly satirical elements, the detailed exposition of Sade's sexual philosophy found in it is fraught with contradictions, in particular with regard to female sexuality, but also to religion with which it is inextricably linked. The sadomasochistic aspects of that philosophy which have come to dominate the popular perception of Sade are essentially derived from Christian guilt about sex and the body. The notion of punishment, of the need to suffer for sexual sins that runs through the whole Christian tradition (a tradition largely attributable to St Paul and St Augustine), links sex and pain erotically to the point where, for some, the two become inseparable: 'c'est par les peines,' Mme de Saint-Ange declares 'qu'on arrive toujours aux plaisirs' (p. 167) / 'it is always by way of pain one arrives at pleasure' (p. 280).

The masochistic side of Sadean sexuality is present in many of Christianity's traditions: in the self-flagellation of the celibate religious, in the so-called 'ecstasies of the saints', orgasmic conditions induced by self-deprivation and self-torture. Though religion and morality are actually inseparable in Sade's thinking, Dolmancé's pamphlet tries to address them separately, and so I shall respect this division in the summary that follows.

On 7 May 1794, Robespierre had declared the republic to be deist and atheism as 'anti-republican'. More than anything else, therefore, the pamphlet represents Sade's reaction against this decree. The deism of 'l'infâme Robespierre' and even of Voltaire (a writer much admired by Sade) must be swept away to be replaced by the paganism of ancient Rome. The first section on religion is therefore primarily intended to demonstrate the kinship of atheism with republicanism, and, indeed, Sade clearly saw that the monarchy was supported by the Catholic Church – if the new republic was to survive, the Church must also be stripped of its power. History teaches that religion has always been in the service of tyranny. Sade's attack on Robespierre and religion would certainly prove to have been prophetic – within a few months, the architect of the Terror had been executed and the cult of the Supreme Being which he promoted began to wither.

As with most political polemics, the arguments presented here depend largely for their effect on rhetorical forcefulness rather than logical consistency. Attacks on Christianity as 'this imbecile' or 'stupid' religion, with Jesus as 'the imposter from Nazareth' and Mary as 'his dirty and disgusting mother', even appear hysterical in tone. Here, as in other dissertations on religion in Sade's work, such bluster undermines objectivity and suggests an obsessive personal investment. There is also evidence of the political hypocrisy that characterises all Sade's writing: both royalists *and aristocrats* are held responsible for the Church's continuing authority, and there are sycophantic expressions of a patriotic republicanism that, in reality, Sade did not wholeheartedly embrace.

The same desire to pass the test of patriotism leads Sade to preach the rule of law and the 'social principles' of charity, heroism, humanity and civic spirit, sentiments that do not chime well with the presentation in the second part of the pamphlet of a morality rooted in pragmatic self-interest. The subtitle for this part is *Les moeurs*, which translates as 'morals' but also as 'manners' or 'customs', and so, while sexual morality is the underlying thread, it runs through every major aspect of the functioning of a republican state, from its laws, systems of education and communication to the rights and responsibilities of individual citizens. In other words, everything in this prospectus for a utopian state is seen in sexual terms – this is indeed the characteristic which, more than any other, marks Sade out as unique among the writers and philosophers of his time – and the dominant theme is individual liberty. Thus, fewer laws will be needed to control a population that serves neither king nor God, but above all, there will be fewer sex crimes for laws to deter and punish because morality is relative, not universal, and often governed by purely pragmatic considerations.

Here, Sade is particularly good at highlighting the hypocrisies of the current regime. In fact, so many of the arguments in this section of the pamphlet strike such a wrily cynical note that Sade's republican vision begins to sound more like satirical fantasy than serious politicking.[16] With monarch and deity gone, only four possible crimes remain: calumny, theft, impurity and murder, all offences against our fellow-men under the monarchy but none of them serious under a republic! Written so soon after the Terror, the irony of this ingenuous-sounding defence of anarchy and violence would not have been lost on the contemporary reader. What can be wrong with calumny, announces the author 'avec la plus extrême franchise'? – 'surtout dans un gouvernement comme le nôtre, où tous les hommes, plus liés, plus rapprochés, ont évidemment un plus grand intérêt à se bien connaître' (p. 219) / 'It is with utmost candour I confess that I have never considered calumny an evil, and especially in a government like our own, under which all of us, bound closer together, nearer one to the other, obviously have a greater interest in becoming acquainted with one another' (pp. 311–12). After the internecine divisions of the preceding years, Sade's understated sarcasm launches a devastating attack on the ideal of republican brotherhood. 'Ne naissons-nous pas tous isolés,' Dolmancé had asked Eugénie earlier, 'tous ennemis les uns des autres, tous dans un état de guerre perpétuelle et réciproque?' (p. 172) / 'are we not all born solitary, isolated? [...] are we not come into the world all enemies, the one of the other, all in a state of perpetual and reciprocal warfare?' (pp. 283–84). Sade pays lip service to the ideals of the Revolution, allowing that, whereas the Christian injunction to love one's neighbour as oneself is contrary to all nature's laws, we might love him as a brother. It is hard to take him seriously when he refers in the very next breath to the closer ties between the citizens of a republican state. Knowing the circumstances in which he wrote the work makes the irony of such passages impossible to ignore.

The justification of theft as an understandable response to the unfair distribution of wealth in society is both prophetically Marxist and scathingly critical of the corruption of the revolutionary regime. As for the 'impure crimes' of prostitution, adultery, incest, rape and sodomy, how can the state expect its citizens to be moral, when the state itself must necessarily behave immorally (by conducting wars) in order to survive? But the irony is especially biting in relation to the 'offence' of murder, a practice legitimised by the Revolution itself: 'N'est-ce pas à force de meurtres que la France est libre aujourd'hui?' (p. 255) / 'Is it not by dint of murders that France is free today?' (p. 332). As Donald Thomas so nicely puts it, however, 'That Sade truly felt an enthusiasm for murder among the stench of blood and the procession of the condemned seems as likely as that Swift, after his *Modest Proposal*, felt an appetite for infant flesh.'[17]

Detailed expositions of the views expressed here can also be found in *Justine* and *Juliette*, where a direct satirical intention is not always so easy to discern. As we have seen, the basis of this message is that individual men and women should be free to indulge their sexual whims, whatever they might be: incest, sodomy, coprophilia, any and all sexual practices are natural and should therefore be legal. The pamphlet reiterates these views, concentrating on the sexual liberation of women in particular. Generally speaking, much of this seems in tune with the liberal-mindedness of modern

Western culture. On the face of it, Sade's pamphlet accords women the same sexual rights as men. Women, too, should be free to indulge their desires, unconstrained by marriage or by the prejudices of superstition. What in our times has come to be known as the nuclear family effectively disappears under such a system, and all children are the responsibility of the state, alleviating women of the burden of child care.[18] If every town of the new republic should have a brothel to satisfy male lusts, then women too ought to have their own 'houses of pleasure'. Now, at a time when any sexually active woman was considered a prostitute or a lunatic, such views were extremely novel.[19]

As I said earlier, however, *La Philosophie* is a complex work and, in addition to the parodic and satirical elements and the strong plea for women's sexual freedom that it contains, it is certainly vulnerable to negative readings, especially in relation to the feminine. Like the Eden which it ironically inverts, Sade's sexual paradise is utopic, and all utopias eventually collapse under the weight of their own contradictions. While on the one hand asserting men's sexual rights over all women, the pamphlet simultaneously and contradictorily asserts that 'Jamais un acte de possession ne peut être exercé sur un être libre' (p. 230) / 'Never may an act of possession be exercised upon a free being' (p. 318), echoing Saint-Ange's assertion in the Third Dialogue that the body of a woman is her property and no one else's: 'fouts ... ton corps est à toi, à toi seule' (p. 70) / 'fuck [...] your body is your own, yours alone' (p. 221). My freedom to enjoy your body can only be bought at the expense of your own freedom if you object to it, and this simple truth exposes the fundamental weakness of Sade's attitudes to sex.

In defence of Sade, one might argue that the notion of compulsory prostitution for men and women is not so much a serious project as an ironic comment on the ultimate impossibility of total satisfaction. Any society in which people are made to accommodate individual desires will clearly be run according to a philosophy of egocentricity according to which the other has no value whatsoever, except as an erotic object,[20] so that if a man wants a woman or child, he is perfectly entitled to take her by force if necessary. At its logical extreme, then, this doctrine of individual licence is seen to justify the most horrific 'crimes' of rape and even of murder, which in Sade's terms are not crimes because they belong to the natural order. To kill is, in fact, to obey nature's first law of destruction. For Sade, women not only have the right to abort, an apparently liberal if not feminist doctrine, but also to dispose of their children after birth.

Sade's atheism is not humanistic, there is neither a divine nor a human spirit in the newborn and so it has no higher status in nature than a germinating grain of corn. Sade's opposition to the death penalty, which many have used as evidence of his underlying humanity, is actually based on a belief that, whereas the individual murderer has the excuse of acting from passion or personal grudge, the state kills in cold blood according to an impersonal law. There is no doubt either that this conception of individual freedom is more beneficial to men than to women. Indeed, men privilege their own pleasures over that of their lovers because this is their nature, for which they are clearly not responsible: 'Il n'est point d'homme qui ne veuille être despote quand il bande' (p. 277) / 'There is not a living man who does not wish to play the despot when he is stiff' (p. 344). This imbalance shows up in the power relationships of Sade's own text. In the end, not only Mme de Mistival but her daughter too are the property of a man who, in the Sixth Dialogue, sends a letter to the libertines, warning them of the mother's impending arrival and issuing final instructions as to the treatment of each. If Sade's religion is of the body, it is of the male body, and the sacrificial victim is female and maternal.[21]

When Mme de Mistival turns up at the door unannounced to 'rescue' her daughter, Saint-Ange pretends to be offended by the inference that she is 'en de mauvaises mains'/ 'in bad hands' – the phrase could not have been better chosen for its ironic effect – and there is talk of throwing her out of the window. It is clear from the outset, therefore, that Eugénie's mother is going to be the victim of the piece, but it is Eugénie herself rather than her libertine mentors who officiates at the sacrifice. Dolmancé, it is true, initiates the scenario of sacrifice by sodomising and whipping Mme de Mistival and generally directs the proceedings, but, after Mistival has been similarly abused by the others, it is finally the daughter who, having fucked and then sodomised her own mother with a dildo, carries out the final sentence. Dolmancé's syphilitic valet, Lapierre, is ordered to rape and sodomise the hapless victim so that she will be infected with his pox, and Eugénie enthusiastically agrees to sew up her vagina and anus to prevent the disease from escaping and to hasten its deleterious effects.[22]

This scene has probably attracted more critical comment than any other in the work, partly because of the wide range of responses – from revulsion to amusement – it seems to elicit, but mainly because it lends itself so easily to metaphorical and symbolic readings, especially of the psychoanalytic variety.

On one level, the scene contains verbal humour and physical comedy that transform its tragic potential into black farce. Though utterly repulsive if read on a realistic level, Eugénie's actions imply a fantastic use of the mother as object that is funny, in part precisely *because* it is so unthinkable. The transformation of living creatures into things for the purposes of visual humour is a notable characteristic of certain modern cartoons, which depict an extreme though sanitised violence from which the victim always recovers. The knockabout comedy of Sade's 'needlework' scene operates in essentially the same fashion: whilst the mother bemoans her fate in a melodramatic yet controlled language that seems at the least to understate the gravity of her situation – 'Oh! juste ciel! quelle horrible condamnation! [...] Oh! ciel! quelle douleur! [...] Ahe! ahe! ahe! [...] Ah! pardon, monsieur! mille et mille fois pardon! vous me faites mourir! ...' (pp. 305–8) / 'Oh, my God! what a hideous damnation! [...] Oh, my God! the pain! [...] Aië! aië! aië! [...] Oh pardon me, Monsieur, I beg your pardon a thousand thousand times over ... you are killing me ...' (pp. 363–65) – Eugénie keeps missing her aim with the needle because of the delirious state of pleasure occasioned by the Chevalier's intimate fondling. Eugénie's irony, as she performs the unthinkable, only serves further to foreground the humour and deflate the horror - 'Cela vaut mieux que de mourir, maman; au moins, je porterais mes jolies robes cet été!' (p. 305) / 'Better that than to die, Mamma; at least

I'll be able to wear some gay dresses this summer' (p. 363) – while the terms in which the mother voices her pain are confusingly similar to Sade's favourite signifier of *jouissance*: 'vous me faites mourir! ...' (p. 308), which translates as 'I'm dying (with pleasure)!' Once the joke is performed, the scene and, indeed, the narrative end with Mme de Mistival's unceremonious dismissal. Thus, the victim lives to recover from an abuse which, though painful and shocking, is, we assume, not irreversible. A humorous response to this and other such scenes of objectification and dehumanisation is only possible because the reader is prevented by the very process itself from identifying too closely with rounded individuals and so from reacting sympathetically when these individuals suffer harm.[23]

In a more serious vein, Freudians have read the scene in terms of the male castration complex, so that, through Eugénie, Sade enacts a deep-seated fantasy.[24] Plaiting and weaving, to which sewing is closely related, are for Freud intrinsically feminine activities, associated symbolically with women's 'genital deficiency', so that, as they weave, women symbolically reproduce the pubic hair with which nature hides what is not there.[25] By strapping on the dildo and using it to rape her mother, Eugénie has already in a sense restored to herself the lost phallus. As she now sews up her mother's genitals, Eugénie might be said, on an unconscious level, to be 'covering up' its absence. Behind Eugénie, therefore, the male author is closing up the wound of castration in order to assuage his castration fears.[26]

Pierre Klossowski reads Sade generally in terms of what he calls a 'negative Oedipal complex', according to which libidinal agression turns itself against the mother in alliance with an all-powerful father. For Klossowski, the same scenario, of which the needle scene is a perfect model, replays itself repeatedly throughout Sade's work: the father collaborates with the child to punish the mother and/or to destroy the family.[27] We remember that, though physically absent, Eugénie's father has given full permission for the mother's chastisement. In orchestrating the whole scene, Dolmancé can be said to deputise for the absent father.

Angela Carter also conducts an interesting and instructive analysis of the scene with reference to Freudianism, and in particular to the 'object-relation' theories of Melanie Klein. Carter sees the mother as a conflation of both parents and, as such, a novel Oedipal object:

> Eugénie enacts the crime of Oedipus in a richly psychotic trance; she both copulates with her mother and effectively murders her. In this bewildering dream, Mother becomes the essential primal object, subsuming both parents to herself [...][28]

For Carter, the daughter's action is essentially about freeing herself from maternal control, about achieving sexual autonomy, whilst remaining within what Lacan calls the 'Father's Law':

> The Sadeian woman, then, subverts only her own socially conditioned role in the world of God, the king and the law. She does not subvert her society, except incidentally, as a storm trooper of the individual consciousness. She remains in the area of privilege created by her class, just as Sade remains in the philosophic framework of his time.[29]

Eugénie is an unconscious persona of the author, who must punish the mother for having brought him into this miserable world.[30] As Carter observes, 'it is the very fact of generation that he finds intolerable' and she pursues her interpretation with reference to Melanie Klein's notion of the 'good breast'. In a Kleinian analysis, Carter argues that Eugénie sews her mother up to prevent the arrival of siblings who might compete for nourishment by the 'good breast', a symbol of the satisfaction of basic human needs.[31] The Sadean libertine unconsciously yearns for total isolation, in which his enjoyment of the world is unhampered by the presence of others.[32]

These psychoanalytically based readings all place the author's unconscious fears and desires at the centre of his text and seem to me to offer considerable insight into the relation between the two, but they do not preclude an interpretation based on the text's consciously stated intentions of sexual liberation. The closing up of the mother's sexual orifices deprives her of her ability to remain sexually active and so prevents her from competing sexually with the daughter, whose orifices have just been opened up. The needle scene is most transparently about the way in which the sexual availability of women depended in Sade's time upon the removal from their mothers of authority in sexual matters. In this sense, it is socially as well as morally transgressive.

In a similar vein but with a somewhat different emphasis, Marcel Hénaff reads this liberation of daughter from mother in terms of transgression of the incest taboo, which for Claude Lévi-Strauss is necessary for the exchange of women by men in the marital contracts of patriarchal society. Abolition of this taboo therefore liberates women and, in particular, incest frees girls from their mothers, whose function is essentially to prepare their daughters to become the wives of men outside the family group. The education of daughters, which, the epigraph implies, will be a dominant aim of the work, is therefore designed to remove them from the monogamous family system founded on male power, and the exchange of women underpinning it is an exchange which crucially depends on the preservation of the daughter's virginity. It is this system of sexual taboos antithetical to libertinage that Sade symbolically demolishes in the 'needle scene', in which the mother's authority over her daughter is decisively broken and the mother is punished for her role as enforcer of sexual prohibitions:

> S'il n'y a plus de filles modèles il n'y aura plus d'épouses fidèles, plus de familles, plus de reproduction normative, plus d'interdits de jouissance.[33]

> If there are no more model daughters, there will be no more faithful spouses, no more families, no more normative reproduction, no more sexual prohibitions.

When the last stitch is in place, Mme de Mistival is expelled from the privileged space of the boudoir, which is infected with a disease generally associated with sexual immorality. The daughter's 'original sin' and the death that it symbolises have been transferred to the mother, and the daughter is at liberty to continue her enjoyment of Sade's paradise of the body.

In spite of Eugénie's sexual liberation, one cannot seriously call Sade a feminist, as some of his more adulatory critics have done. If he wants women to be sexually free, it is, in the end, as Hénaff's analysis suggests, because he wants them to be sexually available. Moreover, as we shall see in greater detail in Chapter 5, his conception of an active female libido is fundamentally male centred. On the other hand, it is just as inappropriate to label him a misogynist. The male imperative to control female sexuality has found expression throughout history in almost every society on earth, and eighteenth-century France is no exception. To accuse Sade of misogyny, therefore, to want to take the needle out of Eugénie's hands and give it to Dolmancé or the Chevalier or any other man is to judge him according to the more enlightened egalitarian standards of our own time.[34] How much more subversive it would have been for one of the men to do the sewing! Such arguments, however, are rooted in modern thinking: it is not that Sade here typically reinforces gender roles – in fact, there are many instances in his fiction when such roles are transgressed – it is simply unremarkable when, like any other eighteenth-century writer, he does not subvert them.

In *La Philosophie dans le boudoir*, as throughout the Sadean *oeuvre*, attitudes to women are ambivalent at best, self-contradictory at worst, and so contribute to the overall complexity of the work. Sade's choice, on this occasion, of an overtly theatrical medium is well suited to the ambivalence of his thought.[35] Theatre is, of course, intrinsically dialogic, lending itself to the expression of different and often opposite points of view, and the absence of a narrator makes it much more difficult to identify an authorial voice or a unified message. The weight of evidence certainly suggests that Dolmancé and Saint-Ange act largely as mouthpieces for the author (and *Français, encore un effort ...* has all the characteristics of an authorial polemic), but the theatrical format (as opposed to the novelistic format of his other major libertine works) more readily accommodates the philosophical dialogue which is Sade's stock-in-trade, facilitating the expression of different viewpoints. When the Chevalier objects to Dolmancé's cruelty, for example, the reader's sympathies are unavoidably engaged, and even though his more humane views are immediately ridiculed as attributable to his youth and inexperience, and Dolmancé wins the argument with Eugénie, there is an implicit acknowledgement that more sober individuals, less corrupted by *libertinage*, might agree with him:

> Le Chevalier. – [...] je garderai ma morale pour ceux qui, moins ivres que vous, seront plus en état de l'entendre.
>
> Mme de Saint-Ange. – Oui, mon frère, oui, oui, ne nous donne ici que ton foutre; nous te faisons grâce de la morale; elle est trop douce pour des *roués* de notre espèce. (p. 275)

> Le Chevalier – [...] I'll save my ethics for others who, less besotted than you, will be in a better way to hear me.
>
> Mme de Saint-Ange – Yes, dear brother, yes, exactly, give us nothing but your fuck; we'll forgo your morals; they are too gentle and mild for roués of our ilk. (p. 343)

The theatrical format also, of course, privileges the physical and the visual, and so is far better suited than prose to the practical demonstration that underpins this work's sex show-style pedagogy: if the message of sexual liberation is to be truly effective, pleasure cannot just be catalogued, it must be staged.[36] It hardly seems necessary to point out that on a live stage the actors are physically as well as audibly present – as Alain Robbe-Grillet says, 'The dramatic character is on stage, this is his/her most important quality: (s)he is present'[37] – indeed, theatre is the *only* medium that allows for this physical presence. But the actors are not the only ones on this textual stage, for, alongside Eugénie, the reader too is implicitly invited to join in the debauchery, and this is an innovation which overturns the classical relationship of the reader with the printed page.[38]

In the activities that function as 'practicals' in her short but intense course in sexual pleasure, both Eugénie and we are presented with an idealised body which is anatomically and aesthetically superlative. This is a body to be admired, coveted and copied, like that of the tightrope walker or trapeze artist: completely lacking the physical flaws that might remind the audience of human mortality. The ironic use of theatrical vocabulary to denote physical *jouissance* reinforces this notion of the body as marvellous spectacle – 'Quel beau spectacle!' cries Eugénie, as the Chevalier covers her with spunk. In the dramatic context in which it is expressed, the word 'spectacle' is literal and self-reflexive as well as metaphorical. Sade in fact pushes 'theatre as spectacle' to its extreme, exposing the naked body to the gaze of the putative spectator, but taking this gaze beyond mere voyeurism, as we have seen, to a point of saturation, past the surface to the internal organs of reproduction. This has the effect of transforming the body into a banal object, to be examined, prodded, measured, turned upside down (comic measuring of penises), and ultimately rendered familiar rather than strange. The *comique de geste* of the characters' physical movements and actions similarly drains them of their erotic/pornographic potential. In other words, there is a comic incongruity in the choice of a formal medium to send an obscene message, between the use of a conventional theatrical vehicle (stage directions, etc.) and its mannered idiom, on the one hand, and its licentious contents, on the other.

Annie Le Brun has linked this 'theatre of the body' with Sade's philosophical thought, characterising his use of the philosophical dialogue in particular as a 'dramatisation of thought', so that ideas become actual physical displays:

> Ainsi, en ce qui concerne le dialogue philosophique, à la différence de Diderot qui sait jouer avec virtuosité de toutes les ressources du genre, Sade, lui, les épuise, et cela jusqu'à ce que la «posture» intellectuelle de chaque interlocuteur se défasse comme celle des corps, pour que la légèreté d'échange d'idées se solidifie en prise de position.[39]

> Thus, where the philosophical dialogue is concerned, unlike Diderot who skilfully manipulates all the genre's resources, Sade for his part exhausts them, to the point at which the intellectual positions of each and every objector fall apart just like the postures of their body, so that the light exchange of ideas solidifies into the taking up of positions.

In *La Philosophie dans le boudoir* and *Dialogue entre un prêtre et un moribond* (*Dialogue between a Priest and a Dying Man*), the word is literally as well as metaphorically made flesh (though given her vehement rejection of the notion of a hidden religiosity in Sade, Le Brun would doubtless not put things quite this way). In her more recent article, 'Sade, or the First Theatre of Atheism', Le Brun takes this notion further, directly relating the physicality of Sade's dramatic dialogues to his atheism:

> the very essence of his genius [...] is to show how, in the drama of desire, the mind transcends the body and the body transcends the mind, giving birth to a completely new theatre – the theatre of atheism.[40]

At a time when the conventional theatre of his day was becoming increasingly abstract (Diderot's *théâtre à thèse* typifies this trend), Sade saw theatre as an essentially material and physical medium, as 'the site of bodily incarnation' and 'the best means of taking free thinking beyond the limits of philosophy'.[41] Whether or not *La Philosophie* is actually performable – and as far as I am aware, its obscenity has so far prevented it from reaching a public stage – is, in a way, irrelevant. What matters is that it is written for performance in the sense that it is spectacular in form, giving physical expression to philosophical ideas.

If *La Philosophie* occupies a central place in Sade's 'theatre of atheism', the use of religious vocabulary here as elsewhere in his writing to denote the sexual parts and activities connected with them is then, in part, heavily ironic. The following speech by Dolmancé exemplifies this technique well:

> Vos voeux vont être exaucés, madame; mais souffrez que je m'arrête un instant aux pieds de l'idole: je veux la fêter avant que de m'introduire au fond de son sanctuaire ... Quel cul divin! ... (p. 152)

> Thy will shall be done, Madame; but suffer me to halt an instant at my idol's feet; I would praise it before entering

> into the depths of the sanctuary ... What a divine ass is this! ... (p. 271)

In an extension of Le Brun's argument, in conclusion I want to argue that this use of language also connotes behaviour that can only be described as a veritable worship of the body, a utopic body of pleasure, as we have seen, that effectively takes God's place. 'Plaisir,' says Dolmancé to Eugénie, should be 'le seul *dieu* de votre existence; c'est à lui seul qu'une jeune fille doit tout *sacrifier*, et rien à ses yeux ne doit être aussi *sacré* que le plaisir' (pp. 43–4; my emphasis) / 'let [pleasure] be [...] the one *god* of your existence; it is to this god a girl ought to *sacrifice* everything, and in her eyes nothing must be as *holy* as pleasure' (p. 204). God and physical pleasure are in fact linguistically synonymous in Sade's text: the libertines almost always call on God when ejaculating, an act of blasphemy that Dolmancé defends and justifies in terms of the joys of transgression, but, equally, a significant juxtaposition of the body with the sacred: 'Ah! sacré nom d'un dieu!' cries the Chevalier as he comes, 'que de plaisirs! ...' (p. 169) / 'Ah, sacred name of the fucking Almighty! what pleasure! ...' (p. 282). It is in the body thus sanctified that the only path to immortality can be found: 'Aurais-tu la folie de l'immortalité?' Saint-Ange asks Eugénie, 'Eh bien, c'est en foutant, ma chère, que tu resteras dans la mémoire des hommes' (p. 71) / 'But have you the madness to hope for immortality? Why then, 'tis by fucking, my dear, that you will remain in human memory' (p. 221). This rhetorical argument in a way carries more weight than Sade's usual, purely materialist, position on immortality, that is, that although our individual deaths are inevitable, we live on in other material forms. The pamphlet rehearses this reasoning, familiar to Sade readers: 'De petits animaux se forment à l'instant que le grand animal a perdu le souffle' and 'La mort [...] n'est donc plus qu'un changement de forme, qu'un passage imperceptible d'une existence à une autre' (p. 253) / 'Little animals are formed immediately a large animal expires' and 'Death is hence no more than a change of form, an imperceptible passage from one existence into another' (p. 331). This more rationalistic argument substitutes nature for God, positing a universe that is in eternal motion. Saint-Ange's speech, however, situates immortality in memories rooted in the physical senses of individuals, a rhetoric that is far more seductive than the rationalistic view because it retains human identity intact rather than dissolving it into the natural world. Saint-Ange's *boutade* thus brings together the main strands of Sade's atheistic philosophy – the body, the senses and the cult of freedom – to constitute the novice's first article of faith. In the inverted Eden of the boudoir, the only transcendence possible is located in bodily *jouissance*, and it is only within the consecrated space of the boudoir that this body is truly, *philosophically*, free.[42]

4

Virtuous Virgins and Lustful Libertines: *Justine* and the Misfortunes of Beauty

There are no fewer than three separate versions of *Justine*, which, like Topsy, grew from a mere infant text of 138 pages to mature some ten years later as a triple-X rated adult entertainment of over 1,000. The original version, *Les Infortunes de la vertu* (*The Misfortunes of Virtue*), not so much a novel as a short story with satirical aims (critics describe it as a *conte philosophique* or 'philosophical tale'), was composed in 15 days in the Bastille in 1787. Largely conventional in style, and, as we shall see, lacking any characteristics that might now be termed obscene, this short, snappy novella could safely be recommended nowadays to most maiden aunts. Some critics have found this first draft of Sade's tale of virtue despoiled to contain an intensity and clarity of vision absent from the two subsequent versions, but it was destined never to reach the reading public in the author's lifetime.[1] The unpublished *conte* was, nevertheless, to grow into the novel-length *Justine ou les Malheurs de la vertu* (*Justine, or Good Conduct Well Chastised*) which appeared in 1791, a year after the author's release from Charenton. Sade claimed that money problems and editorial pressure had forced him to write a 'spicy' best-seller.[2] The editor must have been delighted with the result. *Les Malheurs* was considerably more violent and sexually explicit than *Les Infortunes*, and sold so well that five further editions had to be printed in the space of ten years. While the public's appetite for Sade's first published work was evidently insatiable, critical responses of the time were mixed. An article of 27 September 1792 praises the author's 'rich and brilliant' imagination, while exhorting young people to 'avoid this dangerous book' and advising even 'more mature' men to read it 'in order to see to what insanities human imagination can lead', but then to 'throw it in the fire'.[3]

In spite of the popular success of *Les Malheurs*, Sade's financial affairs remained in the doldrums. Maurice Lever tells us that *Justine* did not make its author any money, nor did any of his other books. It did, however, achieve a *succès de scandale*.[4] This apparent success and the writer's continued impecuniousness doubtless provided sufficient incentive for the composition of the much extended and more openly obscene final version of Justine's adventures, entitled *La nouvelle Justine, ou les Malheurs de la vertu* (*The New Justine*), which appeared six years later in 1797 in a ten-volume edition which also included *l'Histoire de Juliette*. As we shall see, *La nouvelle Justine* is, in a number of important respects, significantly different from the two earlier versions. According to Rétif de la Bretonne and Sébastien Mercier, writing at the time, sales were brisk among the booksellers of the Palais Royal, and it was more than a year before the authorities began to seize copies. Gradually, however, the work and its author were systematically hunted down. Sade was accused of having written 'l'infâme *Justine*' in a press article that appeared in 1800 and, despite his vigorous denials,[5] he was eventually arrested the following year, together with his publisher, Massé, for the authorship of these 'dangerous' and 'detestable' works, and detained without trial at the 'maison de santé de Charenton' until his death in 1814.

In a sense, then, Sade fell victim to his own creation. Perhaps all along, as his narrative became increasingly bolder, more challenging to the censor, the Marquis was unconsciously driven to a point of coincidence with his fictional heroine, for both author and character are acutely aware of their own status as victim. After all, it was not Juliette but Justine who preoccupied him for more than ten years of his own less than happy existence to the point of composing three separate versions of her woeful tale. Such, in fact, was the association of Sade with his less fortunate heroine that he would be known throughout the nineteenth century as the author not of *Juliette* but of *Justine*. This identification of the writer with his ingenuous creation outside of the text can perhaps be explained by what some have seen as an unconscious authorial identification on psychological and emotional levels with the character herself.[6] How justified are we in positing such an identification between author and character? In the first person narratives of *Les Infortunes* and *Les Malheurs*, the young woman often appears to speak with her creator's voice. Sade's appreciation of feminine beauty, for example, certainly shows itself in Justine's all too enthusiastic evocation of the beauty of other young women. There is, moreover, a marked discrepancy in the first two versions between the stereotypes of Justine's initial portrait and the more positive ways in which, through her own words and actions, she is subsequently portrayed. Personality, like gender for Judith Butler, is not a being but a doing. We shall return to Justine's self-presentation presently, but first we need to consider the stereotypes of the author–narrator's perspective.[7]

From the outset, Justine appears to us as a passive creature, destined for martyrdom. A devout young girl of twelve at the beginning of her remarkable odyssey, her religious faith remains implausibly unshaken by the unending catalogue of disasters that befall her throughout her relatively short and miserable existence. Suddenly left orphaned and destitute together with her 15-year-old sister, Juliette, this is how she is first described to us:

> [...] d'un caractère sombre et mélancolique, douée d'une tendresse, d'une sensibilité surprenantes, n'ayant au lieu de l'art et de la finesse de sa soeur, qu'une ingénuité, une candeur, une bonne foi qui devaient la faire tomber dans bien des pièges, elle sentit toute l'horreur de sa position. Cette jeune fille avait une physionomie toute différente de celle de Juliette; autant on voyait d'artifice, de manège, de coquetterie dans les traits de l'une, autant on admirait de pudeur, de délicatesse, et de timidité dans l'autre. Un air de vierge, de grands yeux bleus pleins d'intérêt, une peau éblouissante, une taille fine et légère, un son de voix touchant, la plus belle âme et le caractère le plus doux, des dents d'ivoire et de beaux cheveux blonds, telle est l'esquisse de cette cadette charmante dont les grâces naïves et les traits délicieux sont au-dessus de l'éloquence qui voudrait les peindre et d'une touche trop fine et trop

> délicate pour ne pas échapper au pinceau qui voudrait les réaliser. (*Les Infortunes*, pp. 51–2)

> [...] gloomy and melancholic by disposition yet blessed with surprising gentleness and sensitivity, having none of her sister's artfulness and guile but the ingenuousness, candour, and honesty which were to make her stumble into many traps, Justine felt the full horror of her situation. Her face was quite unlike Juliette's. Where the features of the one were all artifice, cunning, and coquetry, the other's were remarkable for their modesty, refinement, and shyness. A virginal air, large, engaging blue eyes, dazzling skin, a slender, well-shaped figure, a voice to move the heart, teeth of ivory, and beautiful fair hair – so much, in outline sketch, for the younger sister whose simple grace and delightful expression were of too fine, too delicate a stamp not to elude the brush which would capture them entire. (*The Misfortunes of Virtue*, pp. 3–4)

In these few lines, Sade deftly sketches the charm of this 'delicious' young creature in terms of what we would now consider to be a stereotype of feminine beauty (big blue eyes, teeth of ivory, lovely blonde hair). For the modern reader, the same physical features make up another stereotype – the dumb blonde – which is reinforced here by character traits connoting 'girlishness' and vulnerability (ingenuousness, sensitivity, naivety). Like her beauty, these traits can be also read on her physiognomy, at the very surface of her body: modesty, delicacy, shyness and, above all, the 'look of a virgin'. In fact, in line with her creator's materialist thinking, physique and temperament become one in Justine, naivety is graceful, vulnerability attractive, sexual innocence seductive. Justine is the first 'girly girl', the young ingénue so beloved of nineteenth- and twentieth-century theatre and film, a blonde whose dumbness here means ignorance of sexuality, an essential prerequisite of female victimhood.

Justine's physical appearance immediately suggests that this is the part she will play: in Sade's terms, she is primed to be a victim of her own virtue (which will prevent her from enjoying the sexual attentions forced upon her, but which, more importantly, will determine the very nature of her attraction for the men and women who abuse her). She will also be the victim of the religious and social prejudices of a society that places a high value on the status of virginity, and in so doing creates a taboo that cries out to be transgressed. Innocence, virtue, beauty are all synonymous in Justine, who initially at least is nothing more than a cluster of nouns and adjectives. She is simply, we are told, the embodiment of virginal innocence and sensibility, having a potentially erotic vulnerability, 'une ingénuité, une candeur qui devaient la faire tomber dans bien des pièges' (*Les Malheurs*, p. 56) / 'an ingenuousness, a candor that were to cause her to tumble into not a few pitfalls' (*Good Conduct*, p. 459). A construct of Platonic ideals expressed unplatonically in physical terms, Justine exists in abstraction only, as an object promised to the reader's sexual curiosity – until the narrative brings her to life, that is.

In all these respects, Juliette is an exact opposite and, like her sister Justine, her character and temperament are initially expressed in physical terms: not blonde but brunette, with eyes not credulously blue but dark and 'prodigiously expressive'; not timid but spirited, not naive but incredulous, not innocent but wordly wise thanks to the best possible education that a father's untimely ruin will deny her younger sister:

> [...] elle avait été élevée [...] dans un des meilleurs couvents de Paris, où jusqu'à l'âge de quinze ans, aucun conseil, aucun maître, aucun bon livre, aucun talent ne lui avait été refusé. (*Les Infortunes*, p. 51)

> [...] she was brought up [...] in one of the best convents in Paris where, until the age of 15, she was never denied good counsel or teachers nor good books or talents. (*The Misfortunes of Virtue*, p. 3)

When both parents die and the two girls are left penniless orphans, Juliette's only response is the pleasure of being free. Even if we had not already been told at the beginning of the narrative of the fortune that her beauty will help her to amass, we would know from this display of lack of feeling that, far from being a victim, the insensitive and self-serving Juliette will be one of life's winners. Not so the 'sad and miserable Justine'.

Justine's narrative follows more or less the same pattern in all three versions, although in the second and especially the third versions events are narrated in considerably more detail and there are some new episodes and characters. We shall return to the differences between the three *Justines* shortly, but for a thumbnail sketch of Justine's tale up until her reunion with her sister, Juliette (or Mme de Lorsange, as she is by then known), we can do no better than refer to the young woman's own summary of her wretched life, told to her sister, Juliette, and her lover, as she waits to be hanged for a crime she did not commit:[8]

> During my childhood I meet a usurer *(Du Harpin)*; he seeks to induce me to commit a theft, I refuse, he becomes rich. I fall amongst a band of thieves *(led by la Dubois and Coeur de Fer)*, I escape from them with a man whose life I save *(Saint-Florent)*; by way of thanks, he rapes me. I reach the property of an aristocratic debauchee *(the sodomist de Bressac, with whom Justine falls in love)* who has me set upon and devoured by his dogs for not having wanted to poison his aunt. From there I go to the home of a murderous and incestuous surgeon *(Rodin)* whom I strive to spare from doing a horrible deed: the butcher brands me for a criminal; he doubtless consummates his atrocities, makes his fortune, whilst I am obliged to beg for my bread. I wish to have the sacrements made available to me, I wish fervently to implore the Supreme Being whence howbeit I receive so many ills, and the august tribunal, at which I hope to find purification in our most holy mysteries, becomes the bloody theater of my ignominy: the monster who abuses and plunders me is elevated to his order's highest honours and I fall back into the appalling abyss of misery *(Justine is referring to the miraculous virgin of the Sainte-Marie-des-Bois monastery, where she is held captive for six months, along with other young women, by lubricious and murderous Benedictine monks)*. I attempt to preserve a woman from her husband's fury, the cruel one *(Gernande)* wishes to put me

> to death by draining away my blood drop by drop. I wish to relieve a poor woman, she robs me. I give aid to a man *(the counterfeitor Roland)* whom adversaries have struck down and left unconscious, the thankless creature makes me turn a wheel like an animal; he hangs me for his pleasure's sake; all fortune's blessings accrue to him, and I come within an ace of dying on the gallows for having been compelled to work for him. An unworthy woman *(la Dubois)* seeks to seduce me for a new crime *(robbing Dubreuil)*, a second time I lose the little I own in order to rescue her victim's treasure. A gentleman *(Dubreuil)*, a kind spirit wishes to compensate me for all my sufferings by the offer of his hand, he dies in my arms *(poisoned by la Dubois)* before being able to do anything for me. I risk my life in a fire *(started by la Dubois)* in order to snatch a child, who does not belong to me, from the flames *(she slips and the child perishes)*; the infant's mother accuses and launches legal proceedings against me. I fall into my most mortal enemy's hands; she *(la Dubois)* wishes to carry me off by force and take me to a man *(a bishop)* whose passion is to cut off heads: if I avoid that villain's sword it is so that I can trip and fall under Themis' *(she is abused, tortured and condemned to death for arson, theft and murder by a debauched judge)*. I implore the protection of a man *(Saint-Florent)* whose life and fortune I once saved; I dare expect gratitude from him, he lures me to his house, he submits me to horrors, and there I find the iniquitous judge upon whom my case depends; both abuse me, both outrage me, both accelerate my doom; fortune overwhelms them with favors, I hasten on to death. (*Good Conduct*, pp. 736–37; *Les Infortunes*, pp. 179–80; *Les Malheurs*, pp. 405–407; *La nouvelle Justine*, pp. 434–37)

In the first two versions, when she finishes her sad tale, Justine is recognised by her sister Juliette, whose rich and powerful lover succeeds in rescuing her from the gallows, and she goes to live with them in their château.[9] Fate, however, cruelly cuts short Justine's life and her new-found happiness. In a savage metaphor for the sheer perversity of providence, she is finally split asunder by a thunderbolt during a violent thunderstorm. The evolution of this scene and its repercussions in the narrative reflect both the increasingly transgressive sexualisation of *Justine* from one version to the next and, perhaps also, the author's changing attitude to his heroine. In *Les Infortunes*, the bolt enters her right breast and comes out through her mouth, whereas in *Les Malheurs* the bolt exits through her abdomen and in *La nouvelle Justine* through her vagina. Furthermore, in the final version, in which there is no happy reunion, Justine's horrific death is not so much an accident as an event engineered by Juliette and her libertine friends, who sadistically drive her outside as the storm reaches its peak.[10]

The common theme of all three narratives is that the heroine's unreasonable attachment to virtue (and in particular to her virginity) attracts nothing but misfortune, as she is exploited and abused physically and sexually by almost everyone she encounters, and is even framed for crimes of theft and murder. Like Voltaire's *Candide*, which Sade had almost certainly read, *Justine* was originally conceived as a satire, attacking the corruption of contemporary institutions, including the judiciary, banking, the bourgeois-dominated world of finances in general and, above all, the Catholic Church, with divine providence being the principal religious target. In these respects, Sade's *conte* is decidedly Voltairean, but where Voltaire never quite found a satisfactory solution to the problem of physical and moral evil other than to posit the totally implausible concept of an indifferent God,[11] Sade's libertines dismiss belief in a deity altogether and draw somewhat different conclusions from the observation, familiar to Candide, that the virtuous perish while the wicked survive. Candide and his fellow truth-seekers do eventually find a kind of contentment in the simple virtue of hard work. In contrast, Justine is repeatedly reminded of what the author–narrator had told the reader on the very first page: that 'in an entirely corrupted age, the safest course is to follow along after the others' (*Good Conduct*, p. 457). Rousseau's idealistic faith in man's natural goodness is directly challenged in a dissertation delivered to Justine by Roland the counterfeitor: the only truth is the law of the jungle according to which the strong not only survive but flourish at the expense of the weak.[12] In the original version, even Justine herself comes to the conclusion on encountering the monstrous counterfeitor that 'Man is naturally wicked'. The note of optimism on which *Candide* ends is completely absent from the far bleaker vision of life and death that closes *Justine*.

This emphasis on man's wickedness is also to be found in another great work of the time: Choderlos de Laclos's masterly tale of Machiavellian manipulation, *Les Liaisons Dangereuses*, published in 1782, may well have had some influence on the Marquis. In the conception of Justine's character there are distinct echoes of the young, delectable and sexually innocent Cécile Volanges, whom Laclos's libertines, the Vicomte de Valmont and the Marquise de Merteuil, take such pleasure in debauching. Other influences on the writing of Sade's novel can be found among the popular genres of the century: fairy tales, the Gothic novel ('roman noir'), and in particular the *conte moral* or 'moral tale'.

Among fairy-tale elements of a general nature, which clearly detract from any realistic effect, there are giants (Gernande) and magical healing potions, while Justine's unfortunate experiences in the forest at the hands of Saint-Florent, the Comte de Bressac and others seem directly inspired by *Little Red Riding Hood, Hansel and Gretel* and the great many other fairy tales known to Sade from his youth in which a credulous young girl, lost in the woods, too willingly places her trust in those she encounters. More specifically, the vampiric Gernande's secret chamber filled with the bloody corpses of earlier spouses is strongly reminiscent of the tale of *Bluebeard*. Gernande's isolated castle, Roland's mountain fortress and the labyrinthine monastery of Sainte-Marie-des-Bois, together with their sepulchral trappings of torture chambers, skulls and the like, seem to come straight out of the Gothic novel, although the atheistic Sadean version is, of course, completely devoid of the genre's supernatural features.[13] While Sade appears merely to borrow from the fairy tale and the Gothic novel, it is the *conte moral* that undergoes parodic treatment in *Justine*. The 'recognition scene', a stock situation of the genre, in which characters long separated are tearfully reunited, is amusingly counterfeited in the reunion of the two sisters towards the end of the narrative:

– Juliette! est-ce toi que j'entends? dit la malheureuse prisonnière en se jetant dans les bras de Mme de Lorsange ... toi ... ma soeur! ... ah! je mourrai bien moins malheureuse, puisque j'ai pu t'embrasser encore une fois! ...

Et les deux soeurs, étroitement serrées dans les bras l'une de l'autre, ne s'entendaient plus que par leurs sanglots, ne s'exprimaient plus que par leurs larmes. (*Les Malheurs*, p. 408)

'Juliette! is it you I hear?' cried the unhappy prisoner, casting herself into Madame de Lorsange's arms; '... you ... my sister! ... ah, I shall die far less miserable, for I have been able to embrace you again! ...'

And the two sisters, clasped in each other's arms, were prevented by their sobs from hearing one another, and found expression in naught but tears. (*Good Conduct*, p. 738)

The style of the *conte moral* is parodied through excess – the *ton larmoyant* or 'tearful tone', the heavy emphasis on *sensibilité* are clearly recognisable here, as in Justine's frequent lachrymose pleadings for mercy. Most controversially of all, the genre's moral aims are outrageously inverted: whereas the moral tale seeks to edify and improve its reader by extolling romantic love and showing how virtue alone leads to happiness, Sade's narrative demonstrates that virtue leads repeatedly and inexorably to misery and that human relations are motivated mainly by lust or self-interest.[14]

The use of these models drawn from the popular literature of the time clearly has an impact on the verisimilitude of the narrative. Whatever her injuries, Justine always makes a perfect and speedy recovery, often thanks to quasi-magical healing potions: 'Muni d'un flacon d'essence, il m'en frotte à plusieurs reprises. Les traces des atrocités de mes bourreaux s'évanouissent [...]' (*Les Malheurs*, p. 402) / 'He picks up a flask of spirits and several times rubs all my wounds. The traces of my executioners' atrocities vanish [...]' (*Good Conduct*, p. 733); and even the mark of the thief branded on her shoulder by Rodin is completely removed by surgeons following her reunion with Juliette (*Les Malheurs*, pp. 402

and 410). Like the hero or heroine of some modern comic-book adventure story, she extricates herself with astounding ease from all of those mortal perils that beset her. The bloodthirsty Gernande, for example, forgets to lock the door of her prison, and with one bound she is free! (*Les Malheurs*, p. 302). At the level of characterisation, too, there is little concern with *vraisemblance*. That the common thieves, la Dubois and Coeur-de-Fer should discourse like philosophers is unlikely, to say the least. We should, of course, not be surprised by this lack of attention to verisimilitude. Sade's fiction is far from the realism that will come to dominate and in many ways define the novel genre in the nineteenth century. As a writer of the eighteenth century, Sade is simply of his time.[15]

I now propose to consider more closely the differences between the versions which will reveal much about the relationship, not only between the author and his text but also between the author and his intended reader. We shall examine how the complexity of Sade's changing relationship with his creation is revealed in textual but also in paratextual features, where a conscious authorial contempt for his heroine manifests itself more and more openly as if more strongly to suppress an unconscious sympathy.[16] As for the girly girl herself, it is in the words of her own story that we shall look for her.

The change of title is not without significance. While both *Infortunes* and *Malheurs* may be and have been translated by the English word 'Misfortunes', the two French words carry quite different connotations. While *Infortunes* connotes the unfortunate fate suffered by virtue through no fault of its own, the ambiguity of *Malheurs* – ill-luck but also misery, the opposite of *bonheur* – seems to imply that virtue is itself a wretched state, and so anyone embracing it has only herself to blame. The juxtaposition of the heroine's name – *Justine ou les Malheurs de la vertu* – personalises the abstract title of the first version, focusing our attention on Justine as the source of her own misery. This change of emphasis in title is the beginning of an important process of evolution in the presentation of the narrative, culminating in the third and final version, *La nouvelle Justine, ou les*

Malheurs de la vertu of 1797. In 1791, however, the changing title may have begun to reflect a growing boldness in Sade, newly liberated and, at this time, full of optimism with regard to his future as a writer and especially as a playwright, but he was still anxious to please his readers, to convince them of the honesty of his intentions.

The author's preface, addressed to the one reader who appeared to matter to him above all others, the woman who by this time had become his constant companion, the aptly named Constance, offers ample evidence of this concern. This preface is essentially designed to condition the responses, first of Constance, to whom the author speaks directly, and, more generally, of all those morally upright citizens that she, in her sensitivity, indirectly represents.[17] Virtue, he implies, is best served when shown as the pitiful victim of vice, so that the reader will be unavoidably moved by her plight. This hypocritical defence of a virtue, against which Sade has already launched vigorous attacks elsewhere,[18] rests upon a number of subtle rhetorical strategies. Constance is made to feel that the story, dedicated to her, was written for her alone – 'c'est à toi que j'adresse cet ouvrage' / 'it is to thee I address this work' – and that it is, therefore, her reception of the work alone that counts:

> Aurai-je réussi, Constance? Une larme de tes yeux déterminera-t-elle mon triomphe? Après avoir lu *Justine*, en un mot, diras-tu: 'Oh! combien ces tableaux du Crime me rendent fière d'aimer la Vertu! Comme elle est sublime dans les larmes! Comme les malheurs l'embellissent!'
>
> O Constance! que ces mots t'échappent, et mes travaux sont couronnés. (*Les Malheurs*, pp. 51–2)

> Have I succeeded, Constance? Will a tear in thy eye determine my triumph? After having read *Justine*, wilt say: 'Oh, how these renderings of Crime make me proud of my love for Virtue! How sublime does it appear through tears! How 'tis embellished by misfortunes!'
>
> Oh, Constance! may these words but escape thy lips, and my labors shall be crowned. (*Good Conduct*, pp. 455–56)

This intimate mode of address (the dedication is entitled 'À Ma Bonne Amie' / 'To my dear friend'; she is 'tu' rather than 'vous', and there is throughout the personalising use of the vocative, as here in the final sentence) is likely to make all other readers feel, unconsciously at least, that they share this intimacy. Indeed, we cannot help but adopt her intended perspective. Here, as elsewhere in this *dédicace*, we are told with Constance how we will react: 'mes motifs, dévoilés par toi [...]' / 'my intentions, these thou shalt perceive'. The use of apostrophe – 'diras-tu' / 'wilt say' – of rhetorical questioning – 'Aurai-je réussi, Constance?' / 'Have I succeeded, Constance?' – of vocatives and imperatives – 'O, Constance! que ces mots t'échappent' / 'Oh, Constance! may these words but escape thy lips' – is repeated throughout the passage in order to manipulate and seduce. The reader thus represented as the author's closest friend would feel disloyal if he or she were to respond in any other fashion than that prescribed here. Moreover, any attacks upon the work could only come from libertines, whose interest it is to show virtue triumphant; like Molière, his crusading predecessor, its author would then be an innocent victim of injustice and malevolence: 'c'est le Vice qui, gémissant d'être dévoilé, crie au scandale aussitôt qu'on l'attaque. Le procès du *Tartuffe* fut fait par des bigots; celui de *Justine* sera l'ouvrage des libertins' (*Les Malheurs*, p. 51) / 'it is only Vice that trembles when Vice is found out, and cries scandal immediately it is attacked. To bigots *Tartuffe* was indebted for his ordeal; *Justine*'s will be the achievement of libertines' (*Good Conduct*, p. 455). In these few short sentences, Sade the most libertine of writers manages by an extraordinary sleight of hand to become the very opponent of libertinage!

It is clear from a letter written to his lawyer, Reinaud, that in private, Sade was far less self-assured:

> On imprime actuellement un roman de moi, mais trop immoral pour être envoyé à un homme aussi pieux, aussi décent que vous. J'avais besoin d'argent, mon éditeur me le demandait *bien poivré*, et je le lui ai fait capable d'empester le diable. On l'appelle *Justine ou les Malheurs de la vertu*. Brûlez-le et ne le lisez point, si par hasard il tombe

> entre vos mains. Je le renie ... (Quoted by Gilbert Lely, Avant-propos, *La nouvelle Justine*, p. 9)

> They are now printing a novel of mine, but one too immoral to send to a man as pious and as decent as you. I needed money, my publisher asked me for something quite spicy, and I made him [a book] capable of corrupting the devil. They are calling it *Justine ou les Malheurs de la vertu*. Burn it and do not read it if by chance it falls into your hands: I renounce it. (Trans. Lever, *Sade*, p. 382)

The letter betrays an uncharacteristic insecurity and, although it is the very opposite in message and tone of the public dedication to Constance Quesnet, both documents, in their different ways, display a need to be accepted on a moral level and an underlying fear of rejection by others. The scriptor of *La nouvelle Justine* is far less tentative. Annie Le Brun points out that in *Les Malheurs de la vertu* of 1791, Sade is still willing to play the part of the socially virtuous author, 'plein de respect pour nos conventions sociales' (*Les Malheurs*, p. 53) / 'full of respect for social conventions' (*Good Conduct*, p. 457), a phrase which, on the first page of *La nouvelle Justine*, becomes: 'Si, plein d'un respect *vain, ridicule* et *superstitieux* pour nos *absurdes* conventions sociales [...]' (Introduction to *Histoire de Juliette*, pp. 46–7, and first page of *La NJ*; my emphasis) / 'If, full of a *vain, ridiculous* and *superstitious* respect for our *absurd* social conventions'.

In addition to the differences in the 'storm scene' referred to earlier, there is in *Les Infortunes* and *Les Malheurs*, a transparently hypocritical attempt to construct a moral lesson. In a factitious and highly ironic 'happy ending', Juliette and her lover are sufficiently moved by her sister's sudden death to follow the path of virtue to true happiness. Juliette joins a Carmelite convent and becomes the very embodiment of piety, whilst her lover embarks on a successful and exemplary career in government. On the basis of events that directly contradict the lessons in self-interest of the entire preceding narrative, the reader is invited to draw the wholly implausible conclusion that

> le véritable bonheur n'est qu'au sein de la vertu, et que si, dans des vues qu'il ne nous appartient pas d'approfondir, Dieu permet qu'elle soit persécutée sur la terre, c'est pour l'en dédommager dans le ciel par les plus flatteuses récompenses! (*Les Malheurs*, p. 414)

> true happiness is to be found nowhere but in Virtue's womb, and that if, in keeping with designs it is not for us to fathom, God permits that it be persecuted on Earth, it is so that Virtue may be compensated by Heaven's most dazzling rewards. (*Good Conduct*, p. 743)

This conclusion is unconscious hypocrisy at best and a purely pragmatic measure to avoid censure at worst. In stark contrast, the ending of *La nouvelle Justine* shows that Sade has abandoned all former pretences at writing a morally uplifting tale. Neither Juliette nor any of her companions undergoes a Pauline conversion to virtue – quite the opposite in fact – and the reader of *Juliette* is left in no doubt as to the rewards of vice.

These changes are certainly reflected in the paratext of the final version of *Justine*. The new title has a ring of authorial pride about it and is clearly designed to maximise sales – *La nouvelle Justine*, 'nouvelle', newly revised and updated, the latest model, just off the production line, an essential social accessory – and there are impertinent parodic echoes of Rousseau's *La Nouvelle Héloise*. Furthermore, its publication jointly with *l'Histoire de Juliette ou les Prospérités du vice* provides the occasion for a pleasing and self-confident symmetry of titles, whereby the misery of virtue now contrasts directly with the prosperity of vice. The dedication to Constance has been replaced by an 'Avis de l'éditeur' or 'Editor's Foreword', which is actually a fiction fabricated by Sade to explain and justify the new edition, and by an epigraph in the form of a rhyming alexandrine couplet:

> On n'est point criminel pour faire la peinture
> Des bizarres penchants qu'inspire la nature

> There is nothing criminal in painting the portrait
> Of those strange leanings inspired by nature

Gone is the personal address to his friend as reader and to the reader as friend, and with it the desire to please the sensitive and morally virtuous. The classical form of the epigraph suggests the self-assurance of a writer who sees himself as belonging to a reassuringly ancient and respected literary tradition, while the categorical negative, 'on n'est point criminel' / 'there is nothing criminal', anticipates objections to the book rooted in conventional sexual morality. The alleged 'Editor's Foreword' claims that a 'faithless friend', to whom the now deceased author had entrusted the manuscript of his work, had used it to produce the earlier version, 'bien au-dessous de l'original et qui fut constamment désavoué par celui dont l'énergique crayon a dessiné la Justine et sa soeur que l'on va voir ici' / 'far inferior to the original and firmly repudiated by the author of the story of Justine and her sister to be found here'. The title page falsely declares Holland, not Paris, to be the place of publication. Such pretences were commonplace in any eighteenth-century works containing politically or philosophically sensitive material (erotic texts were known at that time as *livres philosophiques*), feints familiar to readers as means of preventing the censor from discovering the true identity of an author, and it is unlikely that many were taken in.

Nevertheless, the protective cloak of anonymity leads Sade to make a number of revealing statements. There is the possibly tongue-in-cheek arrogance of 'le génie de cet écrivain à jamais célèbre' / 'the genius of this ever famous writer', and the more immodestly self-righteous tones employed to defend the work. Here, a significant shift of emphasis has occurred: whereas the dedication to Constance aimed to placate a potentially uncooperative reader, cajoling her into a sympathetic response that the scriptor appeared greatly to value, the author of the foreword projects an apparent lack of any concern about the negative reception of *La nouvelle Justine*, once again anticipating such responses but this time rejecting them out of hand as the reactions of idiots: 'il n'y a que les sots qui se scandalisent' / 'only idiots are scandalised'. Since the *avis*, unlike the *dédicace*, is not conceived as a personal address to the potential reader, it contains less of the rhetorical subtlety that the latter's dialogic form makes possible.

This loss of literary subtlety from one paratext to another in my view reflects the lesser merit, overall, of the final version, as compared with earlier versions.[19] The greater literary merit of the first and second versions is attributable in large measure to a common narrative structure which *La nouvelle Justine* does not share. With the exception of the briefest of introductions and conclusions, narrated in the third person by an authorial voice, both *Les Infortunes* and *Les Malheurs* are first person narratives, offering direct access to the heroine's thoughts and feelings and permitting the development of an unmediated relationship between character and reader, whereas the exclusively third person narration of the final version creates an affective distance between them. An authorial voice dominates *La nouvelle Justine,* directly controlling the reader's responses, telling him what to think of a heroine whose speech is confined within quotation marks and at every turn qualified by an author–narrator's accompanying commentary.

On a stylistic level, too, whereas the third person narrator of *La nouvelle Justine* is free to describe sexual activities in a manner that is direct to the point of vulgarity, the autodiegetic narrator of the earlier versions is obliged to employ euphemisms that make for a more interesting use of language.[20] The circumlocutions and lacunae of this euphemistic style do sometimes appear clichéd in the repetitious use of a particular lexical field. Sade here frequently has recourse to precious metaphors belonging to the amorous discourse of the eighteenth-century novel, in which erotic activities are symbolically expressed in terms less shocking to the sensibilities, such as the botanical or the military. At times, however, this euphemisation of obscene events produces a clever use of language and helps to create nice touches of an ironic humour, born of a contrast between content and form:

> *male erection*: Il se lève, et se montrant à la fin à moi dans un état où la raison triomphe rarement [...] (*Les Malheurs,* p. 74) / He gets up, and exhibiting himself to me in a state over which reason is seldom triumphant [...] (*Good Conduct,* p. 473)

> *enforced fellatio*: son ignominieuse passion s'assouvit dans un lieu qui m'interdit toute plainte (*Les Malheurs*, p. 197) / his ignominious passion is appeased in a fashion that prevented me from complaining (*Good Conduct*, p. 571, adapted)[21]

The linguistic or metaphorical veiling of certain activities may on the one hand be said to protect the innocence of a reader lacking in sexual experience, but it can equally be far more erotic than sexual explicitness.[22] For example, compare this description of the sodomising of a young virgin in *Les Malheurs*, in which the act is euphemistically conveyed by the extended use of military metaphors, with the much less circumspect account of the sodomising of Justine by the surgeon Rodin in *La nouvelle Justine*:

> Quelque énorme disproportion qui se trouve entre la conquête et l'assaillant, celui-ci n'entreprend pas moins le combat; un cri perçant annonce la victoire, mais rien n'attendrit l'ennemi; plus la captive implore sa grâce, plus on la presse avec vigueur, et la malheureuse a beau se débattre, elle est bientôt sacrifiée. (*Les Malheurs*, p. 256)

> Whatever the enormous disproportion between the conquest and the assailant, the latter is not the less in a sweat to give fight; a piercing cry announces victory, but nothing mollifies the enemy's chilly heart; the more the captive implores mercy, the less quarter is granted her, the more vigorously she is pressed; the ill-starred one fences in vain: she is soon transpierced. (*Good Conduct*, p. 617)

> Rodin [...] saisit fortement les reins de la jeune fille, pousse avec violence, et disparaît, jusqu'aux couillons, dans ce cul frais et voluptueux. (*La NJ*, Vol. 1, p. 224)[23]

> Rodin [...] gets a firm hold of the girl's posterior, gives a violent thrust and disappears up to his balls into her fresh, voluptuous arse.

The language may be coarse, but the expression is always grammatically correct: 'il fallait bien que je déchargeasse' / 'I just had to discharge,' cries the monstrous d'Esterval after a particularly nasty act of sodomy (*La NJ*, Vol. 2, p. 160).[24] Such a contrast between the vulgarity and unrestrainedness of content and vocabulary and the classical order and erudition of syntax and grammar cannot fail to amuse the modern reader.

The authorial narrative of the final version certainly provides scope for a more direct brand of humour than the first person narratives of *Les Infortunes* and *Les Malheurs* – Justine does not exactly have much to laugh about – and the overall tone of this narrative is consequently more playful, even if the violence is more extreme. *La nouvelle Justine* is as much a work of black comedy as of transgressive eroticism or sadistic violence. Occasionally, the author–narrator seems ironically to mock his own verbal ingenuity, as with the simultaneously sodomising and sodomised Saint-Florent's cries of orgasmic delight: ' – Ahe! ... ahe! ... s'écrie-t-il (c'est sa passion que nous peignons ici d'après nature)' (*La NJ*, Vol. 2, p. 271) / 'Oh! ... oh! ...' he cries (his passion is depicted here from nature)'. In the main, however, the humour is far less subtle than the ironies of *Les Malheurs*, more visual than verbal, recalling the knockabout sexual farce of Chaucer or Boccaccio. Much of it is simply coarse and puerile, focusing frequently on the size and power of libertine organs: Coeur-de-Fer's erect penis is hard enough to break open a walnut (*La NJ*, Vol. 1, p. 74), while the monk Severino's member 'dépassait la table de six pouces' (*La NJ*, Vol. 2, p. 66) / 'protruded above the table by six inches'. The embedded narrative of Jérôme's first sexual experiences with his sister is full of comic mishaps and misapprehensions, as when both mistake one hole for the other! (*La NJ*, pp. 393–94).[25]

One could argue, therefore, that the linguistic and other constraints on the writing of the first two versions of *Justine*, constraints stemming from fear of censorship and the disapproval of those close to the author, lead to greater creativity.[26] Euphemism forces the use of metaphor and simile, and the writer has to achieve a balancing act between the need to be comprehensible to all readers, which necessarily leads him to rely on commonplaces, and the desire to make those commonplaces his own, hence the ironic constrasts referred to earlier.

In *La nouvelle Justine* and *Juliette*, as in *La Philosophie dans le boudoir* which had appeared two years earlier in 1795, the persuasion of the reader and the rhetoric on which it depends drive the narrative in a far blunter fashion: the reader now undergoes less of a seduction than an instruction, which on occasions seems like a taking by force. The undertaking itself is on a much grander scale than *Les Malheurs*, and the paratextual frame grows accordingly to include significant visual support. *La nouvelle Justine et* L'*Histoire de Juliette, sa soeur* fills ten volumes and nearly 3,700 pages, 'ornés d'un frontispice et de cent sujets gravés avec soin' / 'adorned with a frontispiece and 100 carefully wrought engravings'. In *La nouvelle Justine* alone, there are 40 such illustrations. According to a contemporary newspaper article, these covered one-third of the pages of the novel![27] Though something of an exaggeration, this inflated perception of the number of engravings does nevertheless convey the impact of these volumes on the public of the time. Jean-Jacques Pauvert observes that this was no less than 'la plus grande entreprise de librairie pornographique jamais réalisée au monde' / 'the greatest undertaking of print pornography ever accomplished'.[28]

All these illustrations depict lewd scenes from the novel; all are detailed, explicit and highly obscene, according to conventional definitions of the term, representing naked men, women, children and sometimes animals engaging in orgiastic activity, in which flagellation and sodomy are dominant; some are consensual, many involve force. The male organs are always erect and sometimes in the process of ejaculating. Most of the female figures are in the posture of passive and pleading victims. Inevitably, orgy is represented without the dissertation that underpins it, and the clichés of eighteenth-century pornography (and also, perhaps, of the Sadean myth) reduce Sade's novel to a series of sexual thrills. Settings are mainly interiors, high-ceilinged, tapestry-hung rooms of neo-classical design, markers of an aristocratic wealth, associated with the *ancien régime*, turning the corruption associated with it into yet another commonplace. In the written narrative, Sade's killing machines are described in a verbal complexity that challenges the reader's imagination and intelligence, and in so doing in part transforms their horrific function into a technical and textual exercise, but their visual representation somehow lends them a spurious and banal plausibility, making them immediately and disturbingly realisable. By the very weight of their numbers, as well as by their lascivious realistic detail, these illustrations oblige the reader to see more and to conceive less, and the role of the reader's imagination is severely circumscribed by a visual element that comes to define a narrative it was only intended to support. The convoluted acrobatics of the Sadean orgy thus emerge from the particularity of fantasy to become general blueprints for action. In his discussion of the verbal ingenuity of Diderot's erotic masterpiece, *Les Bijoux indiscrets*, Jean-Marie Goulemot identifies the kinds of mechanism that the *gravures* of *La nouvelle Justine* and *Juliette* undermine:

> [...] the position assigned to the reader is not as constraining as in the pornographic novel, so the process of reading brings its own satisfaction to the desire it creates. There is no need to return to the real world, since the text is entirely closed, relying on the quality of the word play and the capacity of the text to evoke without stating explicitly and to contaminate with salaciousness those words that seemed to be least amenable to such a process. There are no bodies offered up to the gaze, no embraces to be spied upon. The intrusion is entirely linguistic in nature [...][29]

Certainly, as Goulemot goes on to argue, the soliciting of the reader's gaze is a key element of the erotic novel, so that the act of voyeurism is frequently represented, *mis en scène*, within the narrative itself, as sexual activities are viewed secretly through keyholes and windows, etc., and the reader is able to identify directly with the intradiegetic voyeur.[30] Goulemot, however, distinguishes the erotic novel from the libertine novel which 'rests on the art of persuasion' and is therefore essentially a 'work of words and not pictures'.[31] All of Sade's writing, including *La nouvelle Justine*, I would suggest, falls into this latter category. The engravings accompanying this work and *Juliette* in this sense might be said to mislead the potential reader, by transforming the paratext of

Sade's 'roman libertin' into that of a 'pornographic novel' (according to Goulemot's definitions) in which the involvement of the reader is less an intellectual than a physical process. The voyeuristic support of the *gravures*, 'Toutes plus piquantes les unes que les autres' / 'All more spicy than the others' (Editor's Foreword), fulfils the same function as photographic material, found on both the inside and the outside of modern publications, in assisting in the all-important business of marketing and promotion. The final paragraph of the Editor's Foreword goes out of its way to emphasise this aspect of the work and, together with the *gravures*, was almost certainly added at the prompting of the publisher. On the other hand, as Marcel Hénaff points out,[32] no special place is given in Sade's text to voyeurism, which is portrayed in *Les 120 Journées de Sodome* as just one perversion among many others – another reason why Sade's novels might be termed libertine but not pornographic. Consequently, these illustrations are quite unsuited to a work that seeks to convince the reader rather than to seduce him – a process not unlike that of religious conversion.

Three main points emerge from these few reflections about the *Justine* paratexts. Firstly, there is the power of the paratext to influence the manner in which the reader receives the text. In constituting the very text itself for those readers – and there are many – who never get beyond the title pages, it may even bear some of the responsibility for the creation of the myth of Sade as pornographer and little else. Secondly, the changes in and additions to paratextual features from one version of *Justine* to another underline and reflect the evolution of the narrative itself, and perhaps more importantly, the changing relationship of the author/scriptor with his own text. Thirdly, and most controversially, these changes suggest that the constraints imposed on the author by imprisonment, by fear of the censor and by a desire to be understood make for a narrative of greater subtlety which leaves more scope for the imagination of the reader to participate creatively in the act of reading. Unlike the final version, *Les Malheurs de la vertu*, published in 1791 but almost certainly written before Sade's release from prison, benefited from all these constraints to become a work of considerable literary merit, a merit that derives substantially in my view from the importance still accorded by Sade at this time to the morally conventional reader's response.

The constraints associated with *Les Infortunes* and *Les Malheurs*, especially the first person narration, also facilitate the projection of a more sympathetic image of Justine. I should now like to return to the hypothesis of an identification by the author with his heroine.

The writing frenzy that produced the first version suggests an emotional investment in the narrative of *Justine* that is absent from *l'Histoire de Juliette*, which was probably written during Sade's prolonged period of freedom in the 1790s. Jean Paulhan has argued that, if Bressac, Raphaël and the other sadistic libertines of the story might be considered personae of the author, he also identifies masochistically with Justine.[33] It is not hard to share this view of a man, writing in the relentless solitude of his prison cell, tortured by sexual deprivation and by ignorance of the term of his detention, suffering increasingly from eye trouble – a real problem for the writer that Sade had by now become. There is some evidence, too, that the figure of his victim-heroine was drawn from life, which might support the hypothesis of a greater psychological and emotional attachment by the author to Justine than to Juliette. A young female servant at the Sade family château de La Coste, whose real name was Catherine Treillet, went by the nickname of Justine, and it is known that she participated voluntarily in sexual activities with the Marquis, refusing to leave the château with her father. Jean-Marie Goulemot conjectures that she may even have fallen in love with her master, just as the fictional Justine does with the Comte de Bressac.[34] Whatever the truth of their relationship, it does not seem implausible to assume that Sade used the serving girl as a general model for his literary creation, in the same way that other figures and events from his past appear to have inspired particular scenes in the novel.

This biographical information is certainly helpful in evaluating the plausibility of the hypothesis of an identification between author and character, but as I suggested earlier, it is, above all, in Justine's own words and actions that evidence of any such identification should properly be sought.

Notwithstanding her initial portrayal as the brainless and bashful blonde with an unreasonable and unthinking devotion to virtue, Justine actually behaves in an entirely sensible and sympathetic manner. In spite of himself, Sade creates a figure with whom the reader (and perhaps also the author) is drawn to identify. One cannot help feeling, though, that, especially in *Les Malheurs*, the feisty heroine frequently escapes the author's conscious control. The entire story is, after all, centred around Justine, and so she is the focus both of the libertines' attention within the text and of the reader's attention outside it. Justine herself expresses an ironic awareness of the central role that her status as victim gives her: 'Je suis le centre de ces abominables orgies, j'en suis le point fixe et le ressort' (*Les Malheurs*, p. 401) / 'I am the focal point of these execrable orgies, their absolute center and mainspring' (*Good Conduct*, p. 733). The centrality of her role as victim is complemented and, indeed, enhanced by the centrality of her role as narrator. Because it is Justine and not the author–narrator who has charge of the narrative in *Les Infortunes* and *Les Malheurs*, she is able to condemn the libertines for their views and is even accorded the right to put her own case at length, for instance, on the question of God's existence (*Les Malheurs,* pp. 167–69). Since she is the principal narrator, both libertines and fellow victims speak through her, which means that we mostly share a point of view that is opposed to and sometimes mocking of that of the libertines. In the monastery at Sainte-Marie-des-Bois, for example, a fellow captive, Omphale, instructing the newly arrived Justine in the rules of conduct for the girls, tells her how easy it is to fool the villainous monks. The main thing is not to fall pregnant:

> – Sans doute, il est de certaines éponges ... Mais si Antonin s'en aperçoit, on n'échappe point à son courroux; le plus sûr, est d'étouffer l'impression de la nature en démontant l'imagination, *et avec de pareils scélérats, cela n'est pas difficile.* (*Les Malheurs*, pp. 216–17; my emphasis)

> Of course, there are certain devices, sponges ... But if Antonin perceives what you are up to, beware of his

> wrath; the safest way is to smother whatever might be the natural impression by striving to unhinge the imagination, *which with monsters like these is not difficult.* (*Good Conduct*, p. 586)

Contrary to the impressions given by her initial character sketch, she is intelligent and self-assertive in debates with her libertine captors, who always listen respectfully to her arguments and at times even compliment her reasoning. Following a sermon from la Dubois concerning the justification of crime, for instance, Justine is given a strong counter-argument, challenging the logic of the female libertine on her own ground (*Les Malheurs*, pp. 357–58; *Good Conduct*, pp. 697–98). La Dubois seems unable to respond to Justine's powerful and cogent objections, and has to resort to other tactics:

> – Un moment, Thérèse, dit la Dubois en me retenant, si je ne peux vaincre ta raison, que je captive au moins ton coeur. (*Les Malheurs*, p. 359)

> 'One moment, Thérèse,' said Dubois, holding me back, 'if I cannot conquer your reason, I may at least captivate your heart [...]' (*Good Conduct*, p. 698)

Justine's opponents are not just monsters, but redoubtable theorists, which makes her arguments all the more impressive to match their knowledge and rhetoric. Far from being the naive ingénue, Justine, even in her final incarnation, is actually a smart cookie who simply has a disastrous run of bad luck. It is not, as Maurice Blanchot maintains, that the same things happen to Justine as to Juliette, and that their fate depends on how each reacts to similar circumstances.[35] Justine's most horrendous experiences befall her like the bolt of lightning that finally strikes her dead without her first being consulted about her readiness to engage in debauchery: the horrors of Sainte-Marie-des-Bois, the abuses to which Roland and the counterfeitors subject her, Rodin's threat of vivisection would have equally happened to Juliette. As Jean-Marie Goulemot puts it, 'Justine is a tragic victim of evil and not a dizzy ingénue who attracts misfortune by being silly.'[36] If Sade is saying that misfortune 'naturally' strikes the virtuous, then he is positing a *malevolent* providence – in any event, a force of some kind outside the human dimension, the existence of which would clearly be in contradiction with his materialistic atheism. It is not Justine's virtue that makes life difficult for her – she finds ways of justifying to herself her acquiescence in the various sexual acts demanded of her – but what Geoffrey Bennington has called the 'double bind' situations that so frequently confront her.[37] In these situations, which involve the choice between two evils, Justine shows herself to be as much a pragmatist as a *dévote*. One of the best examples of the 'double bind' is the episode at d'Esterval's 'cut-throat' inn in *La nouvelle Justine*, where travellers are routinely robbed and murdered. D'Esterval challenges Justine to help the victims to escape; if she succeeds, she too will be set free, but if she fails, she will remain to witness the deaths of more unfortunates. The problem is gleefully posed by D'Esterval himself:

> Si vous vous échappiez de chez moi, certaine que je continue ce métier, vous emporteriez le regret mortel de n'avoir pas essayé de sauver ceux qui succomberont après votre départ; [...] l'espoir d'y réussir un jour vous enchaînera nécessairement toute la vie. (*La NJ*, Vol. 2, p. 96)

> If you escape from my house, you will take with you the certainty that I will continue my activities and with it the mortal regret that you did not attempt to save those who succumb after your departure; [...] the hope of one day succeeding in this will therefore keep you captive all your life.

Were she to run away and denounce him to the authorities, more would have died before they could take action. This is a moral dilemma that the most brilliant of philosophers would find hard to resolve. Justine frequently finds herself on the horns of similar dilemmas and responds to them as sensibly (and as responsibly) as anyone could or would.[38]

Justine, then, is not so much an attack on the foolishness of virtue as on the very notion of a benevolent providence.

Fate does exist, but it is evil, not good. Sade's universe is consequently more Manichean than materialist, and the responsibility of individuals like Justine for the plights in which they find themselves is diminished as a result. Jean-Marie Goulemot sees Justine's adventures in *Les Infortunes* as a kind of speech in defence of her creator, held prisoner in the Bastille for crimes which, like his heroine, he was forced by circumstances to commit.[39] It is certainly undeniable that the two have a great deal in common. Like Justine, Sade suffered much the same reversals of fortune: loss of wealth and property in the Revolution, being branded a criminal (symbolically in his case), what he saw as the abuses of justice in the magistrates courts – Justine's case of arson and murder is heard by a corrupt and lascivious judge: 'L'affaire alla bon train, conduite par la haine, la vengeance et la luxure; je fus promptement condamnée [...]' (*Les Malheurs*, p. 405) / 'The case was tried in short order; motivated and directed by hatred, vengeance, and lust, the court promptly condemned me [...]' (*Good Conduct*, p. 736)) – the threat of the death penalty, and, not least, the tortures of a captivity whose term was unknown to him. When, in the monastery at Sainte-Marie-des-Bois, Omphale tells Justine that 'ce n'est pas seulement la nécessité d'assouvir les passions de ces débauchés qui fait le supplice de notre vie, c'est la perte de notre liberté' (*Les Malheurs*, p. 203) / 'it is not simply the necessity to sate these debauchees' hungers which is our life's torture, it is the loss of our freedom' (*Good Conduct*, p. 575), we unmistakeably hear the writer's own embittered voice.

By reassuming narratorial authority in *La nouvelle Justine*, Sade distances himself from his heroine, partly so that the narration can become less coy, more sexually explicit, but also perhaps because by 1797 Sade's memory of his long years in prison during the 1780s had faded to the point where he was no longer able to identify himself as a victim. Annie Le Brun's persuasive hypothesis that *La nouvelle Justine* was composed not before but after *Juliette* adds further weight to the view that when he came to revise *Les Malheurs* for a readership seemingly hungry for more sex and more violence his own sympathies had shifted markedly.[40] By then, the model of ideal femininity had already become the ever-triumphant and irrepressibly phallic Juliette.

We have seen, therefore, how a closer authorial identification with the character helped to make *Les Malheurs* a more complex and in some regards more erotic narrative than *La nouvelle Justine*. The 'girly girl' voice of innocence defiled is much sexier than the unalloyed account of that defilement from the dispassionate distance of an extradiegetic third person narrator.

There will always be those who are sexually excited by the violent objectification of women. The pleasure of raping virgins owned by so many of Sade's libertines finds its place in the darkest corners of the male sexual imagination. On the other hand, most of us, like Rétif de la Bretonne, will find the more sadistic scenes of *La nouvelle Justine* morally and physically repugnant.[41] However, I have not avoided *Justine*'s more violent aspects from any censorious impulse, but because, in my view, the novel's real influence is due to the representation of a comparatively non-violent and yet transgressive sexuality.[42] In her seminal essay, *The Sadeian Woman,* Angela Carter rightly recognises in Justine the ingenuous but sexually magnetic blonde, beloved of Hollywood cinema since the 1930s. Carter sees Justine as the prototype of the celluloid female victim, punished just for being a woman – a female Christ paying for the sin of Eve. But many of the film characters played by Greta Garbo or Marilyn Monroe, for example, are less victimal than the men who surround them. 'Girly girls' like Monroe are fetishised by male desire precisely because they represent an inaccessible sexual object. Monroe's innocence is oddly protective, her blissful unawareness of her sexual power a constant source of male frustration. Sade certainly allows his male reader to enact the fantasy of satisfying this desire, but, except in the final version, satisfaction depends much less on the sadistic pleasures associated with violence to the female body than on the fantasy of creating circumstances in which the inaccessible is made accessible. The young heroine is throughout forced by circumstances to submit to the attentions of male libertines, but except in *La nouvelle Justine* the focus is on the enjoyment of her body rather than on the force required to achieve it. She rarely suffers serious physical harm and, when she does do so, recovers quickly and completely from its consequences.

Carter observes that when beauty is made into an object of reverence it inevitably excites abuse, that purity is always in danger.[43] Physical perfection invites transgression, perhaps because we cannot believe that, in an imperfect world, it should be allowed to exist. Yet, transgression, the breaking of rules and crossing of boundaries, is not necessarily a violent activity. And even when pain is involved, the victim's pleasure is not always excluded. In a symbolic verbal enactment of all those erotic fantasies that turn upon the pain–pleasure nexus, the incomparably brutal Rodin, for instance, declares in a memorable line how much he loves to make a weeping girl come (*La NJ*, Vol. 1, p. 221). The consensual as well as non-consensual act of heterosexual and homosexual sodomy – the preference of so many of the libertines – and the monk Severino's ejaculation onto consecrated hosts, both in their different ways exemplify the true nature of transgression, which is less about violence or abuse than about the breaking of taboos, whether religious or sexual (the taboos on sodomy and virginity are particularly challenging because they combine elements of both). Such taboos, one might object, don't exist any more in Western culture: homosexuality is legal, and virginity no longer universally held to be synonymous with feminine virtue. But this is true only to a degree in a society that demonises both the sexualisation of children (even of post-pubescent girls if they are under 16) and the practice of perverse sexual acts.[44] If Justine continues to inhabit and arouse the sexual imagination, it is not because she is the embodiment of victimhood, but because, as a symbolic conjunction of those powerful taboos that still influence our thinking about sex at the beginning of the twenty-first century, she iconically represents the thrill of their transgression.

5

Femmes Fatales and Phallic Women: *l'Histoire de Juliette*

Sade's most violent and most shocking completed work, the marathon picaresque novel, *l'Histoire de Juliette,* was published some time between 1798 and 1801, following the appearance in 1797 of its companion, *La nouvelle Justine.* It was the last straw for the Paris Prefect of Police, Dubois, who was already determined to hunt down the author of *Justine.* Dubois was convinced that both were the work of the same man. Eventually, probably acting on a tip-off from one of the many police informers that haunted the Parisian book trade, police officers of the new and highly censorious Napoleonic régime arrested Sade and his publisher, Nicolas Massé, at Massé's offices on 6 March 1801. Sade was allegedly caught with the manuscript of *Juliette* in his hand. Copies of both works were seized and Sade charged with having written what has been considered to be the most depraved novel of all time. He was immediately imprisoned, first at Sainte-Pélagie, then at the infamous Bicêtre prison, and finally, in the more salubrious surroundings of the lunatic asylum at Charenton where he would remain until his death in 1814.

Juliette and *La nouvelle Justine* provide their reader with an unadulterated account of man's inhumanity to man, and in this sense are the cynical product of their author's personal and painful experience of the Terror and its evil. Geoffrey Gorer called *Juliette* 'the final vomiting of de Sade's disgust and disappointment'.[1] As Gorer's observation implies, the novel represents a savage attack on the corruption of eighteenth-century French society in which money is power, and power facilitates the unrestrained pursuit of pleasure. *Juliette* can also be read, of course, as the barely unconscious expression of a desire for such unfettered freedom – a utopic vision of power that is almost divine in its totality: 'O mon amour,' cries the libertine, Saint-Fond to Juliette,

> comme les crimes sont délicieux lorsque l'impunité les voile, que le délit les étaye, et que le devoir même les prescrit! Comme il est divin de nager dans l'or et de pouvoir dire, en comptant ses richesses: voilà les moyens de tous les forfaits, de tous les plaisirs; avec cela, toutes mes illusions peuvent se réaliser, toutes mes fantaisies se satisfaire, aucune femme ne me résistera, aucun désir ne demeurera sans effet, les lois mêmes se modifieront par mon or, et je serai despote à mon aise. (Vol. 8, p. 350)

> Oh, my love, how delicious are our crimes when impunity veils them, when duty itself prescribes them. How divine it is to swim in gold and, as one reckons up one's wealth, to be able to say, here are the means to every black deed, to every pleasure; with this, all my wishes can be made to come true, all my fancies can be satisfied; no woman will resist me, none of my desires will fail of realization, my wealth will procure amendments in the law itself, and I'll be despot without let or hindrance. (pp. 323–24)

Only the leisured upper classes could afford to use sex recreationally as well as procreationally, and only the political masters of a land could indulge with impunity in a perverse sexuality that privileged rape and murder, manipulating the justice system for their own ends.[2] More generally, *Juliette* has been read as an implicit indictment of male sexuality as utterly selfish, intrinsically violent and fundamentally tyrannical, and yet, paradoxically (or so it seems), Sade chooses a female rather than a male character as the central focus of this sexual tyranny. Indeed, the novel is dominated by the activities of a number of violent and depraved *femmes fatales*.[3]

Sade's longest novel is scandalously provocative with regard to the role and status of women, as well as to a whole range of moral and philosophical issues, and there is no doubt that many will continue to find both the ideas contained within its pages and its outright obscenity unpalatable. On the other hand, it is a work of breathtaking geographical and historical scope and of remarkable scholarship, replete with learned allusions and references and detailed philosophical arguments. But at the simple story level, too, the novel's sheer nervous energy carries the reader along with its heroine as she races through a Europe ruled by sexual deviants and ruthless megalomaniacs. Among its hundreds of characters, we encounter lascivious monarchs and psychotic politicians, atheistic clerics and man-hating lesbians, giants and sorcerers, vamps and virgins. The entirely fictional rubs shoulders with the verifiably historical; the real blends with the surreal (a black mass at the Vatican, the giant Minski's 'human' furniture) to produce a work of layered complexity. Sade's *Juliette* can be read on many levels: as an adult fairy tale and a manual of sexology, as a political and philosophical satire and a Gothic horror, as an Italian travelogue and an eighteenth-century road movie, above all, perhaps, as a terrifying journey into the murkier depths of human eroticism.[4] On all of these levels, *Juliette* goes much further than *Justine*. The narrative moves faster, the crimes are greater, and the reader feels swept along from one location to another to encounter ever more extreme situations and behaviour.[5]

Juliette, we remember, is Justine's beautiful but wicked elder sister, and her opposite in every way. She has, in fact, much in common with Eugénie, the mother-hating apprentice libertine of *La Philosophie dans le boudoir*. Fifteen years old when she and Justine are orphaned, she is Eugénie let out of the boudoir into the great, mad, bad world. Already awakened to the pleasures of the body as well as to its power by the mother superior of the convent where the two sisters had resided before their father's financial ruin, she immediately sets out to make her living as a prostitute, becoming the mistress of two extremely dangerous libertines, Noirceuil and Saint-Fond. The latter is a government minister who abuses his position to line his pockets and to evade the consequences of the rapes and lust murders that he and his associates regularly commit. Under the protection of these two monsters, she embarks with her lesbian lover, the equally bloodthirsty Clairwil, on an epic tour of Europe and especially Italy, encountering en route a series of libertines, each more depraved than the last, and leaving a trail of pillage, death and destruction in her wake. These libertines include a number of historical figures, such as

Catherine the Great, the atheistic Pope Pius VI, and two homicidal siblings of Marie-Antoinette's, Grand Duke Leopold of Tuscany and the wife of the King of Naples. Unsurprisingly given the revolutionary period in which the novel was written, kings and pontifs are seen as surpassing all others in their debauchery and corruption. Eventually, following many gruesome and often gratuitous crimes, which include the murder of her friend Clairwil, Juliette returns considerably enriched to France. There she is reunited with Noirceuil, whose iniquities are seen to be rewarded when the king makes him prime minister, assuring him and his fellow criminals of a glorious future. With a note of self-referential irony, Noirceuil draws the obvious moral from their story:

> Allons, mes amis, réjouissons-nous, je ne vois dans tout cela que la vertu de malheureuse: nous n'oserions peut-être pas le dire, si c'était un roman que nous écrivissions. (Vol. 9, p. 582)

> Come, good friends, let us all rejoice together, from all this I see nothing but happiness accruing to all save only virtue – but we would perhaps not dare say so were it a novel we were writing. (p. 1193)

In continuing ironic vein, Juliette adopts and defends the real author's point of view:

> Pourquoi donc craindre de le publier, dit Juliette, quand la vérité même arrache les secrets de la nature, à quelque point qu'en frémissent les hommes? La philosophie doit tout dire. (Vol. 9, p. 582)

> Why dread publishing it, said Juliette, when the truth itself, and the truth alone, lays bare the secrets of Nature, however mankind may tremble before those revelations. Philosophy must never shrink from speaking out. (p. 1193)

So the novel ends with Juliette stepping out of the pages of her own story to take a cheeky swipe at the censor, who is implicitly positioned as the enemy of truth.

If Justine is Sade's accomplice, then Juliette is none other than Sade himself.[6] Robbing Justine of narrative authority in *La nouvelle Justine*, Sade simultaneously hands it over to her ruthless and successful sister. With the exception of the last few pages, the entire text consists of Juliette's first person narration of the events of her life to her sister Justine and others. Now, on the face of it, such a narrative structure would seem to privilege a feminine perspective as in the first two versions of *Justine*, although this time the female narrator would not be a victim but a member of the libertine master class. As such, while she certainly becomes the sexual object of more or less all the men she meets, Juliette is at the same time an active and self-determining subject, proving herself to be just as calculating, just as immoral and just as cruel as any of the male libertines that surround her. *Juliette* teems with male libertines, but most of them merge in the memory. Even Juliette's leading men, Saint-Fond and Noirceuil, perform a double act that makes them at times indistinguishable as symbols of political corruption. On the other hand, here at last, or so it seems, is the portrait in fiction of an intellectually strong and sexually liberated woman, a female model that the surrealist poet Guillaume Apollinaire found positive enough to describe as the woman of the future, this 'creature that we cannot yet conceive, but which is freeing itself from humanity, which will take wing and will renew the universe'.[7]

This impression of a Sadean narrative with a strong female presence is reinforced by the high profile given to other female libertines – to the witch and poisoner, Durand, and to the man-hating Clairwil, who sees it as her duty to avenge the victims of her sex by murdering as many men as possible. Transparently as part of a wider campaign of rehabilitation of the *divin marquis*, some female critics, notably Annie Le Brun, have made much of this theme of female liberation running along the surface of Sade's novel. According to this perspective, the creator of the omnipotent Juliette was nothing less than a precursor of modern feminism. Sadly, however, this impression is only superficial, for in every important respect, both Juliette and her girlfriends are quite simply male surrogates.

Even at the level of narrative structure, the ostensibly feminine authority of Juliette as narrator is seriously undermined by a complexity of form that privileges numerous male voices. In a variety of ways, the third person authorial narrative, which is of course male in perspective, frames and controls Juliette's own: we remember that, outside of Juliette's narration of her story to Justine, the marquis and the chevalier, is the author–narrator who from time to time interrupts Juliette and finally reasserts himself in the novel's closing pages to describe to the reader directly the eventual fate of his protagonists – Justine's death in the thunderstorm, the elevation of Noirceuil, the survival of Durand, and the continuing prosperity of Juliette – and to draw the morals of his story. But the male authorial presence also makes itself felt in other, more subtle, ways. Numerous intertextual allusions, for example, to contemporary philosophers such as Diderot, Montesquieu, Rousseau, d'Holbach and La Mettrie, as well as to classical writers like Molière and Machiavelli, remind the reader of Sade's erudition and help to ram home his underlying philosophical message – this is also the effect of the many extended dissertations delivered by his libertines (the Pope's defence of murder, for example, is over 30 pages long) and of the travelogue-style passages describing the parts of Italy visited by his heroine, and inspired by Sade's own Italian trip. At the same time, the preponderant metanarrativity of the text constantly refers the reader back to the writing and reading process. We have already noted the ironic self-reflexivity of the novel's ending, as Juliette delights in the thought that one day someone might write the story of her life with the title, *Les Prospérités du Vice*![8] But there are many other self-reflexive passages in *Juliette*, in which Sade's own voice can be distinctly heard – for instance, in the minister Saint-Fond's approval of all libertine books and his praise of their authors:

> [...] j'autorise tous les ouvrages libertins ou immoraux ... je les crois très essentiels au bonheur de l'homme, utiles aux progrès de la philosophie, indispensables à l'extinction des préjugés, et faits, sous tous les rapports, pour augmenter la somme des connaissances humaines.

> J'étayerai les auteurs assez courageux pour ne pas craindre de dire la vérité; je payerai, je couronnerai toujours leurs idées; ce sont des hommes rares, essentiels à l'État, et dont on ne saurait trop encourager les travaux. (Vol. 8, p. 346)

> [...] I authorize the publication and sale of all libertine books and immoral works; for I esteem them most essential to human felicity and welfare, instrumental to the progress of philosophy, indispensable to the eradication of prejudices, and in every sense conducive to the increase of human knowledge and understanding. Any author courageous enough to tell the truth fearlessly shall have my patronage and support; I shall subsidize his ideas, I shall see to their dissemination; such men are rare, the State has great need of them, and their labors cannot be too heartily encouraged. (p. 319)

And of course, the implied male reader's sexual interests are efficiently represented in the text by the marquis and the chevalier, who listen with prurient eagerness to Juliette. During one of the author's interventions, she promises only to tell her audience about the extraordinary debauchery she has experienced 'to avoid monotony':

> – A merveille, dit le marquis, en faisant voir à la société un engin déjà tout gonflé de luxure; mais songez-vous à l'effet que ces récits peuvent produire en nous? Voyez l'état où me met leur simple promesse ... (Vol. 8, p. 146)

> 'Marvellous,' said the Marquis, showing the company an already lust-swollen engine; 'but are you bearing in mind the effect these narrations may produce in us? Behold the condition brought about by the mere promise of what is to come.' (p. 103)

Less subtly perhaps, the author's male point of view surfaces repeatedly in the many footnotes that punctuate the novel: there are 129 of these notes, or roughly one for every eight pages of text. Sade's extensive use of the footnote, and especially of the discursive or erudite note, at a time when the device was rarely employed in fiction, is another innovative formal feature.[9] Lucienne Frappier-Mazur sees the notes as instances of male narration within Juliette's female narrative, reminding the reader of the narrative situation.[10] According to Frappier-Mazur, with a single exception in *La nouvelle Justine*, 'Implicitly all the notes in Sade's *oeuvre* are the work of the author [...] The notes come under the category of an "assumption of authorship" in that they refer to a (fictive) reality and take on the authority of a male judgment standing outside the fiction.'[11] Sade literally under*writes* the spoken dissertations of his characters, which has the double effect of completing the point or argument and drawing attention to the illusion, whereby an essentially written use of language is passed off in the main text as speech.[12]

In addition to the male voice of the author himself, there are also a couple of lengthy male micro-narratives embedded within Juliette's story: Saint-Fond's tale and, especially, the 100-page-long story of Brisa Testa, otherwise known as Borchamps. This narrative embedding sometimes extends to a second level, as for example, with Princess Sophie's story, told by the Princess within Borchamps's own. The effect for the reader is rather like opening Russian dolls to find smaller versions inside, as narratives are found within narratives within narratives within narratives. We note, however, that it is the male *récit* of Borchamps that frames and so structures that of Sophie, in a symmetric mirroring of the author–narrator's control of Juliette's. As well as detracting from Juliette's apparent control of the narrative, this complexity of narrative form might be considered one of the novel's more innovative features.[13]

Juliette herself is essentially a projection of her creator's male psyche.[14] Anatomically female, Juliette nevertheless masculinises herself both physically and mentally. Though physically possessing all the usual Sadean attributes of feminine beauty, her reproductive potential is underplayed. There is a single reference, for example, to her menstrual periods, and although she does give birth to a daughter we are given no details whatever of this event. Moreover, she is completely bereft of any maternal instincts, easily consenting to the horrific murder of her daughter,

Marianne, by Noirceuil, which she herself aids and abets. In the many sexual orgies in which she participates, she never fails to don artificial phalluses in the form of dildos which she actively employs to penetrate both men and other women, although, being the phallic woman that she is, she naturally prefers female victims: 'je n'aime à faire que sur mon sexe ce que cette putain veut faire aux hommes' (Vol. 8, p. 560) / 'I only like doing to my own sex what this whore wants to do to men,' she declares, distinguishing the female targets of her sexual aggression from the male targets of Clairwil's. In fact, Juliette shares all the behavioural traits and sexual preferences of her male sodomist associates, to the extent that only the lack of the appropriate anatomical equipment prevents her from conforming exactly to that model – as she herself confesses at the sight of an exceptionally beautiful female posterior:

> Je ne pus tenir à ce cul divin. Homme dans mes goûts, comme dans mes principes, quel encens plus réel j'eusse voulu brûler pour lui! Je le baisais, je l'entr'ouvrais, je le sondais avec ma langue, et pendant qu'elle frétillait à ce trou divin, je rebranlais le clitoris de cette belle femme: elle déchargea encore une fois de cette manière. Mais plus j'allumais son tempérament, plus je me désolais de ne pouvoir l'enflammer davantage.
>
> – Oh! ma chère bonne, lui dis-je, en éprouvant ce regret, sois sûre que la première fois que nous nous reverrons, je serai munie d'un instrument capable de te porter des coups plus sensibles: je veux être ton amant, ton époux, je veux jouir de toi comme un homme. (Vol. 9, p. 101)

> I could not resist the sight of that divine posterior. Manlike in my tastes as in my thinking, how bitterly I regretted that I was unable to burn some more real incense before my idol. I kissed it, opened it and gazed ecstatically therein, my tongue sounded it and while it thrilled in that celestial hole I refrigged lovely Honorine's clitoris: thus did I wheedle a fresh discharge from her. But the more I aroused her, the greater was my distress at being powerless to arouse her farther still.

> 'Oh, my dearest one,' said I, my heart heavy because of this regret, 'be sure that when next we come together I shall have by me some instrument capable of dealing more telling blows than may a tongue: I would be your lover, your husband, I have told you so: I wish to have you as might a man.' (pp. 699–700)

If her active sexual performances are intrinsically masculine, so too is her status as passive sexual object. Again, sodomy is the order of the day: 'Ils me dévorent, mais à l'italienne: mon cul devient l'unique objet de leurs caresses [...] à peine se doutent-ils que je suis une femme' (Vol. 9, p. 138) / 'They devour me, but in the Italian style: my ass becomes the unique object of their caresses [...] they [...] behave for all the world as if they are unaware I am a woman' (p. 738).

In a more general sense, Juliette displays attitudes and characteristics more recognisably male than female: she is promiscuous, goal-orientated and prioritises reason over emotion. For Marcel Hénaff, Juliette is 'l'impossible Monsieur Juliette', a woman defined in terms of male fantasies and objectives.[15] Her first crime, a street robbery, is committed wearing men's clothes. This is a symbolic and defining moment in Juliette's progress in libertine crime. After that, she is quickly assimilated into the male libertine world, not as the stereotypical female victim – Noirceuil excepts her from that category because of her male spirit and character (Vol. 8, p. 239) – but as a sort of honorary male. She is accepted without difficulty into the male libertine club, *La Société des Amis du Crime*,[16] and commits as many lust murders as any of the men around her.[17] To be truly libertine, Juliette must emulate the sun, ancient symbol of paternal authority and simultaneous agent of creation and destruction: 'Ne vois-tu pas l'astre qui nous éclaire, dessécher et vivifier tour à tour?' Saint-Fond urges her, 'Imite-le dans tes écarts, comme tu le peins dans tes beaux yeux' (Vol. 8, p. 369) / 'Do you not see the star that lights us sometimes give life and sometimes take it away, now vivifying, now withering to dust? Match the sun in thy conduct as thou dost figure it in thy fair eyes' (pp. 343–44). By the end of the first part of her six-part adventures, Juliette's beauty does not merely match but actually surpasses that of the sun – she is 'plus belle que l'astre même' (Vol. 8, p. 241) / 'more lovely than the very sun itself' (p. 209) – and so symbolically superior to the patriarchy that nourishes her.

In every significant aspect of her behaviour, then, Juliette is becoming a kind of 'supermale' libertine. Anatomically, however, she remains female. This is not the case with other female libertines encountered by her. The beautiful nun, Volmar, has a mini-phallus of a clitoris three inches long, while Durand's vagina is 'obstructed', her clitoris 'long comme le doigt' / 'as long as a finger', and she discharges 'like a man'. Both seem able to sodomise women with their clitoris alone: 'Je fus enculée comme si j'eusse eu affaire à un homme,' declares Juliette ecstatically, as she relates her first sexual experiences with Durand, 'et j'y ressentis le même plaisir' (Vol. 9, pp. 427–28) / 'I was buggered as solidly as if I had been dealing with a man, and from it experienced the same pleasure' (p. 1033). Defying nature and reality in every way, Sade's female sex criminals are quite simply the product of male fantasy. This fantasy is on one level a self-protection against castration anxiety – as what Freud calls the 'woman's real small penis', the enormous clitoris of these *femmes fatales* reassuringly restores the lost phallus to the female body.[18]

On another, more erotic level, Volmar and Durand represent the impossible but ideal fusion of the masculine and the feminine that Sade unconsciously craves, creatures of the phallic-anal eroticism that defines his sexual universe. Many of the libertines turn away from breasts and especially the vagina in disgust, preferring to conceive of feminine beauty as purely anal. As he sodomises a female victim, Noirceuil thinks of turning fantasy into reality by cutting away the flesh that separates the vagina from the anal canal and so literally abolishing the former while leaving the latter intact (see Vol. 9, p. 556). Like the anus, the phallus is both literally and symbolically dominant in *Juliette*. The ball-breaking Clairwil loves cocks so much that she cuts one off and has it embalmed to make a dildo out of it! Clairwil's action puts one in mind of the veneration of the body parts of saints and martyrs, hacked off at the moment of death and turned into sacred relics. 'Des vits oui, sacredieu! des vits!' she cries,

> voilà *mes dieux*, mes parents, mes amis; je ne respire que pour ce membre sublime, et quand il n'est ni dans mon con, ni dans mon cul, il se place si bien dans ma tête, qu'en me disséquant un jour on le trouvera dans ma cervelle! (Vol. 8, p. 510; my emphasis)

> Pricks, aye, pricks, those are *my gods*, those are my kin, my boon companions, unto me they are everything, I live in the name of nothing but the penis sublime; and when it is not in my cunt, nor in my ass, it is so firmly anchored in my thoughts that the day they dissect me it will be found in my brain. (pp. 492–93)

For Durand, too, the phallus is nothing less than God himself. When Juliette challenges Durand's assertion that they were 'fucked by God', the sorcerer retorts: 'En est-il un plus puissant que le vit?' (Vol. 8, p. 557) / 'Is there one more mighty than the prick?' (p. 540). All the male libertines are endowed with members of astonishing size. The megalomaniac Noirceuil commands Juliette to adore his erect penis, 'ce vit despote [...] ce dieu superbe' (Vol. 8, p. 218) / 'worship it, this despotic engine' (p. 184), a sentiment echoed by many other libertines. Moberti, for instance, would like the entire universe to cease to exist when he gets hard (Vol. 9, p. 493). Juliette sums up the main message of the novel, and perhaps of all Sade's writing, when she observes how dangerous men are when their cocks are erect (Vol. 9, p. 500).[19]

The phallus, therefore, is deified as substitute for the non-existent God, but it is also the focus of a challenge to nature that some, like Rousseau, have sought to put in God's place. If the phallus is the symbol of all power in the Sadean universe, then the battle between man and nature is a clash of angry phalluses.[20] Like the female libertines of the novel, mother nature is phallic-woman, and attitudes towards her as complex as to women themselves: an awesome force to be worshipped, and yet, at the same time, the image of maternal indifference to be vilified and annihilated.[21] In *Juliette*, there are two powerful images of nature as a destructive force: the thunderbolt and the volcano. In their linearity and projective violence, both are also comparable to the phallus itself.

The thunderbolt-phallus that strikes Justine dead, in the final version of this scene in *Juliette*, enters her body through her mouth and exits through her vagina. So phallic nature restages the loss of Justine's virginity from above as it were, and at phallic man's bidding (at Noirceuil's suggestion, the hapless Justine is exposed to the effects of a violent storm as a way of tempting providence). The novel ends with an event that can be read symbolically as a successful attempt to control nature. As Philippe Roger puts it, '*Juliette* is the story of the mastery of thunder.'[22]

The volcano is a clearer symbol than the thunderbolt of the ambivalence of the libertine relation to nature: fascination and admiration on the one hand, and envy and hatred on the other. Roger's analysis is again illuminating: 'Le libertin aime le volcan parce qu'il aime le crime; mais il méprise l'aveuglement d'une nature sans dessein' / 'The libertine loves volcanoes because he loves crime, but he despises the blindness of a nature without purpose'.[23] The volcano represents the evil side of mother nature, which is its true face, that of a cruel stepmother, indifferent to her children. A universe without laws (which for Sade is synonymous with the indifference of nature), would have the phallic explosiveness of the volcano: 'sans lois, l'univers ne fût plus qu'un volcan dont d'exécrables forfaits jailliraient à chaque minute' (Vol. 9, p. 133) / 'without laws the world turns into one great volcano belching forth an uninterrupted spew of execrable crimes' (p. 732).[24] Like the thunderbolt, the volcano represents a challenge to libertine power: if he can control its energies, then he has bested nature. The pupil will then have defeated the master, since nature is the model for all he does. As sources of phallic violence, libertine and volcano are in fact mirror images of each other. The ejaculations of the libertines are evoked as volcanic phenomena: they are 'eruptive discharges', threatening those around. Sometimes they are directly compared to volcanic eruptions – of Moberti, for example: 'L'explosion de la décharge de ce libertin m'avait donné l'idée d'un volcan; ce n'était plus un homme, mais un tigre, un enragé' (Vol. 9, p. 490) / 'His discharge had been awesome, more like a volcanic eruption than anything else; his comportment was that of a wild animal rather than that of a human being' (p. 1097).

Juliette's imagination is fired by the volcanicity of Italy, which becomes its metaphorical expression. Two volcanoes frame Juliette's progress through Italy – Pietra-Mala in the north and Vesuvius in the south – and can be read as the symbolic expression of her growing sexual, political and intellectual force.[25] At Pietra-Mala, she is excited by the volcano's all-consuming flames and aspires to emulate nature's destructiveness: 'O nature! que tu es capricieuse! ... et tu ne voudrais pas que les hommes t'imitassent?' (Vol. 8, p. 591) / 'O Nature! how capricious you are! ... you must surely want men to imitate you' (my translation; the Wainhouse version gives the line an altogether different meaning: see p. 576). From being a mere pupil of libertinage as she gazes on Pietra-Mala, by the time she reaches Vesuvius, she is a libertine master, capable of the very worst excesses, and of a mind not merely to imitate nature, but to join Clairwil in defying her. Tiring of their companion, Olympe Borghèse, Juliette and Clairwil decide to cast her into the bowels of Vesuvius, for the sexual thrill that the murder will afford them, but also as a direct challenge to nature: 's'il est vrai que cette action outrage la nature, qu'elle se venge, elle le peut; qu'une éruption se fasse à l'instant sous nous, qu'une lave s'ouvre et nous engloutisse ...' cries Clairwil (Vol. 9, p. 413) / 'if what we have done is a true outrage to Nature, then let her avenge herself, for she can if she wishes; let an eruption occur, let lava boil up from that inferno down there, let a cataclysm snuff out our lives this very instant ...' (p. 1017). Juliette triumphantly celebrates their victory over nature's apparent impotence:

> Nous insultions la nature, nous la bravions, nous la défiions: et, triomphantes de l'impunité dans laquelle sa faiblesse et son insouciance nous laissaient, nous n'avions l'air de profiter de son indulgence que pour l'irriter plus grièvement. (Vol. 9, p. 413)

> Through our deed we were insulting Nature, defying her, baiting her; and triumphant in the impunity in which her unconcern left us, we looked to be profiting from her indulgence only in order to irritate her the more grievously. (pp. 1017–18)

Moments later, they are showered by rocks spewn out of the crater. Juliette quips that Olympe is avenging herself –

> – Ah! ah! dis-je sans seulement daigner me lever. Olympe se venge! Ces morceaux de soufre et de bitume sont les adieux qu'elle nous fait, elle nous avertit qu'elle est déjà dans les entrailles de la terre. (Vol. 9, p. 413)
>
> 'Ah ha!' said I, not even deigning to get to my feet, 'Olympia's revenge! These bits of sulphur, these pebbles are her farewell to us, she notifies us that she is already in the entrails of the earth.' (p. 1018)

– a cue for Clairwil to provide the scientific explanation that we would expect from a purely materialist view of nature:

> – Rien que de simple à ce phénomène, me répondit Clairwil. Chaque fois qu'un corps pesant tombe au sein du volcan, en agitant les matières qui bouillonnent sans cesse au fond de sa matrice, il détermine une légère éruption. (Vol. 9, pp. 413–14)
>
> 'Nothing more readily explained than this phenomenon,' Clairwil remarked. 'Whenever a weighty body falls into the volcano, by agitating the matter eternally boiling in its depths, it provokes a slight eruption.' (p. 1018)

This produces a further jest from Juliette: it's just Olympe asking for her clothes! Juliette's flippancy degrades Clairwil's science and shows disrespect to nature as represented by the volcano.[26] If the volcano serves to stimulate Juliette's libertine imagination, it is also a rival to be defied and mastered.

The phallus, then, is at the very centre of *Juliette*'s sexual universe, not only as an essential referent, but as an all-pervasive and deeply signifying image. If we now look more closely at the sexual activities depicted in the novel, we shall see that as perverse practices, often with strongly violent components, they are essentially masculine in nature. Freudian psychoanalysis defines perversion as follows:

> Deviation from the 'normal' sexual act when this is defined as coitus with a person of the opposite sex directed towards the achievement of orgasm by means of genital penetration.
>
> Perversion is said to be present: where the orgasm is reached with other sexual objects (homosexuality, paedophilia, bestiality, etc.) or through other regions of the body (anal coitus, etc.); where the orgasm is subordinated absolutely to certain extrinsic conditions, which may even be sufficient in themselves to bring about sexual pleasure (fetishism, transvestitism, voyeurism and exhibitionism, sado-masochism).
>
> In a more comprehensive sense, 'perversion' connotes the whole of the psycho-sexual behaviour that accompanies such atypical means of obtaining sexual pleasure.[27]

Sade's novel adds many other examples of perversion to those mentioned here by Freud. Indeed, its thousand or so pages contain a veritable catalogue of perverse sexual practices and, together with *La nouvelle Justine*, seem to constitute an attempt by Sade to reconstruct from memory the lost manuscript of *Les 120 Journées de Sodome*. As in *Les 120 Journées*, one is struck by the encyclopaedic breadth of Sade's knowledge of human sexuality, the accuracy of which is born out in many modern studies.[28] When Juliette and Durand set up a brothel in Venice, for instance, we are given thumbnail sketches of the perversions of different clients, closely resembling aspects of the lost work in both format and content (Vol. 9, pp. 473 et seq.).

Clearly, a distinction must be made between activities such as fellatio, cunnilingus, masturbation or even sodomy which, although strictly speaking perverse, could feature positively in any sexual relationship, and perversions that involve some form of non-consensual violence or coercion and have the obsessive character of a fixation. It is the latter category which provokes the most heated responses among readers and which, therefore, deserves our attention here. This kind of sexual perversion is mostly confined to men. Where Sade's text does represent women as behaving in this way (as with the lust murders committed by Juliette and Clairwil), they are being made to function according to a fundamentally masculine sexual model (see above). Even the tribadism (or lesbianism) engaged in by Juliette with her female friends is represented in the text from a voyeuristically male perspective, as the heterosexual male reader is implicitly invited to identify with Juliette. This identification is facilitated by an emphasis in these scenes on phallic-style penetration by strapped-on dildos and on cunnilingus, in which the tongue takes on a particularly phallic character (see, for example, Vol. 9. pp. 63–4). The Sadean orgy does appear to abolish gender boundaries to some degree, reducing participants, whether male or female, to the status of objects for penetration. However, this androgyny is only superficial, since the orgy privileges phallic dominance of the predominantly female and child victim.

Louise Kaplan sees the 'male' perversions – fetishism, transvestism, exhibitionism, voyeurism, sexual masochism, sexual sadism, paedophilia, zoophilia, necrophilia – as

> a way of triumphing over the traumas of childhood. In a male perversion, the strategy admits into consciousness a defensive, phallic-narcissistic exaggeration of masculinity [...] It is the special strategy of male perversion to permit a person to express his forbidden and shameful feminine wishes by disguising them in an ideal of masculinity. Macho genital prowess and the impersonation of fantasized, idealized males are hiding places for the man's humiliating feminine strivings. Moreover, these caricatures of masculinity, based as they are on prowess, aggression, and domination, simultaneously give some semblance of orderly expression to what otherwise would be experienced as a terrifying primitive violence.[29]

We recognise all the perversions mentioned by Kaplan as present in *Juliette* (and to a lesser extent in *Justine*), and her explanation of male perversion as motivated by an underlying fear of the feminine, a concomitant celebration of the phallus, and a need to create order out of the violence of sexual desire certainly seems to fit the Sade case.

As Kaplan rightly observes, male perversion is always fetishistic in one way or another, fetishism exemplifying the perverse strategy whereby a part or a detail always stands for the whole.[30] For Freud, the fetish is a substitute for the woman's (mother's) penis that the little boy once believed in and does not want to give up. Freud also considers the fetish as a defence against the threat of castration (which we have seen to figure significantly in Sade's relation to the feminine). Aversion to the female genitals, says Freud, is never absent in any fetishist.[31] Again, Kaplan provides a useful elucidation of this theory:

> The French analysts say that the term fetish originates in the French word *factice*, meaning 'fictitious' or 'artificial'. The sexual fetish, of course, represents artificial or imaginary genitals, and sexual fetishism is about the creation of fictitious and artificial genitals. The mighty penis in eternal erection, the phallus, is as fictionalized as the shortchanged clitoris or mutilated vagina that the phallus is meant to repair and compensate for. [...] In the mind of the fetishist the damaged female genitals must undergo interminable imaginary reparations to be eternally revived as a phallus. The woman whom the fetishist endows with this fictitious genital is transformed into the proverbial 'phallic woman'.[32]

The fetish does not necessarily have to be an inanimate object such as a leather boot or a black corset (although it frequently does take this form), but can also be a part of the sexual partner's body – her breasts, her ankles, her ears or her feet. The most common Sadean fetish would seem to be the clitoris, which, as we have seen, is dramatically emphasised in the physical portraits of Sade's female libertines. Indeed, 'the woman's real small penis' is the very prototype of fetishism.[33] The Sadean phallic woman, then, is essentially fetishistic: the fetish 'saves the fetishist from being a homosexual by endowing women with the characteristic which makes them tolerable as sexual objects'.[34] Clairwil's human dildo (the monk's severed penis, referred to earlier) is striking as the literal realisation of fetishistic fantasy. At the level of activities, too, most of the Sadean perversions contain strong fetishistic elements.

In addition to what we might call the more commonplace features of the Sadean orgy – sodomy, incest, fellatio, cunnilingus, voyeurism, and even flagellation and other forms of sadistic cruelty leading to murder – the libertines indulge in a number of more bizarre activities: urophilia and coprophilia, necrophilia, bestiality, paedophilia, gerontophilia, olfaction, transvestism, cannibalism. Their presentation in the text is characterised by a preoccupation with voyeuristic detail which is itself a feature of male rather than female eroticism, and by increasingly horrific manifestations of male sexual violence that many readers will find hard to stomach. In the novel's final orgy, for instance, Noirceuil and Juliette hold a libertine 'Last Supper', in which the two reach a climax of murderous depravity: while sodomising one of his sons, Noirceuil has Juliette tear out his heart which he proceeds to devour, simultaneously plunging a dagger into his other son's heart; after he has also sodomised Juliette's own daughter, Marianne, the mother helps Noirceuil burn her alive.[35]

As we saw in Chapter 1, all Sadean sex is based on the principle of transgression. Any perversion is itself, by definition, a transgressive activity, since it exceeds the bounds of 'normal' sexuality, which for Freud has procreation as its sole or primary object. Within Sade's text, the erotic charge depends crucially on the libertines' awareness that they are crossing recognised bounds of behaviour, by infringing moral laws (rape, murder), religious taboos (such as those on sodomy or blasphemy), conventional mores (which may not include sex with the very old or the very young, for example), 'natural' or socially conditioned reflexes of repulsion (urophilia, coprophilia), gender or species boundaries (passive sodomy, transvestism, zoophilia). Often, it is the very contrast – between age and youth, for instance, between piety and blasphemy, or between beauty and ugliness – that the libertines find erotic. Juliette expresses this idea, as she relates the sullying of a very young and beautiful girl by the foul and the fearsome Cordelli:

> Oh, juste ciel! que de contrastes! On ne se fait pas d'idée de cette jolie petite mine intéressante et douce, salement baisée par la figure d'homme la plus rébarbative et la plus effrayante qu'il y eut sans doute au monde, flétrissant, de ses rudes moustaches, les lis et les roses du plus beau teint

> possible, et mêlant d'exécrables blasphèmes aux prières douces et pleines d'onction de l'âme la plus innocente. (Vol. 9, p. 460)

> Oh, God of Justice! what contrasts! Imagine, if you can, that pretty little face, so touching, so sweet; that face being nastily kissed by the most unprepossessing and the grimmest figure of a man to be found anywhere on earth, his bristly moustaches withering the lilies and the roses in the loveliest possible complexion, and with execrable blasphemies replying to the plaintive entreaties of the most innocent soul. (p. 1066)

Sadean transgression also embraces the notion, underlined by the author in footnote, that the more singular the perversion, the more pleasurable it will be (see Vol. 9, p. 147, n.).

Listed below are examples from *Juliette* of some of the more unusual perversions encountered.[36]

Anthropophagy or cannibalism

We are told that the giant, Minski, eats 'only human flesh' (Vol. 8, p. 596), which puts him firmly in the tradition of fairy-tale monsters (*Jack and the Beanstalk*, *Hansel and Gretel*, etc.). There is no indication that this is sexually exciting for him. On the other hand, the anthropophagy of Borchamps, Juliette and her female companions, Clairwil and Borghèse (Olympe) seems to be part of their general sexual degeneracy. In a tongue-in-cheek orgy of excess that almost certainly inspired the set-piece final scene of Peter Greenaway's film, *The Cook, the Thief, his Wife and her Lover*, the libertines have ten post-coitally exhausted men killed and dine off their corpses.[37] Here, Sade indulges his penchant for condensation, as the diners engage simultaneously in cannibalism, coprophilia, sodomy and murder. The episode illustrates well the absurdly surreal qualities of the Sadean orgy and is worth quoting at length:

> Par les ordres du capitaine, vingt hommes s'emparent aussitôt de ceux-là; on les massacre pendant que nous nous branlons, Borghèse, Clairwil et moi. C'est, pour

ainsi dire, sur leurs corps que le souper le plus délicieux nous est offert. Et là, nus, barbouillés de foutre et de sang, ivres de luxure, nous portons la férocité au point de mêler à nos aliments des morceaux de chair, détachés par nos mains du corps des malheureuses [sic] qui sont sur la table. Gorgés de meurtre et d'impudicité, nous tombons enfin, les uns sur les autres, au milieu des cadavres et d'un déluge de vins, de liqueurs, de merde, de foutre, de morceaux de chair humaine. Je ne sais ce que nous devînmes; je me rappelle seulement qu'en ouvrant les yeux à la lumière, je me retrouvai entre deux corps morts, le nez dans le cul de Carle-Son, qui m'avait rempli la gorge de merde, et qui lui-même s'était oublié le vit au cul de Borghèse. Le capitaine, qui s'était endormi la tête appuyée sur les fesses emmerdifiées de Raimonde, avait encore son vit dans mon derrière, et Sbrigani ronflait dans les bras d'Élise ... les victimes en morceaux toujours sur la table. (Vol. 9, p. 320)

The captain issues instructions, twenty of his trusties seize the first ten, and the massacre goes forward while we frig one another, Borghese, Clairwil, and I. It is, so to speak, upon their corpses that a delicious collation is served to us. And there, naked, smeared with blood and fuck, drunk with lust, we carry our bestial ferocity to the point of mixing in our food those morsels of flesh we detach from the bodies of the unhappy women lying upon our table. Gorged on murder and impudicity, we at last all fall asleep amidst cadavers and a deluge of wines, spirits, shit, fuck, and bits of human flesh: I am not sure what happened after that. I simply recall that when I opened my eyes to the light I found myself lying between two cadavers, my nose in Carleson's ass, with whose shit my gullet was filled, and whose prick was wedged in Borghese's ass, where he had forgotten it. The captain, who had gone to sleep with his head pillowed on Raimonde's shit-slimed buttocks, still had his prick in my behind, and Sbrigani was snoring in the arms of Elise ... the victims in pieces still lay on the table. (p. 922)

It is revealing that, whereas the corpses are, of course, male, Juliette erroneously refers to female victims (*malheureuses*). Although, in a kind of negative image of her predominantly male associates, Clairwil is seen exclusively to select male victims, this linguistic slip on the part of the author suggests that the concept of the victim for Sade is still a fundamentally *female* one.

Coprophagy/Urophilia

> Il n'est rien à quoi l'on s'accoutume aussi facilement qu'à respirer un étron; en mange-t-on, c'est délicieux, c'est absolument la saveur piquante de l'olive [...] je vous assure que cet épisode compose un acte de libertinage très sensuel ... (Vol. 8, p. 199)

> No habit is more easily acquired than mard-savoring; eat one, delicious, [...] the effect is somewhat that of an olive [...] one of the culminating episodes of the libertine experience ... (p. 163)

> [...] une d'elles me fit pisser dans sa bouche, pendant que je la gamahuchais; une autre me proposa de nous chier mutuellement sur les tétons, elle le fit, je ne pus le lui rendre; un homme, en se faisant enculer, vint manger l'étron que cette femme avait fait sur mon sein, et il chia lui-même après, en déchargeant dans la bouche de celui qui venait de le foutre. (Vol. 8, p. 458)

> [...] one had me piss into her gullet while I lapped her cunt, another suggested we shit on each other's bubs, she larded mine generously, I was unable to repay her in kind unfortunately; while a man labored in his ass-hole, a second man gobbled up the excrement steaming on my chest; and after that he shat there in turn, as he did so discharging into the mouth of him by whom he had just been sodomized. (p. 438)

> [...] elle me supplia de lui pisser dans la bouche; je lui demandai la même chose: nous nous inondâmes d'urine, et nous avalions à mesure qu'elle coulait. (Vol. 9, p. 337)

> [...] she besought me to piss into her mouth; I asked the same of her, we poured urine into each other, swallowing it as it flowed. (p. 938)

Coprophagy is the act of eating faeces for sexual arousal, while urophilia which is closely related to it refers to the derivation of sexual pleasure from acts involving urine.[38] Coprophagy in Sade has a strongly symbolic resonance, based on the unconscious association which Freud identified between faeces and money. Saint-Fond acquires an immense fortune which only serves to increase his power. This Juliette symbolically acknowledges by eating his shit: 'Something told me he had a burning desire to have me eat his shit, I sought permission to do so, obtained it, he was in ecstasies.' Clearly, Juliette's coprophagy reinforces male dominance. It seems to me that the taste for menstrual blood, mentioned a single time in *Juliette* (Vol. 9, p. 474) is akin to coprophila and urophilia, in that all three concern taboo bodily products (the menses are notable as a religious taboo in the Judeo-Christian tradition), and therefore pleasure in licking and eating them is essentially transgressive – as Durand observes, 'les plus grands plaisirs ne naissent que des répugnances vaincues' (Vol. 9, p. 445) / 'great pleasures are only born from surmounted repugnances' (p. 1051).

Gerontophilia

This is sexual attraction for people of a significantly older age group. Saint-Fond determines to sample the erotic delights associated with old women: 'tu me les chercheras de soixante ans au moins,' he instructs Juliette, 'c'est un caprice: il y a longtemps que l'on m'assure que rien ne fait bander comme la décrépitude de la nature' (Vol. 8, p. 383) / '[I want women aged at least sixty] it's a caprice. I've been many times assured that nothing is quite so stimulating as natural decrepitude' (p. 357). Saint-Fond's 'caprice' appears both to project a positive image of the old as erotic objects and as a welcome inversion of the conventional stereotype (older man paired with younger woman), until we remember that in *Juliette*, as in Sade's other fictions, the latter is the standard model.

Incest

Incest is an abiding preoccupation of Sade's, and one of his most important sexual themes. All the short stories that make up *Les Crimes de l'amour* (*The Crimes of Love*) and the epic epistolary novel, *Aline et Valcour*, deal with incest in one way or another, the commonest form represented being that between father and daughter. In *Juliette*, fathers are often forced to violate their daughters. Juliette herself seduces her own father (Vol. 8, p. 490). In contradiction with the view held by some critics that the Sadean text avoids mother–son incest through hatred of the maternal, this too is represented, less often than other forms but probably in proportion to the relatively low frequency of mother–son incest in real life.[39] The relative rarity of mother–son incest in Sade compared with other forms of incest is less suggestive, I would argue, of avoidance of a taboo (in which case it would never, ever occur) than of authorial identification with the father. Juliette describes some of the activities of the Society of the Friends of Crime:

> [...] je vis des frères enculant leurs soeurs; des pères enconnant leurs filles; des mères foutues par leurs enfants [...] un assez beau jeune homme voulut baiser mes fesses pendant qu'il enculait sa mère [...] (Vol. 8, p. 459)

> [...] I beheld brothers embuggering their sisters; fathers encunting their daughters; mothers fucked by their children [...] a handsome young fellow must kiss my behind while he embuggered his mother. (p. 439)[40]

Masochism

Many of the male libertines enjoy being whipped, but there is a single instance in *Juliette* of female masochism, when a woman expresses the desire to become the victim of a male murderer (Vol. 9, p. 272). This fictional stereotype of a masochistic female victim of a sadistic male corresponds to the classic scenario of pornography. In real life, however, the situation is more complex, with far more men than women fulfilling the masochistic role. Kaplan explains:

> In the sadomasochistic sexual fantasies that make up the bulk of pornographic reading materials and films, women and young children of both sexes are depicted as assuming the masochistic role. These scenarios are usually invented by men and designed for the sexual arousal of men, who unconsciously identify with the person in the submissive (feminine) position. The unconscious aim, as always, is to express yet disguise, even if barely, the man's wishes to be a submissive, denigrated female. [...] when it comes to actual behavior between consenting (or paid) partners, more often than not it is the man who demands that a woman enact the role of the sadistic partner. In that way he can identify with the position of the masochist and fulfill his unconscious and shameful feminine longings without anyone's being the wiser.[41]

Necrophilia

Necrophilia is defined as an erotic attraction to corpses and is extremely rare. Some of the libertines, however, do engage in activities that appear necrophilic in character, but the eroticism seems to derive from the transgressive and fetishistic nature of the act rather than from a specific focus on the dead body as a sexually arousing object. The abbess Delbène, for example, has herself fucked on the corpses of her victims (Vol. 8, pp. 139–40), while Juliette's and Durand's using the bones of their victims as dildos (Vol. 8, pp. 555–56) is a particularly macabre example of the surreal humour of Sade's text. Cordelli, exceptionally, appears to derive pleasure from the very action of fucking and sodomising the corpse of his own daughter, whom he has himself poisoned (Vol. 9, p. 441). But even here, the knowledge of his multiple transgressions – in addition to necrophilia, he commits murder, incest, sodomy and blasphemy (the event takes place in church) – framed by the voyeurism of Juliette and Durand who are watching secretly, seems to overshadow the necrophilic act itself. At the same time, necrophilia is a graphic expression of the libertine's megalomania, in that the dead body's utter defencelessness allows him to enact the fantasy of total domination.

Olfaction

In the Society of the Friends of Crime, Juliette encounters a man who loves sniffing and licking armpits (Vol. 8, p. 459). Braschi, too, loves natural odours and asks Juliette to 'abstain from use of the bidet' (Vol. 9, p. 148). Clearly, olfaction or arousal from strong and often unpleasant smells is closely related to coprophilia and similarly motivated.

Paedophilia

Paedophilia refers to adults being sexually aroused by children. The sexual abuse of children is commonplace in Sade, the tenderness of their age being a particular point of emphasis, as is the horrific pain and damage caused by penetration. The libertines' taste for virgins is probably motivated by the same transgressive and sadistic urges. The nine-year-old Laurette is deflowered by Juliette, wearing a foot-long dildo. The description dwells tellingly upon the effects of the disproportion between the size of the dildo and that of the girl: 'le déchirement est affreux [...] les flots de sang qui jaillissent du brisement de l'hymen, les cris terribles de la victime [...]' (Vol. 8, p. 135) / '[my weapon] provokes some truly awesome stretching and tearing [...] the torrents of blood that leap from the bursting hymen, the victim's lusty screams [...]' (pp. 91–2). The giant, Minski, fucks a seven-year-old girl, whom he strangles to death in the process and then sodomises her corpse (Vol. 8, p. 602). Once again, the emphasis is less on the excitement of sexual congress with a child than on the transgression of a taboo and the pleasures of sadistic cruelty.

Sadism

The perversion for which Sade is famous is central to all the sexual activities represented and takes a variety of forms. Flagellation – mainly of women and children – is a common feature of the Sadean orgy, usually as a preliminary to more horrific forms of violence, and occasionally as a slow and painful method of killing. In a lengthy dissertation on murder, Braschi (Pope Pius VI) insists on the cruelty of method as essential to pleasure: 'ce n'est pas assez de tuer, il faut tuer d'une manière horrible' (Vol. 9, p. 191) / 'killing is not enough, one must kill in hideous style' (p. 791). He proceeds to give a catalogue of examples drawn from history. Kaplan interprets male sadism in terms of a hostility towards 'the female body or any body that represents [...] the weaknesses and femininity he despises and fears in himself'.[42]

Transvestism

We encounter examples of cross-dressing that help to blur further gender boundaries already challenged by Sade's phallic women. In orgies, boys are frequently presented as girls for erotic purposes – 'Six jeunes garçons, de quinze ans, nous servaient nus et coiffés en femmes' (Vol. 8, p. 243) / 'On hand as well were six youths ranging in age from fifteen to twenty; naked, their hair arranged in feminine style, they served the table' (p. 214) – and there is the mock double wedding engineered by Noirceuil, in which the latter dresses as a woman to marry a man, then dressed as a man, marries a catamite dressed as a girl, while Juliette dressed as a man marries a lesbian, then dressed as a woman, marries a lesbian dressed as a man. On one level, this sexual maze symbolically deconstructs all received wisdoms with regard to gender and, as such, is a welcome antidote to the stereotypes that still plague our thinking in this area, as well as to the overall phallicism of Sade's text. This gender-bending is to some extent practised in the orgies, with men adopting the 'female' position in sodomy and bedildoed women playing the active 'male' role, although of course, as we have seen, the phallus is still the yardstick against which all such positions are measured.

Voyeurism/Eavesdropping[43]

The Society of the Friends of Crime provides opportunities to engage in both of these related activities. The questionnaire to which Juliette must provide satisfactory answers if she is to be accepted as a member of the society (Vol. 8, pp. 449–51) consists of a series of prurient enquiries about her sexual history closely resembling those of the Catholic confessional.[44] Elsewhere in the novel, the last confession of a young woman does indeed offer masturbating listeners a few lubricious moments, although on this occasion the reader is not allowed to share the experience. As if to cock a snoop at the excluded reader, Juliette emphasises that she and her friends heard every word! (Vol. 9, p. 523.) Passages like these serve to diminish the text's pornographic status by drawing attention to the means by which pornographic effects are created at the expense of the effects themselves. It is in this sense that Sade's writing may be termed 'metapornography'. Rooms furnished by the society are specially designed to maximise voyeuristic pleasure: 'Ce qu'il y avait de fort régulier dans l'arrangement de ces bosquets, c'est qu'il n'était pas une seule table d'où l'on ne put voir toutes les autres' (Vol. 8, p. 462) / 'Owing to the studied placing of the glades there was not one table from which you could not see all the others' (p. 442).[45] Both voyeurism and voyeuristic eavesdropping or listening are features of male rather than female eroticism – as Kaplan observes, 'Very few reported cases of compulsive sexual voyeurism are of women.'[46]

Zoophilia

Noirceuil claims that zoophilia or bestiality (sex between humans and animals) has been known throughout history and cites examples of current practice. Goats, for instance, were used by the Greeks extensively:

> [...] le bouc est meilleur que sa femelle; son anus, plus étroit, est plus chaud [...]
>
> Le dindon est délicieux, mais il faut lui couper le cou à l'instant de la crise; le resserrement de son boyau vous comble alors de volupté.
>
> Les Sybarites enculaient les chiens; les Égyptiennes se prostituaient à des crocodiles, les Américaines à des singes. (Vol. 8, pp. 221–22)

> [...] the buck surpasses the female of this species: its narrower anal canal is warmer [...]
>
> The turkey is delicious, but you must cut its throat at the critical instant; time the operation carefully, and the

> constriction of the bird's bowels will cause you a fairly overwhelming pleasure.
>
> The Sybarites embuggered dogs; Egyptian women gave themselves to crocodiles; American women appreciate being fucked by monkeys. (pp. 188–89)

As usually happens in the Sadean dissertation, the desire to convince the listener leads to increasingly exotic illustration. This, combined with an activity that in itself has much comic potential, can produce a humorous effect.[47] As if to check the reader's incredulity, the author is driven to add a supporting footnote to Noirceuil's account of 'turkey-sex':

> On en trouve dans plusieurs bordels de Paris; la fille, alors, lui passe la tête entre les cuisses, vous avez son cul pour perspective, et elle coupe le cou de l'animal au moment de votre décharge: nous verrons peut-être bientôt cette fantaisie en action. (Vol. 8, p. 221, n.)

> Several Parisian brothels feature avisodomy; the girl holds the bird's neck locked between her thighs, you have her ass straight ahead of you for prospect, and she cuts the bird's throat the same moment you discharge. Of this fantasy being enacted we may perhaps soon have an example. (p. 189, n.)

True to his word, Sade later provides a thumbnail of the experience in an orgy that also includes a monkey, a large dog and a goat! (Vol. 9, pp. 144–46). On another occasion, King Ferdinand of Naples also refers to the pleasures of goat-fucking, prompting a wry observation from Juliette that if the princes of the House of Austria had only fucked goats and its princesses dogs, the earth would not be infested by their accursed race! (Vol. 9, p. 378.)

Conclusion

Histoire de Juliette, Sade's longest surviving work and most comprehensive manifesto in support of libertinage is indisputably a male-authored book that aims to educate the male reader in a fundamentally male-centred eroticism. In addition to the many orgies that illustrate Sade's peculiarly violent brand of sexuality, the work also contains long, and often tediously repetitive, dissertations on philosophical, religious and political matters, many of which, like those on Christianity and murder, are scandalously provocative, highly controversial and founded on dubious logic. Those readers who find little interest in these disquisitions, preferring to focus their attention instead on the more literary aspects of the work, or even on its erotic elements, may choose to read the abridged edition which is available in French (though not, to date, in English).[48] In contrast, others may wish to follow the conventional path taken by so many Sade critics in the past and concentrate on the philosophy to the exclusion of the sex and violence.[49] Either of these choices involves a suppression amounting to censorship of a part of Sade's text, though, in the case of the former, those who read English but not French may, for the reason just given, have no choice at all.

Yet others, in particular feminist readers offended by the misogyny of the writing or by the phallocentricity of the sexuality represented in the novel, may consider the work too politically incorrect to include in their library or to recommend to friends or students. But to respond in this way is surely to refuse to confront the challenge that Sade poses to current debates on sexuality and, more regrettably perhaps, to deny oneself the many insights that his exploration of the darker corners of the human sexual psyche has to offer. *Juliette* is, first and last, a work of the imagination and no more dangerous than the mind of the person reading it. On this level, it has a unique contribution to make to an understanding of sexual fantasy, including its potential dangers, in two major ways.

Firstly, Sade's novel is the fictional representation of the imaginary that underpins all eroticism, hence the extremeness and implausibility of many of the perversions depicted. As the libertines are forever saying, it is the imagination that is the ultimate source of sexual pleasure. Secondly, when we read *Juliette* and perhaps find ourselves aroused by certain passages, we confirm for ourselves both the erotic power of language and the links between sexual desire and its representation in writing and other media. That eroticism is a form of *écriture* is graphically illustrated in the advice given by Juliette on the most effective path to self-knowledge: in order to discover one's most powerful and most erotic fantasy, one must first abstain from any sexual activity for two weeks, then lie down in a quiet and darkened room, give one's imagination free rein until the point of orgasm; following which, every detail of the fantasy should be written down and the operation repeated the next day, so that the written account may be enlarged and enhanced appropriately (Vol. 9, pp. 42–4). This piece of writing will provide the benchmark for future erotic experiences. If Sade's novel provides more comprehensive proof than his heroine of the sexual force of *language*, it is also, in its unparalleled breadth and narratorial and psychological complexity, one of the most extraordinary examples of sexual *literature* the world has ever known.

6

Sade and Transcendence

> The Marquis is a missionary. He has written a new religion. *Juliette* is one of the holy books
>
> *New York Times Book Review*

If, as we saw in Chapter 1, most of the Marquis de Sade's life is dominated by the struggle to survive (physically throughout 27 long years of imprisonment, legally and morally against the authorities arraigned against him, but also financially, and even philosophically), it is hardly surprising that his work expresses unconscious desires associated with such survival. These desires take a number of metaphorical and symbolic forms: the endless repetitions of style and content, the thirst for a social and sexual utopia, the libertines' ambition to commit the absolute or eternal crime, the hyperboles and excesses that lead eventually to Nietzsche's *Übermensch* or Bataille's sovereign man.[1] At the same time, Sade's painful awareness of the non-existence of a transcendental dimension (especially noticeable in his continual rage against religion) generates both a satirical and ironic humour on the one hand and a histrionic self-dramatisation on the other. I should like to end my introduction to Sade's libertine fiction with a polemical argument. The angry young man who wrote these obscene, violent and deeply pessimistic novels created sexual fantasies in his prison cell to substitute for the sexual realities of which imprisonment deprived him. In so doing, he was also pursuing a dream of immanence – not of the Christian God in his mythical heaven, but an earthly paradise of physical and sexual immortality, a transcendence not of the soul but of the body.

Sade's constant attacks on religion are well known. In *Justine* and *Juliette*, there are lengthy dissertations ridiculing the intellectual basis of Christianity in particular. The arguments are indeed repeated from work to work with very little variation and are very familiar to Sade scholars. There are no absolutes, morality and the laws based on moral notions of right and wrong being culturally and temporally relative. In a direct pre-echo of Nietzsche, in *Juliette* Clairwil draws the conclusion that justifies all libertine behaviour: 'Il est donc égal de se bien ou de se mal conduire' (Vol. 8, p. 411) / 'whether you conduct yourself well or ill, it amounts to the same' (p. 386). Religion is superstitious nonsense, arising from ignorance and primitive thinking, and Christianity a credo for the pusillanimous and the passive, conceived by the weak as a defence against the strong. Such infantile beliefs have no place in a century of enlightenment and reason: 'ils sont évanouis, les siècles d'erreur' (Vol. 9, p. 156) / 'the age of error is past,' (p. 755) Juliette tells Sade's fictional Pope Pius VI, who is as much an atheist as she is. Henceforth, a more enlightened mankind will be guided by the 'flame of philosophy' alone. From Sade's point of view, reason dethrones religion, just as the king is dethroned by the republic.

Sade's libertines never miss a chance to launch attacks on religion, which are as passionate as they are logical. In fact, Sadean atheism has an element of personal hatred expressed as much against the representatives of religion as against its philosophical basis, a hatred that is so powerful that it sometimes even overspills the text's conventional bounds, as for example, in the following authorial footnote in *Juliette*:

> Quels sont les seuls et les vrais perturbateurs de la société? – Les prêtres. – Qui sont ceux qui débauchent journellement nos femmes et nos enfants? – Les prêtres. [...] Qui travaille le plus constamment à l'extinction totale du genre humain? – Les prêtres. – Qui se souille le plus de crimes et d'infamies? – Les prêtres. – Quels sont les hommes de la terre les plus dangereux, les plus vindicatifs et les plus cruels? – Les prêtres. – Et nous balançons à extirper totalement cette vermine pestilentielle de dessus la surface du globe! ... – Nous méritons donc tous nos maux. (Vol. 8, p. 418, n.)

> Who are the true and the only troublemakers in society? The priests. Who are they who daily debauch our wives

> and children? The priests. [...] Who most resolutely labor at the total extinction of the human race? The priests. Who are most sullied with crimes and infamies? The priests. Which are the most malevolent, the most vindictive, the most ferocious men on earth? The priests. And we hesitate to exterminate this pestilential vermin off the face of the earth! ... Why then, we richly deserve everything that ails us. (p. 393, n. 17)

In the words of Noëlle Châtelet, 'Sade wants us to beware above all of what he calls "the tonsured scum"' (Note to *Les Malheurs*, p. 425).

And yet, despite this at times almost hysterical campaign against God, motivated in part at least by what seems to be a strong degree of personal bitterness, the religious appears on almost every page manifesting itself notably in the transgressive pleasures of blasphemy. At the height of their sexual excitement, the libertines invariably fling obscenities at the God they don't believe in but wish to provoke into existing: 'Infâme jean-foutre de Dieu!' cries Noirceuil as he is about to murder Juliette's daughter, 'ne borne donc pas ainsi ma puissance, quand je veux t'imiter et commettre le mal! [...] mets, si tu l'oses, un instant, ta foudre en mes mains, et quand j'en aurai détruit les mortels, tu me verras bander encore à la lancer au sein de ton exécrable existence, pour la consumer, si je puis!' (Vol. 9, p. 575) / '"O infamy on high!" he shouts, "remove these curbs that make me little, when I would imitate thee and commit evil. [...] for one instant, if thou darest, put thy lightning into my hands, and once I have destroyed mortals, thou shalt see my loins grow gladder still as I hurl the bolt that blasts thy execrable existence"' (p. 1185). For many Sade scholars, this is the central and unresolvable paradox of the writing – like women, God is hated but will not go away:

> At the moment of their ecstasy, the libertines shout out a name with hatred: that of God [...] God may be eliminated as a phantom and product of the imagination, but he does not disappear from the Sadean text: he exists as an object of hatred.[2]

The repetitiousness and the vehemence of the Sadean text's opposition to religion, coupled with the preoccupation with blasphemy, suggests that we are perhaps dealing here with a case of Freudian denial (or as Shakespeare might have said, 'Methinks the Marquis doth protest too much!'). Catherine Claude succinctly identifies the psychological processes involved: 'one only fights so ferociously against that which is presumed to exist'.[3] Arguing from a theoretical linguistic base, Chantal Thomas similarly concludes that denial of the concept of God logically presupposes his existence,

> For Sadean negation, as a negation that is a conscious part of his writing, proceeds along the lines of linguistic negation whose characteristic, according to Benveniste, 'is such that it can only cancel what is enunciated, which it must therefore explicitly posit in order to suppress, so that a judgement of non-existence necessarily also has the formal status of a judgement of existence'.[4]

Some, notably Pierre Klossowski, go as far as to interpret this preoccupation with God's existence psychoanalytically as evidence of religious belief that has been inverted or repressed but is nevertheless still present. In his 'Le Marquis de Sade and his Accomplice', Jean Paulhan was perhaps the first to talk about Sade's 'gospel of evil': Sade's books, he avers, 'remind one of the sacred books of the great religions'.[5] Klossowski, however, takes the hypothesis of a Sadean religiosity much further, arguing that the problem of evil is at the centre of Sade's work, which he views synchronically, focusing on the contradictions in his thought. Klossowski's thinking is complex and itself evolves between positions outlined in 1947 and 1967 but, in essence, he identifies a destructive theology in the Sadean text, which he equates with a kind of negative acceptance of God.[6] For Klossowski's Sade, cruelty has a cosmic function and passions a transcendental significance.[7] As Maurice Blanchot puts it, writing in 1949, for Klossowski, 'the concept of God [...] [is] indispensable to the libertine consciousness, and Sade resorts to blasphemy as a means of forcing God to break his silence'.[8]

Without wishing to reduce the religious obsessions of Sade's fiction to an unconscious desire to believe, it nevertheless seems to me that Klossowski is right to infer certain psychological attitudes from them. In the libertines' need to rail against God so persistently, does Sade not appear to reproach God with his non-existence? In fact, if he doesn't exist, there's no point in insulting him: 'mon plus grand chagrin,' declares the libertine eccentric, Moberti, in *Juliette* 'est qu'il n'existe réellement pas de Dieu, et de me voir privé, par là, du plaisir de l'insulter plus positivement ...' (Vol. 9, p. 486) / 'I am only sorry that no God really exists, sorry, that is, to be deprived of the pleasure of insulting him more positively ...' (p. 1093). Passages like this have induced some critics to adopt vaguely similar positions to Klossowski's. Noëlle Châtelet, for instance, seems to echo his view of a negative Sadean theology, when she talks about his 'antitheism' and the 'blasphemous affirmation of an absurd God'.[9]

Less controversially, Béatrice Didier, views Sade's 'antitheology' more pragmatically as method, arguing that, armed with a profound knowledge of the Bible and the theological writings of Catholicism, he uses theology's own tactics against it.[10]

More recently, Annie Le Brun has forcefully challenged the hypothesis of a negative theology in Sade (Klossowski, Blanchot), preferring to see his repeated defence of atheism as a necessarily vigorous response to the dominant theistic codes of Sade's society and to the threat posed by the concept of a deity to intellectual freedom:

> [...] l'insistance blasphématoire de Sade, le souci constant d'empêcher la résurgence, avec l'idée de Dieu, de la notion de limite qui empêche de penser cette «diversité des mouvements ou des façons d'agir [qui] constitue seule la diversité des matières».[11]

> [...] Sade's insistent blaspheming represents a constant concern to prevent the reappearance, with the idea of God, of the notion of limits which would hinder the conception of this 'diversity of movements or ways of acting [that] alone constitutes the diversity of matter'.

In a century and a society in which the freethinker was viewed as being beyond the pale, if not an outright danger to social stability, Sade had little choice from the point of view of his own logic but to mount a strong and continuous attack on religion. As for the obsession with blasphemy, Dolmancé in *La Philosophie dans le boudoir* explains this in terms of its effects on the body:

> [...] dès l'instant où il n'y a plus de Dieu, à quoi sert-il d'insulter son nom? Mais c'est qu'il est essentiel de prononcer des mots forts ou sales, dans l'ivresse du plaisir, et que ceux du blasphème servent bien l'imagination [...] il faut qu'ils scandalisent le plus possible: car il est très doux de scandaliser. (p. 119)

> [...] as of the moment God does not exist, what's the use of insulting his name? But it is essential to pronounce hard and foul words during pleasure's intoxication, and the language of blasphemy very well serves the imagination [...] they must scandalize to the last degree; for 'tis sweet to scandalize [...] (p. 251)

Georges Bataille has written at great length on the importance of transgression in all truly erotic activity and of the role played by the religious in this process: for Bataille, it is the sacred that controls the transgression of all taboos, while it is the tension between the forbidden and its transgression that is the basis of eroticism.[12] This being so, Sade's libertines need something to transgress for their erotic thrills, and in eighteenth-century France religion simply happens to be the source of most taboos. To come onto the host that has been transformed in the mass into the body of Christ is, in this logic, the most shocking of acts conceivable in a society imbued with the Catholic faith, and it is the shock value of the action, rather than its specifically religious content, that excites. When Juliette objects to Clairwil that profanation has no meaning when one does not believe, the latter replies simply that she likes it because it 'turns her on' ('[les profanations] échauffent ma tête') (Vol. 8, p. 471). That transgression requires a sense of sin is a psychological rather than a strictly religious mechanism.[13]

Whether or not motivated by components of a personal psychology, Sade's atheism is not in any case a negative force – the negation of man, God and nature, in the words of Maurice Blanchot in *La raison de Sade* – but a force for intellectual liberation, 'Car, en détruisant l'idée de la cause première, la pensée humaine s'ouvre l'univers *et débouche sur l'infini*' / 'For, in destroying the idea of a first cause, human thinking opens up the universe *and emerges into infinity*'.[14] As Annie Le Brun rightly observes, Sade is indeed the only atheistic philosopher of his time to have a 'physical awareness of the infinite' and it is this novel idea, according to which Sade brings infinity and the body together, that I would now like to explore.[15]

Thinking Infinity

Many, certainly, have seen an aspiration to infinity in Sade's work, although this was infinity as either a product of language or of the mind. Michel Foucault, in *Les Mots et les choses*, saw Sade as standing at the junction between the classical and the modern periods and as signalling the death of representation which is also the death of God. In the modern era, anthropology replaces theology and man becomes his own limit. The anthropological perspective is focused on human finitude, not divine infinity. As the gatekeeper standing between the classical and the modern era, and thereby between theology and anthropology, Sade embodies the tension between classical and modern ways of thinking (or what Foucault calls *epistemes*), and so between infinity and finitude. For Foucault, what Sade does is to apply the structure of the classical *episteme* to the content of the modern, to replace the infinity of a God-centred universe with the infinity of human desire. This is essentially a linguistic event:

> Il faut qu'à l'infini le langage recule cette limite qu'il porte avec lui, et qui marque à la fois son royaume et sa limite. De là, dans chaque roman, une série exponentielle et sans fin d'épisodes; puis au-delà, une série sans fin de romans ...[16]

> Language must necessarily keep pushing back to an infinite degree the limits that it carries within itself and that mark both its realm and its boundaries. Hence, in every novel, an endless and exponential series of episodes; then beyond, an endless series of novels ...

Sade's ambition to 'say everything' about human sexuality (*Les 120 Journées*), to offer his reader an endless variety of postures and combinations, is an equally linguistic affair. Joan De Jean suggests that Sade reduces language to denotation by making it function mathematically and, in search of the perfect system, converts narrative to computation.[17] We saw in Chapter 2 just how important numbers and the totality of symmetrical form are in the Sadean narrative universe. Sade employs the perfection of mathematics and geometry in pursuit of the perfect (and ultimately incorruptible) body. Indeed, it is a desire for totality that, as Marcel Hénaff has argued, leads to obsession with repetition and excess: 'Cette inquiétude de manquer un élément, de laisser une case en blanc, déclenche toute la mécanique du ressassement: reprise des mêmes scènes, des mêmes dissertations, des mêmes arguments' / 'This anxiety about missing out any element, about leaving a box blank, sets off the whole mechanism of repetition: the same scenes, the same dissertations, the same arguments are reprised.'[18] It is not, however, in the repetitiousness of the Sadean text that the infinite is to be found, or even in its numerical and geometric structures – neither bulk nor symmetry make for infinity – but beyond language, in the boundless human imagination, whose power surpasses that of the gods themselves:

> voilà vos fesses, [says Belmor to Juliette] elles sont sous mes yeux, je les trouve belles, mais mon imagination, toujours plus brillante que la nature, et plus adroite, j'ose le dire, en crée de bien plus belles encore. Et le plaisir que me donne cette illusion n'est-il pas préférable à celui dont la vérité va me faire jouir? Ce que vous m'offrez n'est que beau, ce que j'invente est sublime; je ne vais faire avec vous que ce que tout le monde peut faire, et il me semble que je ferais avec ce cul, ouvrage de mon imagination, des

> choses que les Dieux mêmes n'inventeraient pas. (Vol. 8, pp. 538–39)
>
> lo, there is your ass, Juliette, there before my eyes, and beauteous it is to my contemplation; but my imagination, a more inspired architect than Nature, a more cunning artisan than she, creates other asses more beautiful still; and the pleasure I derive from this illusion, is it not preferable to the one which reality is about to have me enjoy? There is beauty in what you offer me there, but only beauty; what I invent is sublime; with you I am going to do nothing that anyone else may not do, whilst with this ass my imagination has wrought, I might do things which not even the gods themselves would invent. (p. 522)

Imagination liberates man from the fixity of bodily identity in the symbolic as defined and determined by language. The limits of the objective body dissolve, for example, as erotic fantasy mixes the masculine and the feminine. In *La Philosophie dans le boudoir,* Mme de Saint-Ange explains to Eugénie that the purpose of the numerous mirrors in the room is to 'multiplier *à l'infini* les mêmes jouissances aux yeux de ceux qui les goûtent sur cette ottomane [...] il faut que *tout* soit en vue' (pp. 40–4; my emphasis) / '*infinitely* multiply those same pleasures for the persons seated here upon this ottoman [...] *everything* must be seen' (p. 203). The point here, Hénaff maintains, is not narcissism, but total visibility and endless visual imagery to feed the libertine imagination.[19] In Sade's writings mirrors function to multiply the body to an infinite degree, so that it is not the body per se that generates pleasure but its representation in an unlimited number of reflected images. That the human imagination opens the door to endless pleasure in transcending the linguistic categories that structure our reality was one of Sade's most valuable insights. As much a poetic as an intellectual notion, infinity expresses itself in the sexual utopianism and unfettered desires of the Sadean man.

Even from a more rigorously scientific or philosophical point of view, there is no doubt that the concept of infinity is not dependent on the existence of a transcendental being – recent discoveries in astrophysics have confirmed the infinity of time and space in the universe – and Sade was just one of a number of materialist philosophers of the eighteenth century who believed in the concept of perpetual motion underlying the concept of infinity. For La Mettrie, who strongly influenced Sade's thinking in this area, the human body is a self-driven machine, perpetual motion making redundant any notion of a motor. If men want to talk about a creator, says the author of the pamphlet, *Français, encore un effort ...* in *La Philosophie dans le boudoir*, then one must tell them 'que les choses ayant toujours été ce qu'elles sont, n'ayant jamais eu de commencement et ne devant jamais avoir de fin, il devient aussi inutile qu'impossible à l'homme de pouvoir remonter à une origine imaginaire qui n'expliquerait rien et n'avancerait à rien' (p. 206) / 'that things always having been what they now are, never having had a beginning and never going to have an end, it thus becomes as useless as impossible for man to be able to trace things back to an imaginary origin which would explain nothing and do not a jot of good' (p. 304).

The infinity of a universe in perpetual motion presents a challenge to the libertine, whose megalomania drives him to aspire to match it and even to destroy it.[20] He perceives a chance of immortality in the commission of a crime of such magnitude that it would have perpetual effects. This fantasy of an impossible crime against nature recurs throughout Sade's *oeuvre*, but is most clearly formulated by Clairwil and by Saint-Fond in *Juliette*:

> Je voudrais, dit Clairwil, trouver un crime dont l'effet perpétuel agît, même quand je n'agirais plus, en sorte qu'il n'y eût pas un seul instant de ma vie, ou même en dormant, où je ne fusse cause d'un désordre quelconque, et que ce désordre pût s'étendre au point qu'il entraînât une corruption générale, ou un dérangement si formel, qu'au-delà même de ma vie l'effet s'en prolongeât encore. (Vol. 8, p. 541)

> 'I would like,' Clairwil answered, 'to find a crime which, even when I had left off doing it, would go on having perpetual effect, in such a way that so long as I lived, at every hour of the day and as I lay sleeping at night, I would be constantly the cause of a particular disorder, and that

> this disorder might broaden to the point where it brought about a corruption so universal or a disturbance so formal that even after my life was over I would survive in the everlasting continuation of my wickedness ...' (p. 525)

> Saint-Fond: Ah! je voudrais, ainsi qu'Hérode, prolonger mes férocités au-delà même du tombeau. (Vol. 8, p. 298)

> Ah, like Herod, I should like to prolong my ferocities beyond life itself. (p. 271)[21]

It is Saint-Fond, however, who extends this fantasy of the perpetual crime to the individual. Alone among the libertines, he believes in God and an afterlife (although for him, any God that exists must be evil). At a textual level, this belief is nothing more than a pretext for the creation of a symbol of infinite human suffering, for what Saint-Fond envisages is dominion over his victim's very soul: in order to

> prolonger ses maux au-delà de l'immensité des siècles [...] il fallait, avec du sang tiré près du coeur, lui faire signer qu'elle donnait son âme au diable, lui enfoncer ensuite ce billet dans le trou du cul avec le vit, et lui imposer pendant ce temps la plus forte douleur qu'il soit en notre pouvoir de lui faire endurer. Jamais, avec ce moyen, [...] l'individu [...] n'entrera dans le ciel. Ses souffrances, de la même nature que celle que vous lui aurez fait endurer en lui enfonçant le billet, seront éternelles; et l'on jouira du plaisir délicieux de les avoir prolongées au-delà même des bornes de l'éternité, si l'éternité pouvait en avoir. (Vol. 8, pp. 394–95)

> make its sufferings last beyond the unending immensity of ages [...] it is necessary to have him sign a pact, writ in his heart's blood, whereby he contracts his soul to the devil; next to insert this paper in his asshole and to tamp it home with one's prick; and while doing so to cause him to suffer the greatest pain in one's power to inflict. Observe these measures [...] and no individual you destroy will enter into heaven. His agonies, in kind identical to those you make him endure while burying the

> pact, shall be everlasting; and yours will be the unspeakable delight of prolonging them beyond the limits of eternity, if eternity there be. (pp. 369–70)

Although dependent on belief in the immortality of the soul, Saint-Fond's fantasy dramatically immortalises the body too by transforming it into an object of eternal pain.[22]

For Annie Le Brun, it is the organic bond between truth and the body that is at the centre of Sade's thought and that too many modernist critics of Sade, such as Georges Bataille and Maurice Blanchot, have underplayed in their emphasis on the linguistic or textual nature of the Sadean phenomenon.[23] As La Dubois insists in *Justine*, physical sensations are the only reality. In her most recent work, Le Brun shows how the physicality of theatre is at the core of Sade's atheistic philosophy, how his theatricality, found in the novels as well as in the many plays, constitutes the first 'theatre of atheism'.[24] Starting from this idea of the fundamentally physical nature of the Sadean universe, I want to suggest that, if the body is at its centre, as Le Brun argues, it is in part because it is seen to displace both God and the perpetual motion of nature.[25] Saint-Fond's exploitation of the body of his victim as a means of access to an eternity of suffering can in this sense be interpreted as a metaphorical expression of the desire for *physical* transcendence. The Sadean libertine's longing for transcendence is not spiritual but visceral, an aspiration not to an afterlife but to an immortality in this life.

This yearning for a 'transcendence of the body' manifests itself in a number of ways; for example, in the portrayal of the body, whether of libertines or of victims, as physically perfect and uncorrupted, like the impeccable body that Christians believe they will regain on the day of the Last Judgement. Such representations do not take place in the libertine imagination, but have a literal and material reality in Sade's text. In that sense, the Sadean body is a transfigured body: to transfigure is 'to change in form or aspect especially so as to elevate or idealise' (*OED*), whilst the noun, 'transfiguration' carries the narrower connotation of 'a change of form or appearance, especially that of Christ' (*OED*).

The Sadean body can be seen to conform more or less to these definitions in a number of ways. The body of the

Sadean victim is always superlative in every sense: if a woman is beautiful, then her beauty is without compare – 'la plus jolie bouche possible [...] la plus belle gorge du monde' / 'the prettiest possible mouth [...] the loveliest bosom in the world' (Rosalie in *Les Malheurs*, p. 150), etc. – while the libertine woman is equally unsurpassable in physical beauty: Clairwil, for instance, in *Juliette*: 'Jamais on ne vit une plus belle taille, jamais une gorge mieux soutenue ... Ces fesses! ah Dieu! c'était le cul de la Vénus adorée des Grecs: je n'en vis jamais de coupées plus délicieusement' (Vol. 8, p. 302) / 'Never has there been such a lovely figure, never such a bosom ... Those buttocks! O God! 'twas the ass of that Aphrodite the Greeks reverenced; I never saw a more delicious cleft' (p. 276, adapted). If the victim is ugly, then her ugliness is equally incomparable. In either case, it is excess that is found attractive. The male libertine, too, may be a physical inadequate (he may have a minuscule penis or be sexually impotent), but otherwise he has sexual equipment of mythical dimensions. Physically idealised, the anus and the phallus are literally objects of worship. Juliette is instructed quite simply to adore Saint-Fond's arse, while in Noirceuil's case, it is his prick that she must venerate:

> Mettez-vous à genoux devant lui, adorez-le, félicitez-vous de l'honneur que je vous accorde en vous permettant d'offrir à mon cul l'hommage que voudrait lui rendre toute la terre ... (Vol. 8, p. 248)
>
> Kneel facing it, adore it, consider the honor I accord you in permitting you to do my ass the homage an entire nation, nay, the whole wide world aspires to render it ... (p. 218)
>
> – Que de crimes me coûte ce vit! s'écria Noirceuil [...] Il n'est aucun objet sur la terre que je ne sois prêt à lui sacrifier: c'est un dieu pour moi, qu'il soit le tien, Juliette: adore-le, ce vit despote, encense-le, ce dieu superbe. Je voudrais l'exposer aux hommages du monde entier [...] (Vol. 8, p. 218)
>
> 'What a tale of crimes that prick has cost me!' cried [Noirceuil], '[...] Upon this globe's whole extent there is

> not a single object I'm not ready to sacrifice to its comfort: this tool is my god, let it be one unto thee, Juliette: extol it, worship it, this despotic engine, show it every reverence, it is a thing proud of its glory, insatiate, a tyrant; I'd fain make the earth bend its knee in universal homage to this prick [...]' (p. 185)

For Moberti, the phallus is quite simply the source of all omnipotence, the greatest force in the universe: 'Je voudrais que l'univers entier cessât d'exister quand je bande' (Vol. 9, p. 493) / 'I would like to have the entire earth stand still when I lift my prick,' (p. 1100) he exclaims. Both organs may be covered in shit – indeed, the libertine requires his victim's anus to be *merdeux* like his own – but this is not seen as a sign of material corruption. Like the body that evacuates it, the turd in Sade is sanctified as an object of desire. Indeed, in *Les 120 Journées* and in *Justine*, the special diets of those required to produce turds for consumption transform them into culinary delicacies. All the body's waste products – faeces, urine, and even menstrual blood – can be eroticised and so venerated as objects of desire. At the same time, no one ever gets sick or old in Sade, and curiously in a libertine society devoted as much to the pleasures of the table as to the joys of sex, obesity does not seem to be a problem.[26] The body's very corruptibility is in this way effectively neutralised, 'bracketed off'.

In other ways, too, the Sadean victim's body is transfigured to fit an ideal of libertine perfection. This ideal is anal-phallic: there is no place for the woman's breasts or vagina and so these are either ignored or even removed, the breasts hacked off, the vagina sewn up. In *Les 120 Journées*, the masters of Silling surgically transform boys into girls and vice versa, transcending the limitations of the 'natural' body: 'Un bougre arrache les entrailles d'un jeune garçon et d'une jeune fille, met les entrailles du jeune garçon dans le corps de la fille et ceux de la fille dans le corps du garçon, puis il recoud les plaies' (p. 500) / 'A sodomist rips the intestines from a young boy and a young girl, puts the boy's into the girl, inserts the girl's into the boy's body, stitches up the incisions' (p. 649); 'Après avoir coupé tout ras le vit et les couilles il forme un con au jeune homme avec une machine de fer rouge qui fait le trou et qui cautérise tout de suite' (p. 507) / 'After having sheared off the boy's prick and balls, using a red-hot iron he hollows out a cunt in the place formerly occupied by his genitals; the iron makes the hole and cauterizes simultaneously' (pp. 655–56). Nature is thus refashioned to suit the megalomania of libertine desire. The Sadean machines that bore more and more deeply into human flesh, stripping the body bare, emptying man of content, seem part of a quest for a hidden transcendence.

Standing Christian theology on its head, Sade presents us with a body that is transfigured or made perfect, not through virtue but through vice. In those cathedrals of the body at Silling and Sainte-Marie-des-Bois, the libertines discharge with an intensity reminiscent of the ecstasies of the saints. If sexuality is the path to transcendence, then orgasm is a transfiguring moment. With their disciples and secret ceremonies, they appear almost like Messianic figures. In *La Philosophie dans le boudoir*, Dolmancé and Saint-Ange put their young novice, Eugénie, through an arcane ceremony of sexual initiation, while in *Juliette* the Society of the Friends of Crime with its articles of faith and codes of loyalty operates like any religious sect. All the libertines deliver sermons on moral, religious and philosophical matters: proselytising is as important an activity in libertinage as in Christianity. Atheism is the Sadean religion and the libertines take every opportunity to convert the unbeliever. On an emotional level, Sade himself certainly perceived atheism in quasi-religious terms: 'If atheism wants martyrs, let it say so,' he proclaimed, 'and my blood is ready', while Bressac, in *La nouvelle Justine*, calls atheism 'le plus sacré de mes systèmes' / 'the most sacred of my systems' (Vol. 2, p. 236). In fact, in its focus on the body, Sadean libertinage is actually not that dissimilar to the Christian faith it so despises. One could even say that Sade does not invert but interprets literally the Christian promise of physical perfection and immortality. Whenever the libertines reveal their bodies, those present are dazzled by what they see, as were the apostles by the transfigured Christ. Just as the mountain was the location of Christ's bodily transfiguration, the volcano in Sade functions in part as a holy place in the cult of the phallic body: in both *La nouvelle Justine* and *Juliette*, volcanoes are the site of a direct challenge to a nature that the libertines aspire to dethrone.

In the Catholic mass that Sade knew so well, the divine is bodily incarnated: this is the meaning of the transubstantiation, when the priest transforms bread and wine into the actual body and blood of Christ. In *Juliette*, the black mass celebrated by Pius VI on the altar of St Peter's in the Vatican, assisted by 'six young girls and six handsome boys' in a parodic echo of the Last Supper, is not a satanic event, but a desecration of the consecrated body of Jesus Christ and a consecration of the libertine body as divine object in its place:

> La messe se disait [...] Dès que l'hostie fut consacrée, l'acolyte l'apporta sur l'estrade et la déposa respectueusement sur la tête du vit papal; aussitôt qu'il l'y voit, le bougre m'encule avec. [...] Sodomisée par le pape, le corps de Jésus-Christ dans le cul, ô mes amis, quelles délices! [...] Nous retombâmes épuisés au milieu des *divins* objets de luxure qui nous entouraient, et *le sacrifice* s'acheva. (Vol. 9, p. 202; my emphasis)

> Mass was said [...] The Host once consecrated, the acolyte brought it up to the stage and respectfully deposited it on the tip of the papal prick; the very next moment the bugger claps it into my bum, wafer first. [...] Sodomized by the Pope, the body of Jesus Christ nested in one's ass, oh, my friends! what rare delight. [...] We fell back exhausted amidst that crowd of *celestial* playthings surrounding us, and *the sacrifice* was over. (p. 802)

We note the use of religious terminology to denote sexual activity – a common feature of the Sadean text – and in particular, the use of the word 'sacrifice' which here refers to the Catholic Mass but in practically all other circumstances in Sade's fiction denotes the murder of a sexual victim. The consistent employment of the vocabulary of religion in Sade for eroticised parts of the body – 'altar' for 'arse', and 'incense' for 'spunk' for example – is not only ironic, but it also lends linguistic support to the image of the body as sacred object.

The priests of Sade's religion of the body are mostly men – Dolmancé, Saint-Fond, Noirceuil or the Pope himself – but in *Juliette*, Durand is the body's high priestess. A sorcerer with supernatural powers, *Durand* displays an ability to *endure*, to come back from the dead, that makes her seem immortal. Among her many talents is the ability to conjure up mythical creatures at will – the sylph, Alzamor, for example. A sylph is an 'elemental spirit of the air', but Alzamor is no ethereal being: a creature of 'prodigious (sexual) vigour', he is summoned, 'le vit en l'air' / 'with his prick in the air', to deflower a young virgin, a task which he proceeds to accomplish 'en deux minutes' / 'in a trice' (Vol. 8, p. 549). The *super*natural Durand symbolises and embodies the Sadean desire for omnipotence: 'Toute la nature est à mes ordres' (Vol. 8, p. 555) / 'All Nature is at my orders' (p. 538). Herself an *un*natural creature (she has an enormous clitoris but a blocked vagina and so can neither engage in orthodox sexual intercourse or make babies), Durand is the androgynous symbol of culture's struggle against nature.

The Sadean libertine's ultimate victory over nature is his victory over death itself, which he transcends by eroticising it: in *Justine*, Roland hangs himself to experience orgasmic pleasures – a real *petite mort* – but cuts the cord at the crucial moment. Like the risen Christ, Roland survives death in a *physical* sense. It is interesting to note in this respect that when Sade himself dreams in his prison cell of his beautiful thirteenth-century ancestor, Laure de Sade, to whom the poet Petrarch dedicated so many poems, her beauty remains unchanged for him, her body uncorrupted: 'The horror of the tomb had not impaired the splendour of her beauty, and her eyes had the same fire as when Petrarch sang of them.'[27] From a psychoanalytic point of view, these visions of a body whose physical perfection has survived the ravages of death are the invention of a psychotic or narcissistic personality as a protection against the threat of physical disintegration – a characteristic of a megalomania that refuses to die.[28]

Conclusion

In the concluding pages of his definitive postmodern study of Sade, Marcel Hénaff hesitates to sanctify the libertine body:

> Le corps libertin c'est peut-être celui du dernier homme dansant sur les dernières ruines du néolithique. On pourrait dire que *L'Histoire de Juliette* y prend un peu les allures de son Évangile et *Les 120 Journées de Sodome* celles de son Apocalypse. Un peu, mais quand même ...[29]

> The libertine body is perhaps that of the last man dancing on the last ruins of the neolithic age. One might say that, to some extent, *The Story of Juliette* thus takes on the aspect of his Gospel and *The 120 Days of Sodom* that of his Apocalypse. But only to some extent ...

It is time to pick up the gauntlet that Hénaff threw down over 20 years ago by bringing together the two dimensions of Sade's writing that critics have for so long deemed incompatible: the enthronement of the body and the thirst for transcendence. In the Gospel According to Sade are four books: *Justine, Juliette, La Philosophie dans le boudoir* and *Les 120 Journées de Sodome*. The figure four seems to have a structural significance in the Sadean text, as we saw in Chapter 2 and as Michel Delon has recently emphasised: in *Les 120 Journées*,

> The quaternary of libertines represents the diversity of sexuality, just as it embodies the four temperaments of Hippocratic medicine [...] and the four social elites of the *ancien régime* (the nobility of the sword, the high clergy, the nobility of the robe and high finance). [...] The quadripartition of the libertines organises the text, since the figure 4 determines the number of spouses, of victims, and of fuckers, as it does the duration of the plot which covers four months, that is, one hundred and twenty days. We find a similar quadripartition in the convent at Sainte-Marie-des-Bois into which Justine wanders to her great misfortune: the four monks correspond to the four temperaments and between them exhibit all aspects of sexuality.[30]

One might conjecture that as the number of the Christian Gospels, the figure four also lends a quasi-religious structure to Sade's four major libertine works.[31] These books were composed at different times in different circumstances, but all were dictated by an author-god, determined to displace other faiths with his own quest for the Absolute.

From the modern reader's point of view, the Sadean cult of the human body offers a number of positive insights. In his promotion of bodily perfection, of sexual athleticism and potency, and even his obsessive concern with dietary matters, Sade may be said more than any other writer of the modern period to have initiated a veritable worship of the body which seems on one level uncomfortably close to our own fanatical pursuit of immortality in the gymnasium and the health food store, as well as in the bedroom. In this sense, he sounds a timely warning for the contemporary Western reader: like any monomania, the current cult of the body threatens to blind its followers to other, potentially rewarding, dimensions of life. At the same time, Sade divinises the singularity of the ugly and the deformed, the decrepitude of old age, and the repulsiveness of bodily waste in ways that might paradoxically help those who have the courage to read him to adopt more reasonable, more realistic and less discriminatory attitudes to the physical and sexual aspects of their existence.

Afterword

Sade's world, as we have seen, is an interior world, a world of castles and dungeons and boudoirs and monasteries in which the reader can feel as trapped as Justine. The writing contains no descriptions of the sun warming the skin, or sweet summer fragrances, or cool sea breezes, and no evocations of wide open spaces – Sade's mountains, forests and volcanoes are physically confining, not liberating, spaces. The claustrophobic sexual arena of the Sadean imagination reflects the loss of physical and sexual freedom the author was forced to endure. The interior spaces of the fiction are projections of the internal world of the mind, as well as stages for the representation of the body. In the dissertations and footnotes and philosophical dialogues that alternate with and seek to justify the acts of extreme violence and sexual abuse conducted by his libertine anti-heroes, Sade invites us to rethink received wisdoms and reinterpret long-standing values, challenging essentialist conceptions of morality and truth. In *Les Mots et les choses* (1966), Michel Foucault maintained that Friedrich Nietzsche was the father of postmodernism, that in his writing lay the origins of the scepticism that is its overriding character:

> Nietzsche marks the threshold beyond which contemporary philosophy can begin to start thinking again; and he will no doubt continue for a long while to dominate its advance.[1]

If this is so, it is in large measure due to the influence of Sade on Nietzsche, for, notwithstanding Sade's aristocratic leanings and hierarchical ways of thinking, the Sadean text contains many thoughts and ideas that we would now consider both Nietzschean and postmodern in character.[2]

One might object that Sade's influence on Nietzsche is most evident in some of his more reactionary ideas.

Certainly, both men were fundamentally elitist: Nietzsche's *Übermensch* or 'superman' is Sade's physically and intellectually superior libertine, a self-determining individual, unbound by moral or social convention, and wholly responsible for the creation of his own value system. However, at the same time, there are unmistakeable echoes of Sadean thought in the deep scepticism and bold iconoclasm of Nietzschean philosophy and its postmodern reincarnations. Friedrich Nietzsche's doctrine of perspectivism, which claims that there are no absolute truths, only historically relative interpretations, is a direct descendant of Sade's moral relativism. Jean-François Lyotard's argument in *La Condition postmoderne* (1979) that all of the 'grand narratives' of Western civilisation, such as those of Christianity and the Enlightenment, have now been demolished, owes a great deal to Nietzsche but also to Sade's atheistic individualism and profound distrust of collective human enterprise.[3] It is true that, along with other philosophers of the Enlightenment, Sade substituted reason for superstition and the gods of religion, but Sadean reason uniquely and scandalously was itself subordinated to the anarchy of bodily desire – for Nietzsche, the Dionysian nature of human beings, and for Lyotard, their libidinal drives, which the Marxist 'grand narrative' completely ignores. The objectification and disciplining of the body that Foucault would identify in the schools, prisons and factories of nineteenth- and twentieth-century society were designed to suppress and control these desires and to socially engineer the body's potential for production in the capitalist system. Such processes are starkly prefigured in the Sadean fragmentation of the physical subject.

If, therefore, at the beginning of the new millennium, Sade is worthy of a place in the corner bookstore and public library, as well as on university and examination syllabuses, it is not only because of the enormous and undisputed influence of his writing and thought over the last two centuries, but also because, in so many regards, the transgressive character of his work once again finds resonance with the current artistic climate: our *fin de siècle* suspicion of modern political credos, the fragmentation of our value systems and the ubiquitous pursuit of sexual ecstasy and physical immortality. Although, like all writers and thinkers, undeniably a product of his own times, Sade raises moral, social and even political questions that are as relevant now and everywhere as they were in eighteenth-century France: the threat of religious fundamentalism, the repression and persecution of non-normative forms of sexuality, the obsession with physical perfection, the sexual motives underlying our fascination with violence, and the emergence of greater pluralism in the way we organise our societies, for example, are all important Sadean themes. And if as the seventeenth-century English philosopher, Thomas Hobbes, famously opined, life is 'nasty, brutish and short', Sade's unvarnished representation of this unpleasant fact is strangely and surprisingly consoling. In summary, Sade deserves to be called a great writer because of the extraordinary modernity of his thinking, because of the breadth of his vision and the novelty of his perspectives, because he alone dares say what others before him considered unsayable, because he says it in a form of some artistic depth and complexity, and perhaps most of all, for the unambiguous warnings he so fearlessly and stubbornly sounds against the ever-present dangers of self-deception and ignorance:

> I authorize the publication and sale of all libertine books and immoral works; for I esteem them most essential to human felicity and welfare, instrumental to the progress of philosophy, indispensable to the eradication of prejudices, and in every sense conducive to the increase of human knowledge and understanding. (*Juliette*)

Notes

Chapter 1

1. The word 'libertinage' had come to mean 'free thinker on religion' by the end of the sixteenth century, but during the next 100 years it gradually took on the secondary meaning of debauchery. By Sade's time then, a libertine was an individual leading a dissolute life, and libertine writing and painting were virtually synonymous with our modern term of pornography. In that they are vehemently anti-religious and depict scenes of debauchery using so-called obscene language, Sade's libertine novels conform to both definitions of the word.
2. Readers of French have access to Chantal Thomas's excellent primer, *Sade* (Paris: Éditions du Seuil, 1994), while readers of English only have the entertaining but very basic *Sade for Beginners* by Stuart Hood and Graham Crowley (Cambridge: Icon Books, 1995).
3. Sade has so frequently become the creature of orthodoxies or critical positions in a way that less controversial writers have not, and readers with an interest in following the critical debate are referred to works mentioned below.
4. In the autobiographical passages of *Aline et Valcour*: see Maurice Lever, *Marquis de Sade: A Biography*, translated by Arthur Goldhammer (London: HarperCollins, 1993), pp. 75 and 576, n. 27.
5. Sade was afflicted by piles throughout his life. It is interesting to relate the suffering that the condition caused him to the pain–pleasure nexus of his anal fixations.
6. Some have argued that Sade's behaviour was no worse than that of many other aristocrats of his day who, when brought before the courts for similar offences, habitually got off scot-free, but that, on this occasion, the Marquis was an unfortunate pawn in a power game between the king and the Parliament: see Francine du Plessix Gray, *At Home with the Marquis de Sade* (New York: Penguin Books, 1999), pp. 98–100 and Lever, *Marquis de Sade*, pp. 159–63.

7. For details of the perversion of coprophilia in Sade's fiction, see Chapters 2 and 5.
8. Memories of this winter orgy probably helped inspire the similar, though far more extreme, situation depicted in *Les 120 Journées*, which Sade would write in the Bastille a decade later.
9. See Chapter 4.
10. The *lettre de cachet* or 'sealed letter' was 'an arbitrary order of arrest or detention, used since the Middle Ages, which could be issued and signed only by the king and was looked on as an ultimate symbol of the monarch's divine right. One of the most arbitrary and detested features of the *ancien régime*, it could imprison any citizen for life without his ever being granted any kind of legal hearing, the length of the prison term depending solely on the king's pleasure and will'. (du Plessix Gray, *At Home*, p. 97).
11. The phrase 'bien poivré' is Sade's editor's.
12. See Joan De Jean, *Literary Fortifications. Rousseau, Laclos, Sade* (Princeton University Press: 1984), p. 264.
13. Sade and Restif de la Bretonne loathed each other intensely. Sade described Restif as a hack writer who churned out potboilers for money, while Restif called Sade a woman-hating monster and wrote *L'Anti-Justine* as a counterblast to *Justine*: see Chapter 4.
14. De Jean, *Literary Fortifications*, p. 274.
15. The phrase is Robespierre's, attacking 'those who make a religion of atheism' in a famous speech made at the Jacobin Club on 22 November 1793 against the anti-religion movement: see Lever, *Marquis de Sade*, p. 461.
16. See Michel Delon, 'Sade, maître d'agression', *Europe*, No. 522 (October 1972), p. 125.
17. See Jane Gallop, *Intersections. A Reading of Sade with Bataille, Blanchot, and Klossowski* (Lincoln and London: University of Nebraska Press, 1981), Chapter 1, and Georges Bataille, *L'Érotisme* (Paris: Les Éditions de Minuit, 1957), 'L'homme souverain de Sade'.
18. *Français, encore un effort si vous voulez être républicains* in *La Philosophie dans le boudoir*, p. 258; *Justine, Philosophy in the Bedroom and Other Writings*, p. 333.
19. Françoise Laugaa-Traut, *Lectures de Sade* (Paris: Armand Colin, 1973).
20. Jean Paulhan, Introduction to *Les Infortunes de la vertu* (Paris: Point du Jour, 1946), pp. ii–xliii, translated as 'The Marquis de Sade and His Accomplice' in *Marquis de Sade, Justine, Philosophy in the Bedroom, and Other Writings* (New York:

Grove Weidenfeld, 1990), pp. 3–36; Pierre Klossowski, *Sade, mon prochain* (Paris: Éditions du Seuil, 1947; rev. edition 1967), translated as *Sade My Neighbour* (London: Quartet Books, 1992); Maurice Blanchot, *Lautréamont et Sade* (Paris: Les Éditions de Minuit, 1963), from which the translated essay, 'Sade' in *Marquis de Sade, Justine, Philosophy in the Bedroom, and Other Writings*, pp. 37–72, is taken.

21. Albert Camus, *L'Homme révolté* in *Essais d'Albert Camus,* (eds) R. Quilliot and L. Faucon (Paris: Gallimard, 'Pléiade', 1965), p. 457; Raymond Queneau, *Bâtons, chiffres et lettres* (Paris: Gallimard, 1950), p. 152.
22. Simone de Beauvoir, 'Faut-il brûler Sade?' in *Les Temps modernes,* December 1951, January 1952; later in *Privilèges* (Paris: Gallimard, 1955); English translation, 'Must we burn Sade?' in *The Marquis de Sade, The 120 Days of Sodom and Other Writings* (London: Arrow Books, 1990), pp. 3–64.
23. Jean-Jacques Pauvert himself offers a fascinating account of what came to be known as 'L'Affaire Pauvert' in *Nouveaux visages de la censure* (Paris: Les Belles Lettres, 1994). See also Jean-Jacques Pauvert and Pierre Beuchot, *Sade en procès* (Paris: Éditions Mille et Une Nuits/Arte, 1999). Readers of English only are referred to Nicholas Harrison, *Circles of Censorship. Censorship and its Metaphors in French History, Literature and Theory* (Oxford: Clarendon Press, 1995), Chapter 3.
24. See note 17 above.
25. Roland Barthes, *Sade, Fourier, Loyola* (Paris: Éditions du Seuil, 1971); Michel Foucault, 'Préface à la transgression' in *Critique* 195–96 (1963), pp. 751–69, 'Le Langage à l'infini' in *Tel Quel* 15 (1963), pp. 44–53, *Les Mots et les choses* (Paris: Gallimard, 1966), pp. 221–24, *Histoire de la folie à l'âge classique,* (Paris: Gallimard, rev. ed. 1972); Jacques Lacan, 'Kant avec Sade' in *Écrits* (Paris: Éditions du Seuil, 1966), pp. 765–90; Gilles Deleuze, *Présentation de Sacher-Masoch* (Paris: Les Éditions de Minuit, 1967); Philippe Sollers, 'Sade dans le texte' in *L'écriture et l'expérience des limites* (Paris: Éditions du Seuil, 1968), pp. 48–66; Marcel Hénaff, *Sade: L'Invention du corps libertin* (Paris: PUF, 1978); Philippe Roger, *Sade: La Philosophie dans le pressoir* (Paris: Bernard Grasset, 1976); Béatrice Didier, *Sade* (Paris: Éditions Denoël/Gonthier, 1976); Angela Carter, *The Sadeian Woman* (London: Virago Press, 1979).
26. Annie Le Brun, *Soudain un bloc d'abîme, Sade,* Introduction to *Sade, Oeuvres Complètes* (Paris: Jean-Jacques Pauvert, 1986); Michel Delon, *L'idée d'énergie au tournant des Lumières* (Paris: PUF, 1988); Chantal Thomas, *Sade, l'oeil de la lettre* (Paris: Payot, 1978), *Sade* (Paris: Éditions du Seuil, 1994); Lucienne

Frappier-Mazur, *Writing the Orgy: Power and Parody in Sade* (Philadelphia: University of Pennsylvania Press, 1996), originally published in French as *Sade et l'écriture de l'orgie* (Paris: Nathan, 1991); Jane Gallop, *Intersections*.

27. *Yale French Studies*, No. 35 (1965), *The Divine Sade*, edited by Deepak Narang Sawhney, *PLI Warwick Journal of Philosophy* (February, 1994), and *Paragraph*, Vol. 23, No. 1 (Edinburgh University Press, spring 2000), edited by John Phillips.
28. du Plessix Gray, *At Home*, p. 360. This indeterminacy seems to be mirrored in a confusion over the very signifiers of Sade's civic identity: registered incorrectly at birth as 'Alphonse' rather than as 'Aldonse', Sade chose to name himself in a number of different fashions, styling himself as 'Marquis' after his father's death instead of assuming the title of 'Comte' as convention dictated, and after the Revolution signing himself variously as 'François Sade' and 'Louis Sade'. Du Plessix Gray sees this oscillation as 'evidence of his elusive sense of identity, or even of a split personality' (p. 367).
29. Camille Paglia, *Sexual Personae. Art and Decadence from Nefertiti to Emily Dickinson* (New York: Vintage Books, 1991), pp. 230–47, (p. 237).
30. Maurice Lever, *Donatien Alphonse François, Marquis de Sade* (Paris: Librairie Artheme Fayard, 1991), English translation: Lever, *Marquis de Sade*; Donald Thomas, *The Marquis de Sade* (London: Allison and Busby, 1992); Laurence L. Bongie, *Sade: A Biographical Essay* (Chicago and London: The University of Chicago Press, 1998); Francine du Plessix Gray, *At Home*.
31. Roger Shattuck, *Forbidden Knowledge: From Prometheus to Pornography* (New York: St Martin's Press, 1996).
32. Sade's libertine novels are certainly obscene according to conventional definitions of the word. As I shall show in the following chapters, however, they cannot be said to be pornographic: see my *Forbidden Fictions: Pornography and Censorship in Twentieth Century French Literature* (London and Sterling, Virginia: Pluto Press, 1999), Chapter 1 for detailed discussion of the use and meaning of terms like 'obscenity' and 'pornography'.
33. Bruno Bettelheim, *The Uses of Enchantment: The Meaning and Importance of Fairy Tales* (London: Penguin Books, 1991; first published by Thames and Hudson, 1976).
34. The so-called 'Moors murderers', Ian Brady and Myra Hindley: see Donald Thomas, *The Marquis de Sade*, pp. 8–14 and 316 for details of the allegations that reading Sade had corrupted Brady and Hindley and inspired them to commit their horrible crimes.

Chapter 2

1. While in prison, Sade had special implements made for the purpose of self-sodomy.
2. The roll is presently in the ownership of a private collector living in Switzerland.
3. Maurice Heine, *Recueil de confessions et observations psychosexuelles*, 1935; quoted by Henri Pastoureau, 'Sadomasochism and the Philosophies of Ambivalence', *Yale French Studies*, No. 35 (1965), p. 50.
4. See Sade's correspondence for August 1789: *Correspondance* in *Oeuvres Complètes*, Vol. 12 (Paris: Cercle du livre précieux, 1967).
5. See, for example, Le Brun, *Soudain un bloc d'abîme*, p. 23.
6. This influence is confirmed, Georges May argues, by Sade's long-standing familiarity with and admiration for Boccaccio's work: see Georges May, 'Fiction Reader, Novel Writer', *Yale French Studies*, No. 35 (1965), p. 10.
7. See Hood and Crowley, *Sade For Beginners*, p. 72.
8. Carter, *The Sadeian Woman*, p. 23.
9. De Jean, *Literary Fortifications*, p. 277. Chapter 6, to which I shall be referring extensively here, contains an excellent exegesis of *Les 120 Journées*.
10. As Angela Carter says, '[Sade] is an extreme writer and he describes a society and a system of social relations *in extremis*, those of the last years of the *ancien régime* in France.' (*The Sadeian Woman*, p. 23).
11. Claude Lévi-Strauss, *Les Structures élémentaires de la parenté* (Paris: PUF, 1949), p. 595.
12. The explosion of the family structure through incest is graphically illustrated in Blangis's story of a man 'qui a foutu trois enfants qu'il avait de sa mère, desquelles il y avait une fille qu'il avait fait épouser à son fils, de façon qu'en foutant celle-là il foutait sa soeur, sa fille et sa belle-fille et qu'il contraignait son fils à foutre sa soeur et sa belle-mère' / 'who fucked three children he had by his mother, amongst whom there was a daughter whom he had marry his son, so that in fucking her he fucked his sister, his daughter and his daughter-in-law, and thus he also constrained his son to fuck his own sister and mother-in-law', and in Curval's tale of a brother and sister 'qui firent projet de se livrer mutuellement leurs enfants; la soeur avait un garçon et une fille, et le frère de même. Ils se mêlèrent de façon que tantôt ils foutaient avec leurs neveux, tantôt avec leurs enfants, et tantôt les cousins germains ou les frères et soeurs se foutaient, pendant

que les pères et mères c'est-à-dire le frère et soeur, se foutaient également' (pp. 431–32) / 'who reached an agreement whereby each would surrender his children to the other: the sister had a boy and a girl, so did the brother. They mixed the pudding in such wise that sometimes they fucked their nephews, sometimes their own children, and sometimes their first cousins, or else the brothers and sister would fuck while the father and mother, that is to say, the brother and sister, fucked one another also' (p. 576). Sade also favours the description, in this and other works, of mock marriages, in which gender differences as well as familial ties are deliberately undermined: see *Les 120 Journées*, pp. 132, 178, 474, 485 and 504.

13. Gallop, *Intersections*, p. 59.
14. Frappier-Mazur, *Writing the Orgy*, pp. 144–45.
15. De Jean, *Literary Fortifications*, p. 280.
16. See Bongie, *Sade*, p. 145.
17. See Maurice Heine, *Le Marquis de Sade* (Paris: Gallimard, 1950).
18. De Jean, *Literary Fortifications*, p. 296, n. 24.
19. Ibid., pp. 275–76, 287.
20. Beatrice Fink refers to the spatial mechanism in the novel which operates in 'patterns of four': see her 'Food as Object, Activity, and Symbol in Sade', *Romanic Review*, No. 65 (March 1974), p. 99.
21. See Peter Cryle, *Geometry in the Boudoir: Configurations of French Erotic Narrative* (Ithaca and London: Cornell University Press, 1994), Chapter 6: 'Taking Sade Serially: *Les 120 Journées de Sodome*', pp. 136–37 and p. 141. The whole chapter considers the use and significance of number in the novel.
22. Ibid., p. 127; my emphasis.
23. See my 'Sade and Self-censorship', *Paragraph*, Vol. 23, No. 1 (March 2000), pp. 107–18.
24. For example, see Donald Thomas, *The Marquis de Sade*, p. 183.
25. Éric Bordas, 'Sade ou l'Écriture de la Destruction: À propos de la structure stylistique des *Cent Vingt Journées de Sodome*', *The Romanic Review*, Vol. 86, No. 4 (1995), pp. 657–80 (p. 659).
26. De Jean draws attention to the linguistic and semantic proximity between 'compter' (to count) and 'conter' (to recount): see De Jean, *Literary Fortifications*, p. 302.
27. Hénaff, *Corps Libertin*, pp. 38–9.
28. Cryle, *Boudoir*, pp. 111 and 113–17.
29. J. Laplanche and J-B. Pontalis, *The Language of Psycho-Analysis* (London: The Hogarth Press and The Institute of Psycho-Analysis, 1985), pp. 35–6.

30. Sylvie Dangeville, *Le Théâtre change et représente. Lecture critique des oeuvres dramatiques du marquis de Sade* (Paris: Champion, 1999), pp. 399–400; see also Lever, *Marquis de Sade*, pp. 469–90.
31. See du Plessix Gray, *At Home*, pp. 185, 231–34, 238–39.
32. Amazingly, it is the excremental rather than the violent elements of *Les 120 Journées* that have led some critics to operate a form of quasi-censorship of this text. Gilbert Lely famously deplored these themes in the work, protesting that coprophagia is an extremely rare perversion. More recently, Noëlle Châtelet contrasts the 'horror' of Sadean coprophilia with the 'happiness in Rabelais's grotesque scatology' ('Le Libertin à table', *Écrire la crise*, pp. 77–8), and Marcelin Pleynet says that coprophagy is what really threatens to make Sade unreadable ('Sade, des chiffres, des lettres, du renfermement', *Tel Quel*, Vol. 86 (winter 1980), p. 29). This judgmentalism on the part of otherwise adulatory *sadistes* tells us more about the prejudices and unconscious anxieties of the critics concerned than it does about the text, but it also seems to me to spring from an inappropriate realist reading of an aspect of the writing that lends itself more fruitfully to symbolic and psychoanalytic interpretations.
33. Bernard Noël, 'La Machine en tête', Introduction to *Les 120 Journées*, p. xi.
34. Lucienne Frappier-Mazur argues that 'the money model structures all the erotic practices' in Sade: see her *Writing the Orgy*, p. 27.
35. Inversion, as we have seen, is a basic principle of Sadean eroticism.
36. Cryle, *Boudoir*, p. 142.
37. Beatrice Fink, 'Lecture alimentaire de l'utopie sadienne', *Sade, écrire la crise*, pp. 175–91 (pp. 189–90).
38. 'Intradiegetic' is a term coined by the French structuralist, Gérard Genette, meaning 'within the narrative'.
39. Sade does not seem ever to have made these marginal notations, the first complete French edition produced by Maurice Heine containing no trace of them. Nevertheless, our attention is still irresistibly drawn in this passage to details of print and page layout and away from content. In the spirit of Sade's original intention, the Wainhouse and Seaver translation from which all English quotations and references are taken follows the example of Pauvert's 1953 French edition in giving the storytellers' narrations in italics.
40. See Marcel Hénaff, 'The Encyclopedia of Excess' in *Sade and the Narrative of Transgression*, pp. 142–70, especially pp. 143–45.

41. Roger, *Pressoir*, p. 79.
42. Jean-Marie Goulemot, *Forbidden Texts: Erotic Literature and its Readers in Eighteenth-Century France* (Philadelphia: University of Pennsylvania Press, 1994), p. 71; first published in French as *Ces livres qu'on ne lit que d'une main* (Paris: Éditions Alinea, 1991).
43. This is true of Sade's writing generally: the dissertations of the libertines have a distracting effect on the reader, whom they aim to inform and persuade rather than seduce.
44. Goulemot, *Forbidden Texts*, p. 42.
45. De Jean, *Literary Fortifications*, pp. 290–91, 323–25.
46. Cryle, *Boudoir*, pp. 206–25.
47. For more detailed discussion of Sadean ellipses, see my 'Sade and self-censorship'.
48. As Jean-Christophe Abramovici points out, 'Paradoxically, there is no other novel by Sade in which the writer addresses the *reader* as much as in this supposedly *unreadable* book' ('Écrire et captiver', *Europe*, 1998, p. 37).
49. For instance, Donald Thomas, *The Marquis de Sade*, p. 180.
50. Chantal Thomas, *Sade*, p. 118.
51. Luis Buñuel was a Spanish surrealist film-maker. Born in 1900, he was famous for his controversial and often anti-clerical films.
52. Pier Paolo Pasolini (1922–75) was an Italian poet, novelist and film director. Pasolini's film uses Sade's horrific fantasies as a metaphor for the many inhumanities perpetrated by tyrants (Hitler, Stalin, etc.) in the twentieth century. Pasolini himself called it a 'parable of what men in power do to their fellow citizens' (quoted by Frappier-Mazur, *Writing the Orgy*, p. 68; see ibid., pp. 68–9 for a more detailed discussion of Pasolini's film).

Chapter 3

1. Donald Thomas, *The Marquis de Sade*, p. 221.
2. Chantal Thomas, *Sade*, pp. 185–86.
3. See Cryle, *Boudoir*, pp. 11 and 20–21 for a more detailed discussion of Chorier's text.
4. This is the principal thrust of Annie Le Brun's work on Sade: see, especially, her *Soudain un bloc d'abîme, Sade*.
5. Chantal Thomas, *Sade*, p. 192.
6. Carter, *The Sadeian Woman*, pp. 127–28.
7. See Chapter 4.
8. This poignant truism is repeated elsewhere in Sade's work: see, for instance, *Histoire de Juliette*, Vol. 8, p. 117.

9. The number seven seems to be a highly appropriate structuring device in a Sadean context: in ancient symbolism, the septenary represents the moral order, whilst in Christian mythology, seven is the number of the capital sins and their opposing virtues; it is also the symbol of pain. (See J. E. Cirlot, *A Dictionary of Symbols* (London: Routledge, 1971), pp. 230–33.)
10. Sade had certainly read Rousseau's *Émile ou l'Éducation* which had appeared in 1762, and which taught that children learn best by playing an active role in the educational process. The emphasis, for Rousseau, is on the practical experience of nature. In Sade's privileging of sexual practice and his constant references to the destructive side of nature as a model for human behaviour, it is hard not to see an implicit parody of Rousseau's optimistic educational philosophy.
11. For a full discussion of public and medical perceptions of both male and female masturbation in the eighteenth century, see Vernon A. Rosario, *The Erotic Imagination. French Histories of Perversity* (New York and Oxford: Oxford University Press, 1997), pp. 13–43.
12. Angela Carter draws attention to Sade's construction of women's sexual role as active as well as passive: 'Women do not normally fuck in the active sense. They are fucked in the passive tense (sic) and hence automatically fucked-up, done over, undone. Whatever else he says or does not say, Sade declares himself unequivocally for the right of women to fuck [...]' (*The Sadeian Woman*, Polemical Preface, p. 27).
13. One of the leisure pursuits that Sade missed in prison was, in fact, the game of hide-and-seek which he loved passionately: see Chantal Thomas, *Sade*, pp. 63–4.
14. Gilbert Lély, 'Avant-propos' to *La Philosophie dans le boudoir* (Paris: U.G.E., 10/18, 1991), p. 10.
15. Didier, *Sade*, p. 55.
16. Philippe Roger points out that some of the best commentators (Huxley, Klossowski) have agreed on the parodic, satirical and critical status of this revolutionary treatise: 'Sade "fictionalizes" ideology to stir, displace, shock. Ambiguity prevails in all of his political declarations.' (Roger, 'A political minimalist' in *Sade and the Narrative of Transgression*, p. 80).
17. Donald Thomas, *The Marquis de Sade*, p. 224.
18. In these respects, Sade can thus be said to have pre-empted Marx by over a century, conceiving notions of social reform that many twentieth-century communist societies have attempted to put into practice.

19. In the 1780s, pre-revolutionary pamphlets had successfully undermined the monarchy's reputation by depicting Marie-Antoinette as sexually voracious: see Robert Darnton, *The Forbidden Best-sellers of Pre-Revolutionary France* (London: HarperCollins, 1996), pp. 225–26.
20. See Chapter 1 for discussion of Sade's philosophy of 'isolisme'.
21. See Chapter 6.
22. Justine is the victim of a similar operation at the hands of Saint-Florent: see *Justine ou les Malheurs de la vertu*, p. 399.
23. For Marcel Hénaff, Sadean victims have no logical existence. This lack of existence is manifest in their silence and their passivity, which Hénaff attributes to the libertine's monopoly of mastery and the impossibility of speaking the victim's suffering: see his 'The encyclopedia of excess' in *Sade and the Narrative of Transgression*, pp. 142–70 (p. 164). One might add that victims don't speak for a third reason: the reader is thus prevented from sharing the perspective of the victim-object and forced to adopt the pleasurable position of the agent-subject.
24. 'Castration complex: Complex centering on the phantasy of castration which is produced in response to the child's puzzlement over the anatomical difference between the sexes (presence or absence of the penis): the child attributes this difference to the fact of the girl's penis having been cut off. [...] The boy fears castration, which he sees as the carrying out of a paternal threat made in reply to his sexual activities; the result for him is an intense castration anxiety.' (J. Laplanche and J-B. Pontalis, *The Language of Psycho-Analysis* (London: The Hogarth Press and The Institute of Psycho-Analysis, 1985), p. 56.)
25. See Freud's essay on 'Femininity' in *New Introductory Lectures on Psychoanalysis* (The Penguin Freud Library, Vol. 2) pp. 145–69 (pp. 166–67), and Nancy K. Miller's comment on Freud's argument concerning plaiting and weaving as a female invention in 'Arachnologies' in *The Poetics of Gender* (New York: Columbia University Press, 1986), p. 289, n. 3.
26. See in particular the final page of Jacques Lacan's somewhat rebarbative essay on *La Philosophie dans le boudoir*, 'Kant avec Sade' in *Écrits* (Paris: Éditions du Seuil, 1966), pp. 765–90.
27. See Pierre Klossowski, *Sade, mon prochain* (1967); Klossowski interprets de Bressac's matricide in *Justine* in similar fashion.
28. Carter, *The Sadeian Woman*, p. 133.
29. Ibid.

30. See the author's Preface, 'Aux Libertins' and my comment on it above.
31. Carter, *The Sadeian Woman*, p. 135.
32. Hence the ambition to destroy the entire universe expressed by so many in his fiction – a megalomaniac fantasy according to which the ego alone exists: see Chapter 6.
33. Hénaff, *Corps libertin*, p. 304.
34. From a modern sociological standpoint, it could be argued that, as seamstresses are traditionally female in gender, Sade is reinforcing gender roles in placing the needle in Eugénie's hands (rather than in Dolmancé's, for example).
35. Drama was also Sade's great passion (see Chapter 1), and the Revolution had given new impetus to the theatre as a powerful medium for the diffusion of ideas: see Sylvie Dangeville, *Le Théâtre change et représente*, p. 52; on the intrinsic theatricality of Sade's writing as a whole, see ibid., pp. 514–15.
36. Jean-Marie Goulemot makes much of the reader's voyeuristic role: see his 'Beau marquis parlez-nous d'amour' in *Sade, écrire la crise*, pp. 119–32; but note also my comment below. For discussion of the staging of sexual activities in *Les 120 Journées*, whose influence on the structure and format of *La Philosophie* is evident in this regard, see Chapter 2.
37. Alain Robbe-Grillet, 'Samuel Beckett ou la présence sur la scène' in *Pour un nouveau roman* (Paris: Les Éditions de Minuit, 1963), pp. 95–107 (p. 95).
38. For Philippe Roger, it is the holes in the text that allow the reader in: see Roger, *Pressoir*, p. 119.
39. Le Brun, *Soudain un bloc d'abîme*, p. 82.
40. Annie Le Brun, 'Sade or the First Theatre of Atheism' in John Phillips (ed.), *Paragraph*, Vol. 23, No. 1 (Edinburgh: Edinburgh University Press, March 2000), pp. 38–50.
41. Le Brun, ibid., p. 44.
42. Characters never change in Sade: they are doomed to be eternally virtuous (Justine) or eternally wicked (Juliette) – the world is 'irredeemably evil' and 'Sade's vision is utterly without transcendence' (Carter, *The Sadeian Woman*, p. 129). So, as Angela Carter observes, Sade has Mme de Mistival faint as she begins to orgasm when her daughter is fucking her with a dildo, because she cannot be allowed to experience sexual pleasure. Otherwise, the corruption of virtue that this would imply would conversely suggest the possibility of redemption from vice, and 'Transcendence would have crept in. [Sade] might even have to make room for hope' (ibid.).

Chapter 4

1. It was not until 1909 that the manuscript came to light thanks to the efforts of Guillaume Apollinaire, and it was eventually published in 1930 by Maurice Heine.
2. See Sade's letter to his lawyer, Reinaud, quoted later.
3. *Journal général de France*, 27 septembre 1792, quoted in Laugaa-Traut, *Lectures*, pp. 37–8.
4. Lever, *Marquis de Sade*, p. 387.
5. In 1801, Sade published an essay entitled *L'auteur des Crimes de l'amour à Villeterque, folliculaire* in response to an article by the critic, Villeterque, accusing him of being the author of *Justine*.
6. Both Jean Paulhan and Noëlle Châtelet have expressed this view.
7. Sade always presents his characters by providing an initial, often detailed sketch. This construction of character, according to which 'doing' follows and is predicated on 'being', seems rooted in Sade's biologically deterministic approach to human nature. In reconstructing Justine through her speech and actions and through other characters' comments on her behaviour, instead of in the predetermined authorial definition of her personality, we are reading the novel against the author.
8. For the convenience of the reader, I have slightly extended this account within italicised parentheses, inserting the proper names omitted by Justine. I have also omitted the French version for reasons of space. Full references to the relevant French editions are given in the main body of the text.
9. If Juliette has not recognised her sister right from the start, it is partly because Justine assumed a false name on leaving the convent – Sophie in *Les Infortunes*, Thérèse in the other two versions – ostensibly in order to hide her real identity.
10. The ending of *La nouvelle Justine* is substantively different from that of the preceding versions. Having escaped from her death cell, Justine encounters Juliette, who takes her back to her château where she recounts her story. Juliette then in turn relates her own life history, to be found in the companion volumes of *l'Histoire de Juliette*, and Justine's death occurs at the very end of the *Juliette* narrative.
11. The only logical explanation, for Voltaire, to the problem of evil was that God had created the universe and, rather like a clockmaker making a clock, had 'wound it up' and then left it to 'run down' on its own.

12. See Chapter 1 for a more detailed discussion of Sade's philosophical ideas.
13. 'Gothic novels', popular in England especially from around the middle of the eighteenth century, were originally fictions depicting cruel passions and supernatural terrors, usually in a medieval setting, although by the nineteenth century any works with a gloomy, violent and horrific atmosphere, such as Mary Shelley's *Frankenstein* (1818), also came to be described as 'Gothic'. Typical examples contemporaneous with Sade are Walpole's *Castle of Otranto* (1764), Ann Radcliffe's *Mysteries of Udolpho* (1794), and M. G. Lewis's *The Monk* (1795), which, according to Gilbert Lely, may itself have been inspired by the *Justine* of 1791: see Lely, 'Avant-propos' to Sade, *La nouvelle Justine* (Paris: U.G.E, 10/18, 1995), Vol. 1, pp. 7–19 (p. 13).
14. For a detailed discussion of Sade's extensive parody of the *conte moral* in the short stories collected under the title, *Les Crimes de l'amour*, and of the important consequences of his parody of the genre for the development of the more sophisticated nineteenth-century *nouvelle*, see Katherine Astbury, 'The Moral Tale and the Marquis de Sade: *Les Crimes de l'amour* as parody of the conte moral', forthcoming in *Australian Journal of French Studies*.
15. The absence of any perceivable attempt to create a realistic effect at the level of plot is one very good reason why, despite its proselytising intentions, it is hard to accept that the Sadean text can seriously be said to influence the reader in the 'real' any more than can the imaginary discourses of the fairy tale or the picaresque novel of the same century, say, or the 'horror' genre of our own (of which the Gothic novel is a direct ancestor). All literature can, of course, be argued to exert influences of different kinds on their readers, but no research of which I am aware has ever been able to prove any direct cause-and-effect relationship. This problem is central to the whole debate concerning the alleged harmful effects of pornography in general: see my *Forbidden Fictions: Pornography and Censorship in Twentieth Century French Literature* (London and Sterling, Virginia: Pluto Press, 1999), Chapter 1.
16. Paratextuality, according to Gérard Genette, is the relationship of a text with what accompanies it (titles, prefaces, notes, epigraphs, illustrations, book covers, etc.) and is one of the privileged sites from which a work can influence the reader: see Genette, *Palimpsestes* (Paris: Éditions du Seuil, 1982) and *Seuils* (Paris: Éditions du Seuil, 1987).

17. Marie Constance Quesnet, nicknamed 'Sensible' by Sade, remained devoted to him, and he to her, for the rest of his life – see Chapter 1.
18. See, for instance, *Dialogue entre un prêtre et un moribond* (*Dialogue between a Priest and a Dying Man*), completed in 1782. Anyone who doubts Sade's hypocrisy should look again at the private letter to his lawyer quoted at the beginning of this chapter.
19. Jean-Marie Goulemot, for his part, considers the first version to be superior to the other two: see his *Préface* to Sade, *Les Infortunes de la vertu* (Paris: Garnier-Flammarion, 1969), pp. 19–36 (p. 35).
20. 'Autodiegetic' is a term coined by Gérard Genette to denote a narrator who is the hero or heroine of his/her own story: see his *Figures 111* (Paris: Éditions du Seuil, 1972), p. 253.
21. Seaver's and Wainhouse's translation reads 'that cannot justify any complaint on my part', an inaccurate rendering that completely misses the saucy ambiguity of the original, and which I have consequently adapted.
22. In her own discussion of these changes of style in the *Justine* narratives, Noëlle Châtelet argues that the use of metaphor is only a 'provisional moment in Sade's writing' and she agrees with Roland Barthes that the 'transgressions of language' (of *La nouvelle Justine* and *Juliette*) are 'revolutionary'. While recognising the potentially transgressive power of linguistic obscenity, I am nevertheless arguing here against Châtelet's implication that Sade's precious and provisional use of metaphor is also of less critical interest. (See *Justine ou les Malheurs de la vertu*, edited by Noëlle Châtelet (Paris: Gallimard, 1981), pp. 431–32, n. 74.)
23. This scene does not appear in the earlier versions.
24. Unfortunately, the rigorous grammaticality of the use here of an imperfect subjunctive in the original French version (*déchargeasse*) does not carry over into English!
25. For a general discussion of humour in the Sadean text, see my article, '"Laugh? I nearly died!" Humor in Sade's Fiction' in *The Eighteenth Century: Theory and Interpretation*, Vol. 40, No. 1 (spring 1999), pp. 46–67.
26. Writing under particular constraints can produce unusual and sometimes exciting results, as the group of modern French writers who made up the experimental group known as OULIPO discovered. One of these adventurous authors, for instance, achieved the remarkable feat of writing an entire novel without using the vowel 'e'!

27. *Courrier des spectacles*, 5 fructidor (23 août 1800); cited by Jean-Jacques Pauvert, 'Notice bibliographique' in Le Brun and Pauvert (eds), Sade, *Histoire de Juliette, ou les Prospérités du vice*, (Paris: Société Nouvelle des Éditions Pauvert, 1987), Vol. 8, pp. 9–31 (p. 27).
28. Pauvert, 'Notice'.
29. Goulemot, *Forbidden Texts*, p. 47.
30. See Chapter 2, n. 38.
31. Goulemot, *Forbidden Texts*, pp. 49–50.
32. Marcel Hénaff, *L'Invention*, p. 124.
33. See Jean Paulhan, 'The Marquis de Sade and his Accomplice'.
34. Préface to *Les Infortunes de la vertu*, p. 22.
35. Blanchot, *Lautréamont et Sade*.
36. Goulemot, *Préface* to *Les Infortunes de la vertu*, p. 34.
37. See Geoffrey Bennington, 'Forget to Remember, Remember to Forget: *Sade avec Kant*' in *Paragraph*, Vol. 23, No. 1 (March 2000), edited by John Phillips, Edinburgh University Press, pp. 75–86.
38. For more examples of 'double binds', see *Les Infortunes*, pp. 73, 91, 95, 169, 178; *Les Malheurs*, pp. 331, 341.
39. Goulemot, *Préface* to *Les Infortunes de la vertu*, p. 26.
40. Annie Le Brun, 'Avant et après Juliette' in Le Brun and Pauvert (eds), Sade, *Histoire de Juliette, ou les Prospérités du vice*, (Paris: Société Nouvelle des Éditions Pauvert, 1987), Vol. 8, pp. 33–52 (p. 48).
41. Rétif de la Bretonne was inspired in 1798 to write *L'Anti-Justine* as an antidote to the cruelty depicted in Sade's works.
42. As Philippe Roger points out, there is actually very little killing in *Justine*: see Roger, *Pressoir*, p. 130.
43. Carter, *Sadeian Woman*, p. 72.
44. In the UK and certain US states, while its homosexual counterpart may have been decriminalised long ago, consensual heterosexual sodomy is still theoretically against the law.

Chapter 5

1. Geoffrey Gorer, *The Life and Ideas of the Marquis de Sade* (New York: W. W. Norton, 1963; first published in London in 1934).
2. A particular target is the widespread use until the Revolution of the infamous *lettre de cachet* which authorised arrest and indefinite detention without trial, and of which Sade had personal experience: see Chapter 1.

3. For Camilla Paglia, the *femme fatale* 'is not a fiction but an extrapolation of biologic realities in women that remain constant. The North American Indian myth of the toothed vagina (vagina dentata) is a gruesomely direct transcription of female power and male fear. Metaphorically, every vagina has secret teeth, for the male exits as less than when he entered. [...] Physical and spiritual castration is the danger every man runs in intercourse with a woman' (*Sexual Personae*, p. 13).
4. Memories of the author's own journey through Italy in the 1770s in the company of his delectable sister-in-law, Anne-Prospère, inpired lengthy descriptions of the Italian cities and countryside visited by Juliette. On the other hand, all locations and landscapes in Sade are described less for their interest as potential tourist spots than for their libertine functionality: Vesuvius, for instance, provides the opportunity for murder, while the columns of St Peter's in Rome are the perfect place to tie up victims.
5. Marcel Hénaff has noted how the transitions between episodes in *Juliette* are effected simply by moving characters and readers from town to town: see his *Corps libertin*, p. 157.
6. See Jean Paulhan, 'Sade and his Accomplice'.
7. Quoted by Laugaa-Traut, *Lectures de Sade* (Paris: Armand Colin, 1973), p. 180.
8. See also Vol. 9, p. 377: Juliette's 'Si jamais ces écrits s'imprimaient [...]'; 'Were these tales ever to be printed, the reader, his imagination heated by the lubricious details strewn throughout, would be enchanted, would he not, to be able to pause from time to time and dwell upon milder, more restful descriptions, framed nonetheless within the bounds of the strictest truth?' (p. 978).
9. See Andreas Pfersmann, 'L'Ironie romantique chez Sade', *Sade: Écrire la crise*, Colloque de Cérisy (Paris: Éditions Pierre Belfond, 1983), pp. 85–98 (p. 91). The footnote in the novel was a relatively recent phenomenon at the end of the eighteenth century, and the *note d'érudition* or 'erudite footnote', in particular, represents a more original model. Philippe Roger also sees the use of footnotes as a salient feature of the Sadean novel, tracing their growing preoccupation with libertinage from novel to novel, culminating with the predominance of this subject in the notes of *Juliette*: see Roger, *Pressoir*, p. 75.
10. Frappier-Mazur, *Writing the Orgy*, p. 147.
11. Ibid., p. 149.
12. Since footnotes are a typographical convention and, as such, a quintessentially written and indeed printed use of

language, Frappier-Mazur is therefore able to link speaking with the feminine and writing with the masculine (ibid., p. 151), the implication being that the female storyteller is seen to need the male author's written seal of approval. One might object, however, that this feminist reading polarises the masculine and the feminine too simplistically, ignoring the many notes that lend support to the views of male libertines, whose narratives/dissertations are embedded within Juliette's own (for example, Brisa Testa's (Borchamps') lengthy autobiographical tale). Moreover, Sade appears on occasions to forget that his heroine is speaking, rather than writing, for instance, 'c'est aussi de cette époque que je vais vous la peindre avec la cynique franchise qui caractérisera toujours mes *crayons*' (Vol. 9, p. 84; my emphasis) / 'from here on I shall describe it in the cynically frank style which will always be the hallmark of my *writing*' (p. 682; adapted).

13. Other distinctive features of the narrative in *Juliette* include the question and answer format of the quizzing of Juliette by the President of the Société des Amis du Crime (Vol. 8, pp. 449–51) and Borchamps's similarly structured interrogation by the templars (Vol. 9, pp. 261–63), although this dialogic format does not lead to the generation of multiple perspectives – all of the text's narrative voices are simply different manifestations of the author's. Béatrice Didier rightly observes that, whether mediated by character or narrator, the discourse of all Sade's works is constituted by a single authorial voice (Béatrice Didier, *Sade* (Paris: Denoël/Gonthier, 1976), p. 201).
14. Pierre Klossowski sees Juliette as androgynous: see his 'Sade, or the philosopher-villain' in *Sade and the Narrative of Transgression*, pp. 33–61 (p. 56 et seq.).
15. See Hénaff, *Corps libertin*, p. 310; see also, on this point, Luce Irigaray, '«Françaises» ne faites plus un effort' in *Ce Sexe qui n'en est pas un* (Paris: Les Éditions de Minuit, 1977).
16. The Society of the Friends of Crime is in one sense a parody of the numerous secret societies that flourished in France during the revolutionary years.
17. Sex crimes are committed almost exclusively by men. Even those few women, like Myra Hindley or Rosemary West, who have been found guilty of them in recent times, have invariably been under the influence of a svengali-like male. As Freud says, 'Women show little need to degrade the sexual object' (quoted by Paglia, *Sexual Personae*, p. 247).
18. Sigmund Freud, 'Fetishism' in *Three Essays on Sexuality* (London: Pelican Books, 1984), pp. 351–57 (p. 357).

19. Any doubts that the obsessive phallicism of Sade's text is not also shared by the author himself are dispelled by the footnote in which he describes to us with relish the pleasures of penis masturbation: Vol. 8, p. 474, n.
20. Catherine Cusset draws attention to the representation of the Sadean erection as an expression of anger: see her 'Sade: De l'imagination libertine à l'imaginaire volcanique' in *French Forum*, No. 18 (1993), pp. 151–63 (p. 152).
21. For a discussion of links between the mother and nature in Sade, see my 'Sade and the Female Body', in *The South Central Modern Languages Association Journal*, special issue: 'The Form of Violence: Use and Abuse of Gender in French Literature and Culture', edited by Owen Heathcote (forthcoming, spring 2001).
22. Roger, *Pressoir*, p. 148.
23. Ibid., p. 161.
24. In *La nouvelle Justine*, Almani, the chemist whom Jérôme encounters on Mount Etna, encapsulates this ambivalence in a single line: 'J'aimerais une mère semblable! Non, je l'imiterai mais en la détestant'(Vol. 2, p. 45) / 'Could I love such a mother? No, I shall imitate her but with hatred.' When he masturbates into the volcano's lava, he is symbolically making the phallic mother nature his mistress, establishing dominance over her. For a discussion of this scene in the context of Sadean attitudes to the feminine, see my 'Sade and the Female Body'.
25. See Cusset, 'De l'imagination libertine', pp. 156–57.
26. Catherine Cusset reads this scene somewhat differently, in my view misinterpreting Juliette's remark about the stones as superstitious rather than jocular. Curiously, moreover, in an otherwise useful article, Cusset takes no account of the volcano's phallic character: see Cusset, 'De l'imagination libertine'.
27. Laplanche and Pontalis, *The Language of Psycho-Analysis*, p. 306.
28. See, for example, Brenda Love, *The Encyclopedia of Unusual Sexual Practices* (London: Greenwich Editions, 1999).
29. Louise J. Kaplan, *Female Perversions: The Temptations of Emma Bovary* (New York: Anchor Books, 1991), p. 12.
30. Ibid., p. 34.
31. Freud, 'Fetishism', pp. 352–53.
32. Kaplan, *Female Perversions*, p. 35.
33. Freud, 'Fetishism', p. 357; see also Richard von Krafft-Ebing, *Psychopathia Sexualis* (London: Velvet Publications, 1997), p. 21.

34. Freud, 'Fetishism', p. 353.
35. The horror of the Sadean text is in some degree attenuated by the surreal black humour that accompanies it: see my '"Laugh? I nearly died!": Humor in Sade's Fiction'.
36. For the reader's convenience and in true Sadean spirit, these examples are listed in alphabetical order.
37. See Beatrice Fink, 'Sadean Savouries in Peter Greenaway's *The Cook, the Thief, his Wife and her Lover*' in John Phillips (ed.), *Paragraph*, Vol. 23, No. 1 (March 2000), pp. 98–106.
38. Urine, certainly, but other bodily fluids too play a central role in the Sadean orgy: 'Le foutre, les liqueurs éjaculées des godemichés, le sang, nous inondaient de tous côtés; nous nagions dans leurs flots' (Vol. 9, p. 374) / 'Spunk, the liquids ejaculated from the dildos, blood inundated us from all sides; we were swimming in them.' Against the background of ambivalent attitudes to the maternal that run through Sade's writing, one might conjecture that such scenes express an unconscious desire to return to the fluidity of the mother's womb.
39. See, for example, Frappier-Mazur, *Writing the Orgy*, p. 46.
40. For more examples of mother–son incest in Sade's fiction, see *La nouvelle Justine*, in which Séraphine's brother, de l'Aigle, has long wanted to 'do to his mother what his father, Siméon, does to her' and the mother, Pauline, is more than willing to oblige (*La NJ*, Vol. 2, pp. 304–306), and the short story, 'Florville et Courval' in *Les Crimes de l'amour*, in which the ironically named Saint-Ange rapes his mother, the unfortunate Florville.
41. Kaplan, *Female Perversions*, p. 28.
42. Ibid., p. 27.
43. Gaëtan Brulotte coins the term *ouïr*, an Old French verb meaning 'to hear', for this hitherto unnamed erotic activity: see his *Oeuvres de chair: Figures du discours érotique* (Québec: Les Presses de l'Université Laval, 1998), pp. 408 et seq.
44. This is unsurprising given Sade's Catholic upbringing. The purpose of confession in the Catholic Church is the absolution of sins, but it also provides the celibate priest with many opportunities for vicarious sexual thrills. A remarkably similar set of questions to those posed to Juliette were used in 1697 by priests hearing the confessions of the Tarascan tribe in Western Mexico: see the 'Confessions' entry in Love, *The Encyclopedia of Unusual Sexual Practices*, pp. 69–70.
45. This arrangement recalls the adroit disposition of mirrors for the same purpose in *La Philosophie dans le boudoir*: see my discussion of this passage in Chapter 6.

46. Kaplan, *Female Perversions*, p. 30.
47. See my '"Laugh? I nearly died!": Humor in Sade's Fiction'.
48. *Les Prospérités du vice* (Paris: U.G.E, 1969).
49. Timo Airaksinen's, *The Philosophy of the Marquis de Sade* (London and New York: Routledge, 1995) is an excellent example of this approach.

Chapter 6

1. The *Übermensch* or 'Overman' was for Nietzsche the man surviving after God's death. There are striking resemblances between Sade's and Nietzsche's thinking, and there is little doubt that the nineteenth-century German philosopher was strongly influenced by Sade. Bataillean 'sovereignty' 'is the opposite of servility [...] sovereignty may be said to be the determination to have done with ends and live entirely in the instant. It represents an existence freed from worry [...]' (Michael Richardson, *Georges Bataille* (London and New York: Routledge, 1994), pp. 38–9).
2. Catherine Cusset, 'Sade: de l'imagination libertine à l'imaginaire volcanique' in *French Forum*, Vol. 18, (1993), pp. 151–63 (p. 153).
3. Catherine Claude, 'Une Lecture de Femme', *Europe*, No. 522 (October 1972), p. 64.
4. Chantal Thomas, *Sade, l'oeil de la lettre* (Paris: Payot, 1978), p. 94.
5. Jean Paulhan, 'The Marquis de Sade and His Accomplice', p. 10.
6. See Pierre Klossowski, *Sade mon prochain* (1947) and the revised version of 1967.
7. Pierre Klossowski, 'A Destructive Philosophy' in *Yale French Studies*, No. 35, p. 72.
8. Blanchot, *Sade*, pp. 58 and 61; adapted from *Lautréamont et Sade* (Paris: Les Éditions de Minuit, 1963).
9. See Michel Delon, 'Sade, maître d'agression' in *Europe*, No. 522 (October 1972), p. 124.
10. Béatrice Didier, 'Sade théologien', *Sade: Écrire la crise*, Colloque de Cérisy (Paris: Belfond, 1983), pp. 219–40 (p. 220). With regard to biblical allusion, one should, in any case, be aware of the enormous influence of the Bible on Western literature, whose texts must position themselves in relation to it. Edward Saïd offers an illuminating analysis of the central and dominant place occupied by the Bible in the genealogy of all texts in his *The World, the Text and the Critic* (Harvard University Press, 1983). This analysis is especially

relevant to eighteenth-century French society in which theological considerations inform practically every area of life, and in which all writing is in some way influenced by scriptural models.

11. Le Brun, *Soudain un bloc d'abîme*, p. 79.
12. See Bataille, *L'Érotisme*, pp. 76, 79–80. Bataille's theory that the divine and violence are linked is also relevant to a reading of Sade's representation of the body: see ibid., p. 201.
13. Philippe Roger discusses the paradox of Sadean transgression at length, seeing the increasingly horrific nature of libertine crimes in *Juliette* in terms of a quest for the absolute: see Roger, *Pressoir*, pp. 124–32.
14. Le Brun, *Soudain un bloc d'abîme*, p. 63; my emphasis.
15. Ibid., p. 81.
16. Michel Foucault, 'Le langage à l'infini' in *Tel Quel*, (autumn 1963), p. 51.
17. De Jean, *Literary Fortifications*, p. 305.
18. Hénaff, *Corps libertin*, p. 73.
19. Ibid., p. 129.
20. Chantal Thomas has pointed out that for Sade the prisoner, whose opportunities for physical movement were strictly limited, the movement of the body is replaced metaphorically by the movement of writing: 'La liberté d'un immaîtrisable mouvement de glissements, de déplacements, de métamorphoses hante toute l'écriture de Sade et sa vie'/ 'The freedom of uncontrollable movement, as manifest in slidings, displacements and metamorphoses haunts all of Sade's life and work' (*L'Oeil de la lettre*, pp. 100–101). We might add that, in a Lacanian perspective, insatiable desire and the metonymic movement of language are closely linked.
21. Similar ambitions are expressed by Durand in *Juliette* (Vol. 9, p. 434), by Curval in *Les 120 Journées* (p. 200), and in *La nouvelle Justine* by Jérôme (Vol. 2, p. 42), Verneuil (Vol. 2, p. 207) and Dorothée (Vol. 2, p. 243).
22. Catherine Cusset supports this reading when she sees the act of sodomy here as 'sanctifying the bottom' which 'opens the gate to an infinity of suffering' ('Sade: Critique of Pure Fiction' in *The Divine Sade*, pp. 117–18). Frappier-Mazur rightly argues that Klossowski places too much importance on this speech in his attempts to 'rescue Sade from atheism': see her *Writing the Orgy*, p. 118, n. 67.
23. See Le Brun, *Soudain un bloc d'abîme*, p. 277.
24. Le Brun, 'Sade, or the First Theatre of Atheism'.
25. Sade's libertines come to insult nature, just as they used to insult God, competing with nature for the vacant throne that

God has left behind. See my 'Sade and the Female Body' in *The South Central Modern Languages Association Journal*, special issue: The Form of Violence: Use and Abuse of Gender in French Literature and Culture, edited by Owen Heathcote (forthcoming in spring 2001).

26. See Beatrice Fink's work in this area: for example, 'Lecture alimentaire de l'utopie sadienne', *Sade: Écrire la crise*, pp. 175–92.
27. Marquis de Sade, *Lettres à sa femme*, 17 February 1779; edited by Marc Buffat (Paris: Actes Sud, 1997), p. 79.
28. Laure represents the ideal mother that Sade never had: see Chapter 1 for details of the Comtesse de Sade's absences from her son's life.
29. Hénaff, *Corps libertin*, p. 322.
30. Michel Delon, 'Le corps sadien' in *Europe*, No. 835–36, 'Sade. Le Grand Guignol', (November–December 1998), pp. 23–4
31. The three Sadean heroines – Eugénie in *La Philosophie dans le boudoir*, Justine and Juliette – are on one level parodies of the iconic female figures of the Bible: respectively, Eve, the Virgin Mary and Mary Magdalen.

Afterword

1. Michel Foucault, *The Order of things*, trans. Alan Sheridan (London: Pantheon, 1970), pp. 353–54; originally published in French as *Les Mots et les choses* (Paris: Gallimard, 1966).
2. I suggested in Chapter 1 that this characteristic of the writing helps explain the enthusiasm of postmodernists for Sade.
3. Nietzsche's contemptuous view of Christianity, with its gloomy emphasis on guilt and sin, as a credo for the passive and the weak, is clearly influenced by Sade: see Chapter 1. Indeed both Sade and Nietzsche exhibit a very personal response to religion, the former reacting against the puritanical myths and anti-sex bias of Catholicism, the latter against a strict Lutheran upbringing; 'I call Christianity the one great curse, the one enormous and innermost perversion, the one great instinct of revenge for which no means are too venomous, too underhand, too underground and too petty – I call it the one immortal blemish of mankind' (Nietzsche, *The Anti-Christ*, Section 62 (1888), in *The Viking Portable Nietzsche*, 1954, p. 656).

Select Bibliography

1. Primary Texts

Les 120 Journées de Sodome (Paris: P.O.L., 1992).
The One Hundred and Twenty Days of Sodom, compiled and translated by Austryn Wainhouse and Richard Seaver (London: Arrow Books, 1990).
La Philosophie dans le boudoir (Paris: U.G.E., 10/18, 1991).
Philosophy in the Bedroom in *Marquis de Sade, Justine, Philosophy in the Bedroom, and Other Writings*, compiled and translated by Richard Seaver and Austryn Wainhouse (New York: Grove Weidenfeld, 1990).
Les Infortunes de la vertu (Paris: Garnier-Flammarion, 1969).
The Misfortunes of Virtue and Other Early Tales, translated by David Coward (Oxford: Oxford University Press, 1999).
Justine ou les Malheurs de la vertu (Paris: Gallimard, 1981).
Justine, or Good Conduct Well Chastised (1791) in *Marquis de Sade, Justine, Philosophy in the Bedroom, and Other Writings*, compiled and translated by Richard Seaver and Austryn Wainhouse (New York: Grove Weidenfeld, 1990).
La nouvelle Justine, Vols 1 and 2 (Paris: U.G.E, 10/18, 1995).
Histoire de Juliette, ou les Prospérités du vice, Oeuvres Complètes, Le Brun and Pauvert (eds), (Paris: Société Nouvelle des Éditions Pauvert, 1987), Vols 8 and 9.
Juliette, translated by Austryn Wainhouse (London: Arrow Books Ltd, 1991; translation, 1968).
Les Prospérités du vice (Paris: U.G.E., 1969).
Dialogue entre un prêtre et un moribond, Oeuvres Complètes, Le Brun and Pauvert (eds), (Paris: Société Nouvelle des Éditions Pauvert, 1987), Vol. 1.
Dialogue between a Priest and a Dying Man in *Marquis de Sade, Justine, Philosophy in the Bedroom, and Other Writings*, compiled and translated by Richard Seaver and Austryn Wainhouse (New York: Grove Weidenfeld, 1990).
Correspondance in *Oeuvres Complètes*, Vol. 12 (Paris: Cercle du livre précieux, 1967).
Lettres à sa femme, edited by Marc Buffat (Paris: Actes Sud, 1997).

Marquis de Sade: Letters from Prison, translated by Richard Seaver (London: Harvill Press, 2000).

2. Secondary and Critical Reading

Abramovici, J-C. 'Écrire et captiver: La lecture piégée d'*Aline et Valcour*', *Europe*, No. 835–836, November–December 1998, pp. 34–42.

Airaksinen, T. *The Philosophy of the Marquis de Sade* (London and New York: Routledge, 1995).

Astbury, K. 'The Moral Tale and the Marquis de Sade: *Les Crimes de l'amour* as parody of the conte moral', forthcoming in *Australian Journal of French Studies*.

Barthes, R. *Sade, Fourier, Loyola* (Paris: Éditions du Seuil, 1971).

Bataille, G. *L'Érotisme* (Paris: Les Éditions de Minuit, 1957).

de Beauvoir, S. 'Faut-il brûler Sade?' in *Les Temps modernes*, December 1951, January 1952; later in *Privilèges* (Paris: Gallimard, 1955); English translation 'Must we burn Sade?' in *The Marquis de Sade, The 120 Days of Sodom and Other Writings* (London: Arrow Books, 1990), pp. 3–64.

Bennington, G. 'Forget to Remember, Remember to Forget: *Sade avec Kant*' in Phillips, J. (ed.), 'Sade and his Legacy', special edition of *Paragraph*, Vol. 23, No. 1 (March 2000), pp. 75–86.

Bettelheim, B. *The Uses of Enchantment: The Meaning and Importance of Fairy Tales* (London: Penguin Books, 1991; first published by Thames and Hudson, 1976).

Blanchot, M. *Lautréamont et Sade* (Paris: Les Éditions de Minuit, 1963).

Bongie, L. L. *Sade: A Biographical Essay* (Chicago and London: The University of Chicago Press, 1998).

Bordas, E. 'Sade ou l'Écriture de la Destruction: À propos de la structure stylistique des *Cent Vingt Journées de Sodome*', *The Romanic Review*, Vol. 86, No. 4 (1995), pp. 657–80.

Brulotte, G. *Oeuvres de chair: Figures du discours érotique* (Québec: Les Presses de l'Université Laval, 1998).

Camus, A. *L'Homme révolté* in *Essais d'Albert Camus*, R. Quilliot and L. Faucon (eds) (Paris: Gallimard, 'Pléiade', 1965).

Carter, A. *The Sadeian Woman* (London: Virago Press, 1979).

Châtelet, N. Préface, Notes and Annexes to Sade, *Justine ou les Malheurs de la vertu* (Paris: Gallimard, 1981), pp. 9–48 and 415–38.

—— 'Le Libertin à table', *Sade: Écrire la crise*, Colloque de Cérisy (Paris: Éditions Pierre Belfond, 1983), pp. 67–83.

Cirlot, J. E. *A Dictionary of Symbols* (London: Routledge, 1971).

Claude, C. 'Une Lecture de Femme in Europe', No. 522 (October 1972), pp. 64–70.

Cryle, P. *Geometry in the Boudoir: Configurations of French Erotic Narrative* (Ithaca and London: Cornell University Press, 1994).

Cusset, C. 'Sade: De l'imagination libertine à l'imaginaire volcanique', *French Forum*, No. 18 (1993), pp. 151–63.

—— 'Sade: Critique of Pure Fiction' in Sawhney, D. N. (ed.), *The Divine Sade, PLI Warwick Journal of Philosophy* (February 1994), pp. 117–18.

Dangeville, S. *Le Théâtre change et représente. Lecture critique des oeuvres dramatiques du marquis de Sade* (Paris: Champion, 1999).

Darnton, R. *The Forbidden Best-sellers of Pre-Revolutionary France* (London: HarperCollins, 1996).

De Jean, J. *Literary Fortifications. Rousseau, Laclos, Sade* (Princeton University Press, 1984).

Deleuze, G. *Présentation de Sacher-Masoch* (Paris: Minuit, 1967).

Delon, M. 'Sade, maître d'agression' in *Europe*, No. 522 (October 1972), pp. 123–27.

—— *L'idée d'énergie au tournant des Lumières* (Paris: PUF, 1988).

—— 'Le corps sadien' in *Europe*, No. 835–36, 'Sade. Le Grand Guignol', (November–December 1998), pp. 23–4.

Didier, B. *Sade* (Paris: Éditions Denoël/Gonthier, 1976).

—— 'Sade théologien', *Sade: Écrire la crise*, Colloque de Cérisy (Paris: Éditions Pierre Belfond, 1983), pp. 219–40.

Fink, B. 'Food as Object, Activity, and Symbol in Sade', *Romanic Review*, No. 65 (March 1974).

—— 'Lecture alimentaire de l'utopie sadienne', *Sade: Écrire la crise*, Colloque de Cérisy (Paris: Éditions Pierre Belfond, 1983), pp. 175–91.

—— 'Sadean Savouries in Peter Greenaway's *The Cook, the Thief, his Wife and her Lover*' in Phillips, J. (ed.), 'Sade and his Legacy', special edition of *Paragraph*, Vol. 23, No. 1 (March 2000), pp. 98–106.

Foucault, M. 'Préface à la transgression' in *Critique*, 195–96 (1963), pp. 751–69.

—— 'Le Langage à l'infini' in *Tel Quel*, 15 (1963), pp. 44–53.

—— *Les Mots et les choses* (Paris: Gallimard, 1966).

—— *The Order of things*, trans. Alan Sheridan (London: Pantheon, 1970).

—— *Histoire de la folie à l'âge classique* (Paris: Gallimard, rev. ed. 1972).

Frappier-Mazur, L. *Writing the Orgy: Power and Parody in Sade* (Philadelphia: University of Pennsylvania Press, 1996); first published in French as *Sade et l'écriture de l'orgie* (Paris: Nathan, 1991).

Freud, S. 'Femininity' in *New Introductory Lectures on Psychoanalysis*, The Pelican Freud Library, Vol. 2, pp. 145–69.
—— 'Fetishism' in *Three Essays on Sexuality*, The Pelican Freud Library, Vol. 7 (London: Pelican Books, 1984), pp. 345–57.
Gallop, J. *Intersections. A Reading of Sade with Bataille, Blanchot, and Klossowski* (Lincoln and London: University of Nebraska Press, 1981).
Genette, G. *Figures 111* (Paris: Éditions du Seuil, 1972).
—— *Palimpsestes* (Paris: Éditions du Seuil, 1982).
—— *Seuils* (Paris: Éditions du Seuil, 1987).
Gorer, G. *The Life and Ideas of the Marquis de Sade* (New York: W. W. Norton, 1963; first published in London in 1934).
Goulemot, J-M. Préface to Sade, *Les Infortunes de la vertu* (Paris: Garnier-Flammarion, 1969), pp. 19–36.
—— 'Beau marquis parlez-nous d'amour', *Sade: Écrire la crise*, Colloque de Cérisy (Paris: Éditions Pierre Belfond, 1983), pp. 119–32.
—— *Forbidden Texts: Erotic Literature and its Readers in Eighteenth-Century France* (Philadelphia: University of Pennsylvania Press, 1994); first published in French as *Ces livres qu'on ne lit que d'une main* (Paris: Éditions Alinea, 1991).
Harrison, N. *Circles of Censorship. Censorship and its Metaphors in French History, Literature and Theory* (Oxford: Clarendon Press, 1995).
Heine, M. *Le Marquis de Sade* (Paris: Gallimard, 1950).
Hénaff, M. *Sade: L'Invention du corps libertin* (Paris: PUF, 1978).
—— 'The Encyclopedia of Excess' in Allison, D. B., Roberts, M. S. and Weiss, A. S. (eds), *Sade and the Narrative of Transgression* (Cambridge: Cambridge University Press, 1995), pp. 142–70.
Hood, S. and Crowley, G. *Sade for Beginners* (Cambridge: Icon Books, 1995).
Irigaray, L. '«Françaises» ne faites plus un effort' in *Ce Sexe qui n'en est pas un* (Paris: Les Éditions de Minuit, 1977).
Kaplan, L. J. *Female Perversions: The Temptations of Emma Bovary* (New York: Anchor Books, 1991).
Klossowski, P. *Sade, mon prochain* (Paris: Éditions du Seuil, 1947; rev. edition 1967), translated as *Sade My Neighbour* (London: Quartet Books, 1992).
—— 'A Destructive Philosophy' in *Yale French Studies*, No. 35 (1965), pp. 61–79.
—— 'Sade, or the philosopher-villain' in Allison, D. B., Roberts, M. S. and Weiss, A. S. (eds), *Sade and the Narrative of Transgression* (Cambridge: Cambridge University Press, 1995), pp. 33–61.
von Krafft-Ebing, R. *Psychopathia Sexualis* (London: Velvet Publications, 1997).

Lacan, J. 'Kant avec Sade' in *Écrits* (Paris: Éditions du Seuil, 1966), pp. 765–90.

Laplanche, J. and Pontalis, J-B. *The Language of Psycho-Analysis* (London: The Hogarth Press and The Institute of Psycho-Analysis, 1985).

Laugaa-Traut, F. *Lectures de Sade* (Paris: Armand Colin, 1973).

Le Brun, A. *Soudain un bloc d'abîme, Sade* (Paris: Jean-Jacques Pauvert, Gallimard/Folio, 1986).

—— 'Avant et après Juliette' in Le Brun and Pauvert (eds), Sade, *Histoire de Juliette, ou les Prospérités du vice* (Paris: Société Nouvelle des Éditions Pauvert, 1987), Vol. 8, pp. 33–52.

—— 'Sade, or the First Theatre of Atheism' in Phillips, J. (ed.), 'Sade and his Legacy', special edition of *Paragraph*, Vol. 23, No. 1 (Edinburgh: Edinburgh University Press, March 2000), pp. 38–50.

Lély, G. 'Avant-propos' to *La Philosophie dans le boudoir* (Paris: U.G.E., 10/18, 1991), pp. 5–11.

—— 'Avant-propos' to Sade, *La Nouvelle Justine* (Paris: U.G.E., 10/18, 1995), Vol. 1, pp. 7–19.

Lever, M. *Donatien Alphonse François, Marquis de Sade* (Paris: Librairie Artheme Fayard, 1991); English translation: Lever, M. *Marquis de Sade: A Biography*, translated by Goldhammer, A. (London: HarperCollins, 1993).

Lévi-Strauss, C. *Les Structures élémentaires de la parenté* (Paris: PUF, 1949).

Love, B. *The Encyclopedia of Unusual Sexual Practices* (London: Greenwich Editions, 1999).

Lyotard, J-F. *The Postmodern Condition: A Report on Knowledge*, trans. G. Bennington and B. Massumi (Minneapolis: University of Minnesota Press, 1984), originally published in French as *La Condition postmoderne: rapport sur le savoir* (Paris: Gallimard, 1979).

May, G. 'Fiction Reader, Novel Writer', *Yale French Studies*, No. 35 (1965), pp. 5–11.

Miller, N. K. 'Arachnologies: The Woman, The Text and The Critic' in Miller, N. K. (ed.), *The Poetics of Gender* (New York: Columbia University Press, 1986), pp. 270–95.

Nietzsche, F. *The Anti-Christ*, Section 62 (1888), in *The Viking Portable Nietzsche*, 1954.

Noël, B. 'La Machine en tête', Introduction to Sade, *Les 120 Journées de Sodome* (Paris: P.O.L., 1992), pp. i–xi.

Paglia, C. *Sexual Personae. Art and Decadence from Nefertiti to Emily Dickinson* (New York: Vintage Books, 1991).

Pastoureau, H. 'Sadomasochism and the Philosophies of Ambivalence', *Yale French Studies*, No. 35 (1965), pp. 48–60.

Paulhan, J. Introduction to *Les Infortunes de la vertu* (Paris: Point du Jour, 1946), pp. ii–xliii, translated as 'The Marquis de Sade and His Accomplice' in *Marquis de Sade, Justine, Philosophy in the Bedroom, and Other Writings* (New York: Grove Weidenfeld, 1990), pp. 3–36.

Pauvert, J-J. 'Notice bibliographique' in Le Brun and Pauvert (eds), Sade, *Histoire de Juliette, ou les Prospérités du vice* (Paris: Société Nouvelle des Éditions Pauvert, 1987), Vol. 8, pp. 9–31.

—— *Nouveaux visages de la censure* (Paris: Les Belles Lettres, 1994).

—— and Beuchot, P. *Sade en procès* (Paris: Éditions Mille et une Nuits/Arte, 1999).

Pfersmann, A. 'L'Ironie romantique chez Sade', *Sade: Écrire la crise*, Colloque de Cérisy (Paris: Éditions Pierre Belfond, 1983), pp. 85–98.

Phillips, J. *Forbidden Fictions. Pornography and Censorship in Twentieth Century French Literature* (London and Sterling, Virginia: Pluto Press, 1999).

—— '"Laugh? I nearly died!" Humor in Sade's Fiction' in *The Eighteenth Century: Theory and Interpretation*, Vol. 40, No. 1 (spring 1999), pp. 46–67.

—— 'Sade and Self-censorship' in Phillips, J. (ed.), 'Sade and his Legacy', special edition of *Paragraph*, Vol. 23, No. 1 (Edinburgh: Edinburgh University Press, March 2000), pp. 107–18.

—— 'Sade and the Female Body', *The South Central Modern Languages Association Journal*, special issue: 'The Form of Violence: Use and Abuse of Gender in French Literature and Culture', edited by Owen Heathcote (forthcoming, spring 2001).

du Plessix Gray, F. *At Home with the Marquis de Sade* (New York: Penguin Books, 1999).

Pleynet, M. 'Sade, des chiffres, des lettres, du renfermement', *Tel Quel*, Vol. 86 (winter 1980).

Queneau, R. *Bâtons, chiffres et lettres* (Paris: Gallimard, 1950).

Richardson, M. *Georges Bataille* (London and New York: Routledge, 1994).

Robbe-Grillet, A. 'Samuel Beckett ou la présence sur la scène' in *Pour un nouveau roman* (Paris: Éditions de Minuit, 1963), pp. 95–107.

Roger, P. *Sade: La Philosophie dans le pressoir* (Paris: Bernard Grasset, 1976).

—— 'A political minimalist' in Allison, D. B., Roberts, M. S. and Weiss, A. S. (eds), *Sade and the Narrative of Transgression* (Cambridge: Cambridge University Press, 1995), pp. 76–99.

Rosario, V. A. *The Erotic Imagination. French Histories of Perversity* (New York and Oxford: Oxford University Press, 1997).

Saïd, E. *The World, the Text and the Critic* (Harvard University Press, 1983).

Shattuck, R. *Forbidden Knowledge: From Prometheus to Pornography* (New York: St Martin's Press, 1996).
Sollers, P. 'Sade dans le texte' in *L'écriture et l'expérience des limites* (Paris: Éditions du Seuil, 1968), pp. 48–66.
Thomas, C. *Sade, l'oeil de la lettre* (Paris: Payot, 1978).
—— *Sade* (Paris: Éditions du Seuil, 1994).
Thomas, D. *The Marquis de Sade* (London: Allison and Busby, 1992).

Index